Late Arrival

Late Arrival

The Story of Jim 'Winkie' Kirk, RNZAF

Zane Kirk

An imprint of
MENTION THE WAR PUBLICATIONS

First published in the United Kingdom in 2018 by Mention the War Ltd. Leeds LS28 5HA, England.

Cover design: Topics – The Creative Partnership www.topicdesign.co.uk

A CIP catalogue reference for this book is available from the British Library.

ISBN 9 781911 255352

Contents

Acknowledgements

Zane (left) and Jim Kirk in 2006

Writing this book would not have been possible without the contributions, great and small, from many sources, and I am extremely grateful to the following people: Pat Grant, Pam Jackson, Charlotte James, Keith Janes, Lois Cherrington, June Barraclough, June Maaka, Margie Maaka, Barry Marks, Rod MacKenzie, Fernand Nedelec, Bernard Leighton, Kate Beaumont, Daniel Dunbar, Benjamin Norris, Kevin Norris, Larry Grauerhol, Elva Loveridge, Jackie Crow, Cheryl Carbol, Marilyn Fowler, Naomi Lakritz, Geoff Warren, Tim Frank, Ian White, Edouard Reniere, Leroy Kirk, Claude Francois, Jean Magne, Josh Jackson, Denis Bergerot, John Swale, Ron Mayhill DFC, Christopher Brooks NZDF, Dena Rush, Larry Busby, Jean-Claude Schwartz, Peter Wheeler QSM.

A very special thanks to John Thorpe for his constant encouragement, Gerard Lebel, whose tireless efforts did so much to help tell my father's story, Debbie Close for all her help, and to my partner Daphne for her patience and encouragement.

Chapter 1: The Naivety of Youth

Jim Kirk had a short war.

In hindsight that turned out to be a blessing, but at the time he didn't think so. In fact, young Jim had stewed so much over the thought of the war ending before he had a chance to enlist, he got himself down to the RNZAF recruiting office the day before his eighteenth birthday, which just goes to prove that naivety really is the privilege of youth.

He didn't join the air force because he had any great ambition to fly, although the idea had a certain appeal, nor did he habour any lofty idealism, or anything as patriotic as wanting to fight for king and country. Adventure aside, he wanted to see Canada.

Employed as an apprentice butcher with Smart & Son in Christchurch, Jim had reached the age of sixteen and a half when the war started, and he looked forward to the day when he could join up and embark on a great adventure. One of the shop's regular customers, a woman to whom he made frequent home deliveries, helped fuel his appetite for adventure.

'Her son had been training with the RNZAF in Canada for some time,' Jim explained. 'She would read me his letters and show me photographs of him in his air force uniform standing against a backdrop of fir tree covered mountains. His descriptions of Canada and the Canadian people made such a strong impression on me that I developed a single-minded determination to see the country for myself.'

Unable to afford the passage out of his own pocket, and with his mother never going to support such a foolhardy venture, Jim figured his only hope of realizing his dream was to enlist in the RNZAF and hopefully get sent to Canada under the BCATP (British Commonwealth Air Training Plan).

At the recruiting office in McKenzie Arcade, he waited enthusiastically for his turn to be interviewed by a tough-as-nails sergeant sitting behind a large desk. Finally, the grizzled NCO beckoned him over and looked him up and down without even asking his name.

'What a grumpy so and so,' Jim reflected

'How old are you?' The sergeant grunted.

'Seventeen.'

Jim thought his enthusiasm would impress the sergeant no end, so needless to say he found himself taken aback when instead of presenting him with an application form, the sergeant slammed his hand down on the desk.

'Stop wasting my bloody time! Get off with you and don't come back until you're eighteen.'

Being a shy sort, and with the sergeant looking so surly and seemingly so important, Jim withered inside. But it didn't quash his enthusiasm and he returned early the next morning to find the sergeant sitting at the desk looking more fearsome than ever.

'I thought I told you to come back when you're eighteen.'

'I have.'

'You have what?'

'Come back when I'm eighteen. It's my birthday today.'

'Smart bugger.'

The sergeant took Jim's details and had him fill in the appropriate form. Jim wasn't sure what to expect next but he didn't think it would be to be told to go home and wait.

The sergeant said, 'You'll hear something in due course.'

He didn't elaborate on how long 'due course' meant and as the days turned into weeks Jim began to think his application had been thrown in the rubbish just to spite him. He'd almost given up hope when 6 weeks later he received an aircrew application form and an accompanying letter from the Air Ministry informing him that he'd been enrolled in an RNZAF pre-entry correspondence course.

He raced his application down to the recruiting office where he found a far more accommodating sergeant than the grumpy blighter he'd initially encountered. He scrutinized Jim's application.

'Pilot, eh? Everyone wants to be a pilot.'

Jim had only ticked 'pilot' as his preferred trade because it seemed like the right thing to do. But being the pragmatic type, he realized that with less than two years secondary schooling under his belt, he didn't stand much chance. Air Observer also appeared to be a long shot, and not one he had any real interest in, so he pinned all his hopes on the last option - air gunner.

Air gunners weren't held in the same reverence as pilots, or even observers for that matter, but Jim figured they still did a pretty important job which, with a little imagination, could be glamorous in its own unsophisticated way.

On the application, he came across the question, 'Have you any knowledge of internal combustion engines, construction of aircraft, mechanics, or electricity?' It reminded him of an incident from years earlier when his younger brother Frank had put a concoction in his hair tonic that had made his hair go rock-hard.

'I had to go to school in the cold air of a Christchurch winter morning with my hair sticking up all over the place,' Jim laughed when telling this story years later. 'I was terrified it would snap off. When I got home, I took my revenge by wiring up Frank's metal frame bed to a light bulb socket.'

On the application, he answered the question in typically dispassionate fashion; *'Practical knowledge of electricity, not theoretical!'*

'You've got your first correspondence assignment?' asked the sergeant.

Jim nodded. 'Yes, sir.'

'I'm not a sir, I'm a sergeant. You have much to learn, my son. Off you go then and get stuck in. Good luck. You'll be in the air force before you know it.'

The pre-entry course consisted of 21 assignments which arrived fortnightly. Study provided a challenge for Jim as he still had work during the day which left little free time. On top of that, academia had never been his forte for a couple of reasons. First, he'd had an extremely fragmented education, having to change schools every few weeks as the family constantly moved to wherever his mother could find work to support him and his younger siblings, brother Frank and sister Pat. It came as no surprise to find Pat and Jim bunking at the local playground rather than trying to make yet another group of friends.

Second, he suffered a short concentration span as a result of Frank accidentally hitting him in the head with the sharp end of an axe during a game of cowboys and Indians. When he looked back on his childhood, it amazed him that he had lived long enough to even volunteer for war service. An axe in the head wasn't his first brush with an untimely demise.

Jim had been born prematurely and his life expectancy had been measured in hours rather than years. Without the life-saving graces of an incubator at her disposal, his mother had nestled her tiny new born son in a sock drawer stuffed with cotton wool soaked in warm olive oil. This, Jim assumed, accounted for his diminutive size.

If his small stature had ever burdened him, he never mentioned it. Later, fighting for his life in the night sky over Europe, he would count it as a blessing. What had once threatened his life would, 21 years later, save it.

Having survived his introduction into the world, and a game of cowboys and Indians that had proved a little too realistic, his brother Frank then nearly extinguished his life yet again. Being chased by Jim, he bolted through a gate and slammed it shut behind him A protruding bolt stabbed Jim in the chest. A few inches to the left and it would have pierced his heart.

Knowing he would need more than just a basic grasp of mathematics if he wanted to get through the course assignments, Jim enrolled himself in the appropriate class at night school. Even air gunners required some depth of intellect.

Halfway through the correspondence course a letter from the Air Ministry dropped through the letter box. Fearing he hadn't achieved the required standard on his assignments, Jim opened the letter with dread. He needn't have worried. It was merely to inform him that the correspondence assignments were being discontinued and he would have to report to West Christchurch High School for night classes three nights a week to complete the pre-entry course.

11

His nocturnal studies hadn't progressed very far when another more ominous letter arrived. He had slogged through the pre-entry assignments for almost a year only to be called up to the army.

Jim's mother felt only relief because in one of her weaker moments, and against her better judgement, she had signed his air force application, giving the air force permission to send her precious first born overseas. Jim's dream of getting to Canada seemed destined to die a few miles down the road at the gates of Burnham army camp.

On board the train to Burnham, Jim sat next to a strapping lad who introduced himself as Patrick Giles.

'Call me Paddy,' he said. 'Everyone does.'

Paddy had followed a similar path as Jim into the army, working through the RNZAF pre-entry course in the evenings and working as a delivery boy for Christchurch grocer A. L. Walton during the day.

'What's your handle?' he asked Jim.

'Aubrey, but everyone calls me Jim or Jimmy.'

'Why's that?'

'All the kids used to call me Little Jimmy Boy and it just sort of stuck.'

Jim's size amused Paddy. 'You remind me more of Wee Willie Winkie,' he laughed.

Burnham army camp appeared to be a predictably regimented place with ugly weatherboard buildings surrounded by dry, dusty grounds and tall pine trees. The new recruits were marched to the camp barber for the obligatory short back and sides and then to the quartermaster's store for an itchy khaki uniform. It seemed their lives were destined to be spent standing in queues. Queues for uniforms; queues for jabs; queues for meals; queues for washing; queues for the latrines.

'You name it, we queued for it,' Jim recalled. 'Whenever we saw a queue, we joined it just in case we were missing out on something.'

At the quartermaster's store uniform sizes were calculated by nothing more than an experienced glance from a tall, unsmiling corporal. When Jim reached the front of the queue the corporal widened his eyes theatrically. 'What have we got here?'

Paddy slapped Jim on the shoulder. 'This is my mate, Winkie. As in Wee Willie Winkie.'

'Bloody hell, and I thought one size fitted all.' He looked at Jim. 'Unfortunately, we don't supply nightgowns, son.'

'What is it with NCOs?' Jim wondered aloud as he and Paddy departed with their new kit.

'They're God's gift to the army, Winkie,' Paddy laughed. 'And don't you forget it.'

It didn't take long for Jim's new nickname to catch on. One morning on parade he dropped his rifle. A heinous crime. The corporal screamed loud enough for the entire camp to hear, 'Winkie! Pick up that bloody rifle!'

As Jim fell into the routine of army life his resentment at having his Canadian dream scuttled reduced to a simmer. Burnham might not have been Canada but nonetheless he reveled in being away from home for the first time. He enjoyed the spirit of camaraderie and the sense of purpose in the way things were done, even if some of the regulations seemed rather ridiculous.

For example, every morning on parade the corporal demanded any man who hadn't shaved was to step forward. Jim didn't shave every morning. He didn't need to, so he unwittingly stepped forward, straight into the lion's den.'

'And why haven't you shaved, Private Winkie?'

'I don't need to, corporal.'

The corporal exploded 'Don't need to?'

'I only do it twice a week.'

Like a scene straight out of *It Ain't Half Hot Mum*, the corporal pushed his face within an inch of Jim's, barely able to contain himself. 'From now on you'll shave every morning whether you bloody well need to or not!'

In hindsight, Jim realized that such apparently idiotic regulations were designed to instill a thorough sense of discipline. If he couldn't follow an order to shave every morning then how would he cope following orders on the battlefield?

Obnoxious corporals aside, army life unfolded without complication with plenty of square bashing under the steely gaze of grizzled sergeant majors, miles of running in flat-soled sandshoes, and sufficient route marches in hobnailed boots to make sure everyone gained and maintained a high level of fitness. Having never handled anything bigger than a boy scout knife before, Jim found a particular thrill in being entrusted with a weighty .303 rifle. He would have spent hours blasting away on the range if they'd have let him.

The Bren Gun gave him even more pleasure. An uncomplicated lightweight machine gun, it had a good rate of fire and proved easy to maintain. Being mechanically minded, he found he could strip and reassemble one faster than any other man in his barracks. If he had to go into a battle the Bren gun would be his choice of weapon. As it turned out it would be some time before he went into battle, and when he did it wouldn't be with a Bren gun.

He'd been at Burnham about six weeks when one morning he and Paddy found their names on the daily routine orders detailing them to pack their bags and report to Ohakea air base for ADU (aerodrome defense unit) duties and a recommencement of their RNZAF pre-entry studies. His mother wasn't very happy, but Jim was over the moon.

'We couldn't wait to get to Ohakea,' he reflected. 'We'd heard the air force bods had clean sheets on their beds and got to wear nice shoes.'

13

Only after arriving at Ohakea on 30 May 1942 did Jim finally complete his Attestation for Service for Duration of War. At 19 years and 68 days old he joined the RNZAF as an AC2 (Aircraftsman 2nd Class) the lowest form of air force life.

He and Paddy spent further hours standing in queues filling out more forms and undergoing dental and medical examinations. At the stores they were issued shapeless, mish-mash uniforms comprised of khaki tunics displaying blue air force eagles on the shoulders and belted at the waist like a sack of potatoes. Blue cotton shirts, khaki shorts, long blue socks, black shoes and blue forage caps adorned with white flashes denoting their lowly status as trainees, completed the ensemble. In this army-cum-air force clobber they felt like neither one thing nor the other.

Every aerodrome in the country had a defense unit like the one at Ohakea. A trainee's job was to patrol the airfield perimeter and guard the dispersed aircraft against saboteurs and other undesirables.

For the next five months routine ruled Jim's life, with aerodrome defense duties being alternated with a continuation of pre-entry studies. One week the recruits would carry out ADU duties in the morning, then spend the afternoon on their pre-entry course. The following week they would study in the morning and do ADU in the afternoon. This appeared to be the extent of the air force's imagination when it came to providing variety.

Away from the base, Ohakea township offered few attractions, and the distance to the larger town of Bulls made it difficult to get to regularly. Square bashing and PT provided the only real distraction from the classroom and ADU.

Accepting he didn't have the qualifications to be a pilot or an observer, Jim applied himself to the pre-entry work needed for air gunnery. If he washed out, he feared he would be back in the army, but he passed all his exams.

When his posting to an Initial Training Wing in Rotorua came through, he discovered, that with no direct entry for air gunners, he had been re-mustered as a Wireless Operator/Air Gunner (WOP/AG) with the emphasis on wireless. He had mixed feelings. 'Not that I had any disinterest in radios,' he confessed. 'But I thought it would mean more time twiddling knobs than pulling a trigger. On the bright side, most wireless training took place in Canada.'

With the enticing thought that he was one step closer to fulfilling his dream, he headed to Rotorua with Paddy.

Chapter 2: The Making of An Airman

'What makes a good airman?'

A question put to Jim and his fellow recruits by the ITW station commander in his welcoming address. The answer: patriotism, discipline, physical fitness, clean living and technical skill, all attributes the young men would need in the not too distant future. It must have all sounded rather melodramatic for chaps who'd never been closer to the war than a Movie Tone newsreel or the front page of a newspaper.

Following the station commander's speech, Jim and Paddy spent the first day queuing for pay books, ration books and new identity cards. They were blood typed and given medical and dental checks before being marched to the stores where they were issued brand new air force blues. In contrast to the ill-fitting clobber they had made do with at ADU, ITW demanded a correct appearance at all times. The men were thoroughly scrutinized in their new uniforms, and if any alterations were needed it resulted in a quick trip to the station tailor.

Jim and his fellow recruits paraded feeling like proper air force bod at last, even if they were at the bottom of the heap, a fact made painfully obvious by the hated white flashes in their caps. They looked forward to the day they could throw them in the rubbish.

Most ITWs had fairly basic accommodation. Bedding usually consisted of straw filled palliasses atop creaky wooden bunks crammed into wooden huts that leaked cold breezes through a myriad of cracks and slits. Rotorua, however, had such a severe lack of on-base accommodation that recruits and training staff were boarded in local hotels and boarding houses staffed by civilians. Lectures were held at various places around town which meant a smart march from one location to the next. If you could tolerate the aroma of the Sulphur mud pools, Rotorua wasn't a bad posting.[1]

The new arrivals were formed into flights of thirty men, a number considered a practical number for lectures, and two men were elected in each flight to represent and exercise control over their group. In reality, this meant nothing more strenuous than marching the flight to meals and making sure everyone attended lectures on time. The system not only nurtured friendship and camaraderie but also built discipline and instilled the air force's traditions.

In the lecture rooms, seasoned instructors imparted their profound knowledge while inviting questions and testing their charge's attention with occasional discussions. Some subjects were taught with the use of film while others relied on a series of photographs.

---

[1] See Author's notes, Chapter 2 The making of an Airman

In the classroom, getting to grips with the complications of navigation, astronomy and Morse code left Jim wishing he'd been more diligent at school. He disliked Morse from the get-go. All those dits and dots ringing in his ears convinced him he didn't want anything to do with being a wireless operator.

The recruits practiced with all sorts of firearms. Thanks to his army training Jim displayed reasonable proficiency and he didn't have any problem with the rudimentary air gunnery training they received, which included skeet shooting at clay targets to improve their 'aiming off'.

'It basically meant shooting ahead of a moving target in the hope it flew into your line of fire,' Jim explained.

More excitingly, the young men were introduced to the Browning .303 machine gun which armed most British bombers and fighters of the time. They stuffed cotton wool in their ears and lay prone, firing at cardboard targets and sand bags.

Jim lamented, 'They didn't trust us to go anywhere near their precious aircraft, so we could only wonder what it might be like to fire a machine gun in flight. Letting loose a few rounds in the sky would have been a welcome distraction from the constant study.'

The recruits may not have been allowed up in an aircraft at that stage, but they were shown how to don a parachute harness. The instructor demonstrated the correct method on a hapless recruit.

'If you don't get it tight enough,' he grunted, yanking the straps tighter than necessary, 'you'll fall out of the bloody thing.'

He then demonstrated how to affix the Observer type parachute, a chunky brown canvas pack stuffed with yards of life preserving silk. Each of the pack's four sides had a handle, making it easier to grab in an emergency, and the large rip cord handle on the front could be positioned to the left or right side to accommodate both right and left-handed individuals. One simply had to rotate the pack to reverse the position of the handle. On the back of the pack there were two D rings that hooked onto the parachute harness by means of a pair of spring-loaded clips.

'Do we get a few practice jumps?' asked one chap.

'We're spending too much money on you to risk that sort of carry on,' snorted the instructor.

'But what if we have to use the bloody thing?' someone else demanded.

'Then it will be as a last resort, lad. You'll probably be dead before you get the chance.'

A nervous titter spread through the group, but the instructor didn't laugh and neither did Jim. Even before this scant training he had resolved never to bail out of an aeroplane. He had tried defying the laws of gravity once before when, as a boy, he'd jumped off the garden shed roof with a deployed umbrella. Needless to say, things had ended miserably when the umbrella folded inside out and dropped him to earth like a shot duck.

True, an old umbrella didn't have the aerodynamic characteristics of a parachute, which the instructor assured the recruits had a 99.9% chance of opening, but Jim still didn't trust them, and he certainly didn't fancy being the poor blighter who accounted for the remaining 0.1%. The thought of jumping from several thousand feet with only a thin patch of material between life and certain death only solidified his vow never to bail out.

The brief parachute training accounted for only a fraction of the curriculum taught on the intense ITW course. With so much crammed in, Jim could only recall one weekend of leave. But the hard work and swat paid off when he passed the course and received the news that he had been posted to a wireless school in Canada.

Although going to Canada had been Jim's dream, he harboured serious doubts about wireless training. But he didn't want to say anything in case it jeopardized his chances of making the trip. Besides, he couldn't let Paddy make the voyage alone. He would get to Canada, he decided, and then tell them what they could do with their wireless training.

On December 19 1942 all the men destined for Canada were issued rail passes and sent home on two weeks special leave to enjoy Christmas before travelling back to Auckland for embarkation.

Despite his mother being none too happy about her cherished son being sent half way around the world, she gave him a good Christmas. Not knowing when, or even if, she would ever see him again, she gave him her blessing and presented him with a greenstone to remind him of home and family.

Jim travelled with Paddy up to a transit depot in Auckland[2] where they joined a lot of other chaps marking time. They did the usual administration guff, had a final kit inspection, and then boarded a little Dutch ship called the Bloemfontein for a two-week voyage across the Pacific to San Francisco. From there they would take the train to Canada.

On 10 January 1943, Jim and Paddy set sail with 186 other men bound for Canada 'under training' for attachment to the Royal Canadian Air Force. Of their number, 41 (28%) would never see New Zealand again.

---

[2]   No.1 Depot at Parnell near Mechanics Wharf.

Chapter 3: Dots and Dashes

Registered to the United Netherlands Company, the *Bloemfontein* had served primarily as a cargo ship before the war but could accommodate about one hundred first class passengers. Not that Jim and Paddy were afforded any such luxury, being bunked in the bowels of the ship where the undulating motion of the waves induced a fair amount of sea sickness.

Having been at war with Japan for just over a year, the trainees were drafted in two-hour shifts each day to man the *Bloemfontein's* 3 and 4-inch guns plus several machine guns. As it turned out there were no submarine alerts and nothing to shoot at. Aside from gun duties, they were kept busy with bouts of physical training, card games and letter writing.

When they arrived in San Francisco they found themselves in a vibrant, colourful world where they had difficulty believing a war raged in Europe. They had just enough time to do some souvenir shopping before being loaded onto trucks to be carted down to the ferry for a short trip across to Oakland. There they boarded a train bound for Edmonton, Canada.

The train meandered through the fir tree covered mountains of Oregon and Washington before crossing into Canada with a stop in Vancouver. The young men from the far side of the world were struck by a winter landscape that looked dangerously bleak and majestic in the same instant. They were only in Vancouver long enough to stretch their legs before chugging off to Edmonton, Alberta with stops at Blue River, Banff, Jasper and Kamloops.

Sometimes the Rockies rose spectacularly against the bluest skies Jim had ever seen, while at other times their soaring peaks protruded theatrically through low-hanging clouds that choked the valleys and mountain passes in ethereal, vaporous mists. Canada was every bit as immense and as stunning as Jim had imagined.

A good insight regarding travel across Canada on the Canadian Pacific Railway can be garnered from an article printed in Contact magazine.

'*...Carriages on the C.P.R. are high and of generous proportions, which give an impression of space and roominess. Comparisons between these and the accommodation on the New Zealand railways, provokes speculation as to how many of the latter could be placed inside the C.P.R. carriages... The very best meals are served, but the drawback to the New Zealanders was having ice served with practically everything, like it or not. A feat for the uninitiated is to try and drink a glass of milk as the train negotiates a curve. In all probability, the man next door receives an unexpected drink instead.*

The first main stop was Banff Springs and we were allowed an hour's break to visit the famous Banff Springs Hotel. There the air was very different, cool, crisp and invigorating, whilst the scenery was marvellous. This afforded us the first opportunity of conversing with the Canadians and we were intrigued with their accent, although the speech of many Canadians is identical with that of the average New Zealander. There was some little amusement on both sides as our slang and their equivalent just did not mean the same thing, and at times there was a rather awkward silence.'

In Edmonton, Jim and Paddy marked time at No.3 "M" (Manning) Depot, waiting for their wireless school postings to come through. Manning stations were dispiriting places and Edmonton proved no exception. Newly arrived from the balmy conditions of a New Zealand summer, the trainees suddenly found themselves bundled up in heavy great coats and comical fur-lined hats with side flaps to protect their ears. They wore the flaps tied up most of the time because it looked less ridiculous than walking about impersonating Elmer J. Fudd.

A large indoor stadium, well heated by natural gas, suggested there would be plenty of time spent on physical exercise or drills, but everyone's worries were unfounded and they only ever gathered there to be entertained by visiting acts like American singer Kate Smith.

'What a big woman,' Jim recalled. 'She dwarfed the two MPs who minded her but she sang like an angel.'

In Canada, the Newzies, as the New Zealand airmen were called by the Canadians, couldn't believe the quality and quantity of food available, or that they could help themselves to as much as they liked, although it came with a warning not to pile their plates with more than they could eat. The beef steaks were best Jim had ever had.

'Later, when he got to England,' he reminisced, 'we found the beef rather tough and stringy, and we ungraciously complained. At least until we found out they were serving us horse meat! After that we politely declined whenever steak appeared on the menu.'

Jim and Paddy didn't have to hang around too long before they were posted to No.2 Wireless School in Calgary, Alberta. The prospect of wireless training had loomed like a black cloud over Jim's great adventure ever since Rotorua. By the time he reached the wireless school he would supposedly have had a good grounding in navigation and the basics of radio transmissions, but if he believed he might have been even minutely ready he was only fooling himself. He felt like a fraud, almost as if he'd stowed away to see the world and the consequences be damned.

En route to wireless school he and Paddy met Jock Biggar and Frank Jenkins, fellow Newzies who had been at Ohakea and Rotorua at the same time, although on different courses. They had also sailed on the *Bloemfontein,* but with so many men aboard it came as no surprise that they hadn't crossed paths with Jim and Paddy.

Jock, a cherub faced young farm hand from Wanganui, had a quiet, unassuming quality that fitted well with his ability to enjoy a drink and the occasional social smoke.[3] He and Jim formed a tight friendship that lasted until Jock's death two years later.

Frank Jenkins from New Plymouth had been cut from an entirely different cloth. At twenty-nine years old he had well and truly surpassed the average age (twenty-two) for aircrew selection. With eight years in the territorial army behind him, he applied for aircrew because he thought he might like the idea of flying. In civvy street his last job had been as a tractor serviceman with Dominion motors in Wellington.

Frank loved motorbikes and boasted proficiency in dismantling and assembling all makes and models without assistance, including magnetos, generators and lighting. He also loved the girls and got more dates and mail than everyone else put together. Girls from all over sent him an inexhaustible supply of chocolates and cigarettes, and his sister Elva pampered the daylights out of him.

The following excerpt is from a letter Frank wrote to Elva in 1943.[4]

'Dear Elva, I still have several Canadian girls write to me and now and then send me cigarettes. I don't roll my own anymore as the tobacco here isn't too good. Besides, I have got out of the habit of smoking hand-mades. Can you send a rich fruit cake as they go down very well? Put lots of fruit in it and it will stand up to the trip much better. A Waaf and I ate all the little chocolates.'[5]

One of the Medical Officers ungraciously suggested Frank suffered from emotionally instability and had no motivation, ambition or drive, but that overlooked the fact that Frank just didn't care for authority.

Later, when he and Jim were flying operationally, they were issued bulky Taylor Suits, but Frank decided he'd look better in one of the Irvine flying jackets the pilots wore. He argued that he needed something stylish to get dates with the Waafs.

When he found out gunners weren't entitled to such a jacket he stormed over to the store, kicked in the door and demanded one, or else! He nearly ended up on fizzer but he got his jacket. On more than one occasion he had his pay docked for being absent without leave. He didn't so much walk to the beat of his own drum as stomp.

The wireless school, located in the old Calgary Technical College situated at the top of a hill on 10th Street, sat surrounded by open fields. Flying, if anyone got that far, would be conducted from RCAF Shepard, about 9 miles

---

[3] One of Jock's medical reports stated that he displayed good motivation but needed PT.

[4] In 1998 Elva Loveridge gave Jim a collection of Frank's wartime correspondence.

[5] Frank Jenkins letter to Elva Loveridge, 1943.

from the college. There they would be flying in powerful North American Harvards, whose distinctive guttural engine noise could be heard from miles away. Jim would watch them grunt across the wide blue skies on clear days and wonder how he would cope when the time arrived.[6]

The trainees were quartered in wooden barracks at the west end of the college away from the classrooms in the main building whose daunting façade reflected the opulence of Victorian prosperity. The imposing building, dominated by twin towers either side of an ornate front entrance, bristled with hundreds of windows that stared down on Jim like accusing eyes. He felt like the place had his measure before he even walked through its ominous doors.

His plan to tell his instructors that he'd change his mind and didn't want to be a WOP came to naught when he had a portentous realization one night as he sat in the lounge watching Paddy and a few other blokes writing letters home.

'Crikey, Paddy,' he said. 'It's just occurred to me that if I tell them I don't want to be a WOP they might chuck me on the first boat home and it'll be me you're writing to.'

'Well, I've got enough letters to write without adding you to the list,' Paddy said.

So, Jim put his head down and hoped like heck the mysterious world of Morse would miraculously make sense.

Before the war minimal emphasis had been placed on wireless training, but the outbreak of hostilities created an urgent need for wireless operators to be part of bomber command aircrews, their main function being to maintain contact with base stations using continuous wave Morse Code.

With the introduction of more sophisticated equipment, and the complexities of overseas bombing operations, the initial twenty-week training period for wireless operators increased to twenty-eight weeks. Towards the end of the classroom theory, trainees were tested in aircraft simulators, small cubicles set up with aircraft wireless equipment that simulated the restricted work space in an aircraft. They sat in the cubicle and communicated by Morse Code with an instructor while in-flight conditions were replicated as best as possible. Canadian Gordon L. Diller attended No.2 Wireless School in the last months of the war:

Our instructors were all sergeants, well drilled in dealing with raw material, and very competent and efficient. The same instructors were with us for the duration of the course, and generally I look back on them with fondness ...I recall our Morse instructor would talk back and forth with great speed, in Morse, with instructors in other classrooms, while we were supposed to be practicing on our own. As we became more efficient, we began to understand

---

[6] See Author's note, Chapter 3 – Dots and Dashes. Note 1.

more and more so they switched from Morse to railway code, which none of us could understand. We were required to be able to send and receive at a speed of 20 words a minute, by the time of graduation, and could try 25, which most tried and passed, receiving an appropriate certificate.

A good indication of your Morse proficiency was when you were able to send and receive a message without having to consciously think about the process. I remember one sergeant in particular, although not for his instructing, as he was not one of ours, used to spend a lot of time in a small room at the back of our Morse practice room from which various noises would emit. For a while we were puzzled as to what he was doing. It turned out he was busily making heart-shaped, clear plastic pendants with the Royal Canadian (RCAF) crest embedded inside, which he sold to the trainees eager to impress the girls. He had a pretty good business going, whether surreptitiously or with the tacit consent of the authorities!

As we progressed through the training program, gradually increasing our Morse speed and accuracy, learning the intricacies of the procedure, and being able to recognize aircraft silhouettes in 1/50th of a second, the time finally came to introduce us to the type of equipment currently used on operations, how it was interconnected with its various peripherals and how to operate it.

Once we had mastered these operations, it was time to progress to the 'next-to-real-thing', the dreaded outstations. This involved a room filled with small, completely enclosed cubicles, into which the trainee (victim)crawled and the door was closed behind. Inside this dimly lit enclosure was all the equipment that would normally be encountered in a typical wireless operator's position in an aircraft - transmitter, receiver, bathtub-type Morse key, direction finding equipment, intercom, trailing antenna reel, and J switch (used for antenna switching).

Once inside, we carried out exercises simulating an actual mission, sending and receiving messages, taking bearing, logging each action and responding to demands for 'colour of the day' (supposedly from allied ground forces) which we responded to in great haste. Being tardy to this demand or responding with the incorrect colour resulted in a blast of simulated, friendly (?) anti-aircraft fire, which took the form of a loud cracker-type devise cunningly installed by the instruction staff and detonated with great glee, filling the cubicle with smoke and the smell of gunpowder.

Be assured this seldom happened more than once to a student - we were quick learners. The noise from the explosion was certainly audible throughout the room and the other cubicles and served to alert and motivate the other students to be speedy and accurate. This was probably one of the minor reasons for the dreaded label for outstations. But the main reason was if you

22

didn't do well here, your further progress, or even continuance, was in some doubt.' [7]

Jim struggled to get anywhere near the minimum receiving and sending speed of eighteen words per minute, while Paddy could bang out up to twenty-five, and he continued to suffer through the hours of lectures on radio theory, learning about IF circuits, oscillators and wires which, while interesting to a point, were hardly riveting.

Despite the dread of what might happen to them if they didn't pass the course, Jim and his friends remained in high spirits. Away from lectures they horsed around in the snow and indulged in long bike rides. They were entertained by very accommodating Canadian families who made a total fuss over them and were every bit as gracious and generous as Jim had been led to believe from the postcards and letters he'd read back home.

In Calgary, he met a girl named Margaret O'Neil whose family hosted him a number of times. Photographs of the time suggest they had a very close friendship.[8]

Most weekends the trainees were left to their own devices with a good supply of Canadian whiskey on hand, although Jim never touched the stuff. Away from the grind of training, he and his friends found plenty to amuse themselves. Bikes were provided on the station and they took the opportunity to explore the countryside and meet the locals[9]. Sometimes they'd take the train to Banff or Lake Louise and on one occasion they travelled to America, staying at Grand Coulee in Washington state.

In his typically Spivey way, Frank met a family in Grand Coulee who grew rather fond of him and ended up sending him truckloads of chocolates, cakes and cigarettes after he moaned to them about the tiresome lack of just about everything on base.

Jim also grabbed the opportunity to attend the Calgary Stampede, billed as the greatest cowboy show on earth, and on another occasion represented New Zealand against Australia in ice hockey.

'The only criteria for selection was being able to stay upright on the ice for more than two seconds at a time,' said Jim. 'Nobody told us were going to be the half-time entertainment during an important Canadian league playoff game. The crowd were witness to a spectacular shamble on ice. We even managed the pretense of a fight.'

In the shadows of the bright times lurked the ever-present bane of Jim's life - Morse Code. Once trainees managed to get through a good chunk of theory and some simulator exercises in the out-stations, they could look forward to

---

[7]Gordon L. Diller, 1945.

[8] See Author's notes, Chapter 3 – Dots and Dashes. Note 2.

[9] See Author's notes Chapter 3 – Dots and Dashes. Note 3.

getting up in the air to put it all into practice, but Jim couldn't even manage the out stations let alone being crammed into a Harvard or Fort Fleet packed with radio equipment. The very idea scared the living daylights out of him.

As it turned out he never flew during his time at wireless school. 'I had enough trouble tapping out Morse in a classroom let alone trying to concentrate while being bumped around in an aircraft,' he said.

Yet there are plenty of photographs of him and his mates in the snow bundled up in flying gear.

'That's because we had calisthenics every morning after breakfast,' he recalled. 'And we had to wrap up in our Teddy Bear suits because of the cold.'

Jock and Frank feared no better at Morse and it became painfully obvious that none of them were going to help win the war with a wireless set. Fearing their failure would mean a transfer back to the army, they pro-actively requested re-mustering as straight air gunners. They forwarded their requests to their C.O. who seemed only too glad to get rid of them.

Signing off their Form 5044s (R.C.A.F. Suspension Reports) the C.O. highlighted their inability with Morse. In Jock's case, he also mentioned that being left handed, Jock appeared handicapped by difficulty in writing while Jim and Frank received reports that suggested they had tried hard but had no inclination in that direction.

While they were pleased to leave the world of Morse behind them, Jim and his friends were even happier to learn the air gunner's course lasted a mere six weeks, which meant they'd be operational a lot sooner. Nobody bothered telling them that that might not be something to look forward to.

Jim hoped to be posted to the same AGGTS (Air Gunnery Ground Target School) as Jock and Frank but when his posting to No.2 AGGTS at RCAF Trenton, Ontario came through at the beginning of August 1943 he found he would be going alone.

'Better get yourself a French dictionary,' Jock said. 'They speak froggie there,'

'And go and do something useful,' Paddy said. 'I expect to see an air gunner's wing the next time I see you.'

Everyone put on their best stiff upper lips but nothing could alleviate the gloomy goodbyes that had to be said. They agreed to keep in touch, but in reality, they had no idea when, or if, they'd ever see each other again.

Home on leave before departure to ITW, Rotorua (Kirk Collection).

Home on embarkation leave, Dec 1942 (Kirk Collection).

Preparing for kit inspection prior to embarking for Canada (Kirk Collection).

Taking a break in the Rockies en route to Edmonton. (Kirk Collection).

27

Left: Stop over in Banff. Right: Wireless School accommodation (photos Kirk Collection).

Souvenir from San Francisco, in the snow at No. 2 Wireless School, Calgary. (Kirk Collection).

Chapter 4: Taking Up Arms

#2 AGGTS[10] at Trenton, Ontario opened in April 1942. The academic school remained in operation until October 1943, during which time it graduated 1,900 air-gunner trainees.

Jim had already covered the basics of air gunnery at ITW but at Trenton he got down to the nitty gritty. But before he or any of his fellow trainees could be trusted to fire live rounds from an aircraft in flight they first had to learn about their weapons and shooting tactics, and at an Air Gunnery Ground Training School, as the name suggests, their feet remained firmly planted on the ground. Regular clay shooting encouraged good hand-eye coordination and many hours were spent on turret manipulation and getting familiar with a number of different gun turrets including the Bristol Mk III, the Bolton Paul, and especially the Fraser Nash which equipped most RAF heavy bombers at the time. Jim, being a practical type, found this stuff right up his alley.

Part of the gunnery course involved target practice in turrets mounted on rudimentary wooden platforms that tracked along on wheels as the trainees sat inside firing 850 rounds at targets placed at a distance of 25 yards. 1100 rounds were fired at stationary cardboard cut-outs representing German night fighters placed at a distance of 250 yards.

Like clay shooting, it promoted hand-eye coordination, but as far as preparing them for combat, Jim thought it counted for little. Cardboard cut-outs had the endearing quality of not being able to shoot back.

A couple of weeks after arriving at Trenton, Jim heard that Jock had been posted to #1 AGGTS at RCAF Jarvis, Ontario and at about the same time Frank turned up at Trenton.

'Bloody typical,' he grumbled. 'Why couldn't they have posted us at the same bloody time?'

'That's the air force for you, Frank.'

'Been up yet?' he asked Jim.

'Flying? Fat chance.'

'Too bad. If you'd hung around at wireless a couple more weeks you might have got the chance.'

'Really?'

'Yeah, I got a couple of hours. Bit of a jolly while I stooged around waiting for a posting. Don't worry, Winkie, you didn't miss out on much.'

The fact that Frank had already taken to the air, albeit briefly, gave Jim the resolve to put the bind of the armourer's lectures and ground firing exercises behind him and get up in the Fairey Battles that awaited him at his next posting

---

[10] Air Gunnery Ground Training School.

– No.3 Air Gunnery School at RCAF MacDonald near Portage Le Prairie, Manitoba.

Jim's air gunner course at RCAF MacDonald began on 20 September 1943. Nothing in his training had promised as much excitement as firing a machine gun from an aircraft in flight.

The intake comprised a few Kiwis, Aussies and Englishmen who, like Jim, were wireless school drop-outs, but the majority were Canadians who'd arrived directly from the RCAF Centre in Quebec.

There were a couple of corporals and a sergeant who'd transferred straight from ground duties but most of the trainee gunners were still lowly LACs with the white propeller blade insignia on their sleeves and the hated white flash on their forage caps. On more than one occasion an exasperated instructor could be heard to yell, 'You with the white flash, the cream of the air force, you've gone sour!' It felt like it would be a long time before any of them would be able to swap the flash and their detestable rank for a set of brand-new sergeant stripes.

Unlike the wooden slat huts he'd lived in previously, Jim's accommodation at MacDonald turned out to be a corrugated-iron Nissan hut. His roommates were mostly Canadians who liked to live in a furnace with all the windows closed. The Kiwis and Aussies struggled to cope with this and promptly opened all the windows again, only for the Canucks, who could only tolerate the cooler air for a few minutes, to slam them shut once more and stoke the heat up even higher. Jim found this bizarre because he thought Canadians would have been well used to the cold.

The huts generated a generous amount of static electricity, accentuated by the metal framed beds, and when the lights went out there would often be a spectacular display of fireworks and a descent zap as chaps climbed into bed.

Jim made good friends with a couple of the Canucks, Bill Lamb and Edward Kisilowsky. As nobody could ever get their tongues around Ed's surname, they just called him the Mad Russian. Both Bill and Ed were only 19 when they were later killed on air operations.

Day one of the course saw the trainees sorted into groups for more lessons and lectures, much of which had been encountered at wireless school or ITW. Rehashing what Jim considered elementary stuff taxed his patience, but it needed to be covered for the Canadians who'd come directly from the RCAF Centre.

Periods of physical fitness were undertaken in a hangar specially converted for the task. It was a gloomy place in the autumn but it beat doing a march or a run in the frigid conditions outside.

Aircraft recognition, which had been discussed briefly at ITW and wireless school, received more in-depth analysis with dozens of aircraft silhouettes, friendly or otherwise, having to be committed to memory. As part of the end-of-term exam the trainees were shown 150 silhouettes and given no longer than 10 seconds in which to correctly identify each one. Taking any longer in a combat situation could mean the difference between life and death.

There were also technical details to memorize, such as the armament of the enemy aircraft. Jim considered this interesting but rather pointless when it came to facing a German fighter. To have any hope of shooting one down he would probably have to wait until it got close enough for him to count the rivets on its wings, and that would be nigh impossible. German fighters were equipped with 20 mm or 30 mm canons capable of extinguishing his young life from a range of 1,000 yards, while his .303 Brownings were only effective up to 600 yards. His primary job would be to identify enemy aircraft and alert his skipper to take evasive action before the German pilot spotted them.

Tremendous excitement arose when the trainees learnt they were finally advancing to air-to-air shooting from a Fairey Battle II. A sturdy beast, providing a solid platform for learning the fundamentals of air gunnery, the Fairey Battle had come to the end of its operational life as an effective fighting machine. It had been proven obsolete as early as 1940 when in May that year, as part of the Advanced Striking Force, Battles of 12 Squadron had been given the unenviable task of destroying bridges across the Maastricht River in France as part of a rearguard action to hold off the advancing German troops.

The Battles were hopelessly outclassed by both Luftwaffe fighters and accurate anti-aircraft fire. Not a single one survived. Posthumous Victoria Crosses were awarded to Flying Officer Garland and his observer, Sergeant Gray, for their gallantry. Their gunner, a lowly LAC named Reynolds, went to his death with them and received nothing.

'A good reason to get a set of sergeant stripes on my arm,' Jim remarked many years later.

Unlike the standard version of the Battle in which the gunner fired from an open cockpit, the Battle II had an enclosed rotating turret to provide protection against the elements.

Jim had to reign in his eagerness to start firing live ammunition in the air because the new boys weren't trusted with anything more dangerous than a cine camera attached to a Vickers Gas Operated (VGO) machine gun for their orientation flights

After gearing up Jim made his way with the other trainee gunners to the gunnery flight crew room where they drew their parachute harnesses, a vital piece of equipment.

'What about a parachute?' someone asked.

The request met an exasperated groan. 'Don't they tell you guys anything? Parachutes are in the aircraft.'

Jim wandered off with his harness draped over his shoulder to check the blackboard and see who he had been paired with. The usual method had two trainees go with a long-suffering staff pilot whom Jim suspected would have preferred to be flying ops rather than wet nursing a bunch of eager beavers who thought they were the cat's whiskers. He found his name chalked up alongside Ed Kisilowsky, The Mad Russian.

They plodded out to the flight line bundled up in layers of kapok. The Battles waited with engines running and props lashing out a wild turbulence of wind and noise. Common sense dictated an approach from the rear of the aircraft but apparently from time to time some bods forgot. The instructors were only too pleased to repeat the gruesome story of an unfortunate trainee who had walked into a spinning prop.

'If you're going to be that bloody stupid, don't expect us to pick up the pieces.'

The pilot of their Battle was eager to crack on and gave his passengers the hurry up. They ducked under the wing and struggled into the cramped fuselage via the entry hatch in the floor. Ed climbed aboard first and went into the turret while Jim squirmed to make himself comfortable in the cramped fuselage. Before he had a chance to get settled, the pilot let the brakes off. The Battle trundled down the runway with Jim and Ed hanging onto whatever they could find.

Up until the moment they surged into the air, Jim hadn't considered the possibility of air sickness. But as soon as the wheels left the ground and the Battle began to climb not even the enchanting sight of the Manitoba landscape, spreading out below, as if to remind him of the fertile patchwork of the Canterbury plains, was enough to distract him from a swelling nausea in his stomach.

In level flight he could tolerate the hideous qualm but when the pilot banked or hit an air pocket, he began to feel seriously ill. Fortunately, it didn't result in anything messy.

'Give it a go,' Ed cried over the noise of the engine, as he slid himself out of the turret and into the fuselage. Looking as grey as a ghost, Jim gave him the thumbs up and struggled around him into the turret where he discovered all the classroom theory and ground turret exercises in the world suddenly counted for very little. What might have been a relatively simple exercise on the ground became a completely different ball game in the three-dimensional environment of air combat.

'I dare say my first attempts with the cine camera produced nothing more than a lot of shaky footage of empty sky,' he laughed.

The trainees never saw the results of their cine gun exercises. Their instructors viewed the footage and then stuck it away in some dark vault. A rather poor show, considered Jim.

When they were declared competent to handle live ammunition, the real training began. Over the following weeks things settled into a familiar pattern as they checked the blackboard each morning to see who they had been paired

32

to fly with, drew a few hundred rounds of ammunition from the armoury, and made their way out to the aircraft lugging a hefty ammo box between them.

Air to air shooting had another Battle tow a drogue, which looked like a long windsock, while the trainee's pilot approached from different angles for the gunners to get off their shots. Their efforts were recorded by dye-coloured ammunition. Each gunner used a different colour dye so there could be no argument over which bullet holes belonged to whom. With every fifth round being a tracer that glowed in flight, the gunners could track the trajectory of their shots. Later, on ops, the norm would be one round of tracer followed by three standard rounds and then an armour piercing round.

The two trainee gunners took turns with the gun. The first man into the turret had the privileged if somewhat overstated title of No.1 gunner. After blazing away at the drogue, he vacated the position for the No.2 gunner. The flights usually took place over a lake so any stray bullets would fall harmlessly into the water. In winter, the lake would blend seamlessly with the surrounding snow-covered prairies making it impossible to see. Some of the trainees wondered if the staff pilots even knew where they were over an often-featureless landscape.

Jim and Ed flew together on their first live firing exercise. Ed, a calm, competent bloke, always prepared to engage first in any new exercise, took the No.1 position. Jim sat huddled in the cramped confines of the fuselage with a nauseating concoction of cordite, petrol and hot oil filling his nostrils as the Vickers machine gun rat-tat-tatted over the noise of the engine.

When his turn came, he struggled into the turret with a disturbing qualm in his stomach. He found it bad enough trying to load the guns, clear blockages, and fire at a moving target let alone doing it while battling to keep his breakfast down. With the pilot seemingly unable, or unwilling, to fly straight and level, the canvas bag that was attached to the gun for catching spent ammunition links soon became his new best friend. He let off a few bursts at the drogue with no concern about accuracy. He just wanted to get back on the ground. Ed thought it a great joke.

Strangely, the moment they landed, Jim's air sickness disappeared. He decided not to mention it in case they grounded him, but a lot of green faces in the flight crew room afterwards suggested he hadn't been the only casualty. As the weeks went by, he managed his air sickness to some degree by not eating prior to flying, and consequently he made a much better fist of hitting the target.

Despite having reached its use-by date as a front-line fighting machine, Jim developed a fondness for the Battle's pugnacious reliability, and as he built up his flying hours his confidence and ability grew. He had been at MacDonald for a month when one evening, while having a snooze in the lounge, someone kicked him in the leg.

'Oi, Winkie, you lazy little so and so.'

33

He opened his eyes to find Frank standing over him with a devilish grin.

'Christ,' Frank laughed, 'I seem to be following you all over Canada, Winkie.'

'Frank, great to see you. When did you get in?'

'This afternoon. But you know this lot, we've been doing the usual admin rubbish most of the day.'

He sat down and lit a cigarette. 'Have you heard from Jock or Paddy?'

'Nothing since I last saw you at Trenton.'

'They could be anywhere,' Frank said. 'Who knows how these things work. Bloody air force.'

A couple of weeks later, on a miserable rainy afternoon, with all flying cancelled, they were in the lounge enjoying some free time when the door swung open and Jock walked in with a big cherub grin on his face. 'I didn't think I'd see you blokes again,' he laughed.

'Jock,' Jim said. 'Where the heck did you get to?'

'They sent me to Jarvis for ground school,' he said. 'What's happening?'

'Nothing at the moment,' Frank said. 'But usually when it's raining, they drag us into a hangar for a bout of PT or another bloody VD[11] lecture.'

'Crikey Winkie, you must be almost set for graduation,' Jock said.

'I hope so. I can't wait to finish this training.'

'That bad?'

'No, the training's fine. I just don't want the war to end before it's too late to see any action.'

'There'll be plenty of action where I intend going,' Frank said forthrightly.

'Where's that?' Jim asked.

'Bomber Command of course,' Frank said. 'Lancasters with any luck. That's what I want.'

Some of the boys on Jim's course had already discussed life after training, and the Lancaster seemed to be everybody's preference. They'd heard a lot of encouraging stories about its reliability. What they hadn't been told about was the terrible loss rate among Lancaster crews.

However, before they could get anywhere near a Lancaster, or any other type of bomber for that matter, they had to finish training. On the ground, they faced exams on a variety of subjects including guns, pyros and ammo, plus practical tests on turrets and guns, and an oral exam on sighting. Other exams covered signals and aircraft recognition. A total of 1000 marks were up for grabs. Most of them managed a comfortable pass mark of between 600 – 800. Many of the subjects only required a 50% pass mark.

Trainees were also assessed on qualities of character and leadership for prospective gunnery instructor's roles but Jim didn't fear so well. He was deemed 'NOT AT ALL SUITABLE'. Not that it concerned him in the

[11] See Author's note, Chapter 4 – Taking Up Arms.

slightest. He wanted to be operational, not instructing. By the time graduation arrived he felt confident that he would make a valuable contribution to any crew.

The night before their passing out parade the graduating gunners enjoyed a magnificent banquet. It would be the last time they'd have to wear the propeller insignia on their sleeves and the dreaded white flashes on their caps.[12] The next day the wing commander greeted every one of them in turn with a salute, a handshake, and a few words of encouragement and presented them with their wing. Considering a course graduated every two or three weeks, Jim wondered how the wing commander managed to maintain his enthusiasm and keep his congratulatory remarks so sounding fresh and original.

'He made each of us feel like the most important person in the world.'

Jim graduated on 29 October 1943, 18 months since his enlistment at Ohakea, and two and half years since walking into the recruiting office in Christchurch. Getting his air gunner wing and sergeant stripes marked the greatest achievement of his young life.

The only niggle came after graduation when some of the Brits, Kiwis and Aussies complained about the special treatment the Canadians received. Not only were they paid more, but at the graduation they received a more impressive air gunner brevet with a larger more stylized wing as opposed to the cheap standard issue version handed out to everyone else.

They also received preferential treatment when commissions were handed out. Everyone had been encouraged to apply for a commission but usually only one or two from each course were considered. However, on Jim's course almost all the Canadians received a commission, including his mates Bill Lamb and Ed Kisilowsky who were both commissioned as pilot officers.

Jim hadn't bothered applying for a commission but he did later acquire a New Zealand air gunner's brevet that was equally as stylish as the Canadian one. He had it until it got buried in someone's back garden, but that's another story.

The newly qualified gunners headed to the nearest photographic studio to have their new hard-earned station in life preserved for posterity. The photographs in Jim's leather-bound photo album depicted young men in immaculate uniforms, all exuding an intrepid confidence and devilish charm. In a tragic indictment of the consequences of war, many of the photographs were later poignantly marked with a tiny cross denoting those of his friends who were killed, including Bill Lamb and Ed Kisolowsky.

After graduation, many of the newly promoted air gunners were posted to Y Depot in Halifax, Nova Scotia for embarkation to the UK. It turned out to be a posting in name only. While they may have been attached to Y Depot, they

---

[12] At one time a rumour had spread that the white flash in the cap was a warning that the wearer had VD.

ended up hanging around MacDonald for a couple of more weeks until receiving orders to travel to a TP (Trainee Post) in Halifax.

Jim said another goodbye to Jock and Frank. Once again, he had no idea when, or if, he would see them again.

'Of course, you will,' Frank laughed. 'Bad pennies, mate. Bad pennies.'

The huts at No. 2 Wireless School in the winter of 1943. (Both photos: Kirk Collection).

In the background a snow clearing truck clears paths between the Huts at No.2 Wireless School.

The main building at No.2 Wireless School. Airmen unknown. (Kirk Collection).

Jim (left) with fellow trainees and their gracious host Marjorie Marks. (Kirk Collection).

L-R: Jock Biggar, Jim, Paddy Giles (kneeling) & Snow Robertson.(Kirk Collection).

Everybody in flying gear except Paddy Giles. No.2 Wireless School. (Kirk Collection).

Jim with his friend Margaret O'Neil in Calgary, Alberta, 1943. (Kirk Collection).

Frank Jenkins (left) with friends, Calgary 1943. (Kirk Collection).

Geared up. No.2 Wireless School, Calgary, Alberta. (Kirk Collection).

41

Jim's best friend, Jock Biggar. killed on air operations, 12.09.1944 (Kirk Collection).

Paddy Giles and Jim. No.2 Wireless School in the Spring of 1943. (Kirk Collection).

Frank Jenkins, 1943, Gunnery & Bombing School (Kirk Collection).

Left: Ed Kisilowsky. Right: Bill Lamb Both were aged 19 years at the time and were KIA in 1944 (photos Kirk Collection).

Left: Jim & Ed Kisilowsky 1943 Right: Jim & unknown friend 1943 (photos Kirk Collection).

44

Chapter 5: A Strange Sort of Marriage

Jim boarded the *Mauretania* in Halifax, Nova Scotia and sailed for England. Despite making the voyage without convoy protection, the ship arrived unscathed in Liverpool nine days later on 2 December.

He boarded a train crowded with Kiwis and Aussies for the long journey to the south coast where Brighton's Grand and Metropole Hotels had been taken over by No. 11 (RAAF) PDRC and No. 12 (RNZAF) PDRC.[13]

The impressive façade of the Grand Hotel lived up to the name but the same couldn't be said for its wartime interior. The plush carpets, tapestries, velvet drapes and elegant fittings had been cleared out long ago. The airmen walked about on bare floorboards, and swank hotel beds had been replaced by standard RAF bunks. At night, drab blackout curtains hid windows crisscrossed with air raid tape. Any ideas Jim entertained of being served high-end meals in the once posh dining room were quickly dispelled. With typical military austerity, the dining room had been turned into an uninspiring mess with long wooden tables and bench seating.

Jim faced the uncertainty of not knowing how long he'd be in Brighton. It could be days, weeks, or months before his posting came through. The movements and transitions of men in wartime England seemed to have no rhyme or reason. On the bright side, he had a reunion with Paddy who had been in Brighton since October waiting for a posting to an Advanced Flying School.

They found limited entertainment in the seaside town. The beach, plugged with mines, and littered with barbed wire, had been off limits for years and the pier remained out of bounds, even though the threat of invasion had long since passed. They visited the Royal Pavilion and were occasionally ordered to stride out on a cherry march through the tight, meandering cobble-stoned alleys of

---

[13] (RAAF) Personnel Despatch and Reception Centre was the receiving station for Royal Australian Air Force aircrew arriving in the UK. 11 P.D.R.C relocated from Bournemouth to Brighton in May 1943, occupying both the Grand and Metropole Hotels. The unit also occupied facilities at RAF Charmy Down, Somerset. 11 P.D.R.C closed in March 1946.

No 12 (RNZAF) Personnel Despatch and Reception Centre was the receiving station for Royal New Zealand Air Force aircrew arriving in the UK. It was established in Brighton at the end of May 1943 and existed alongside 11 P.D.R.C in the Grand and Metropole hotels. It closed down at the end of May 1944 but reopened again in October 1944 before finally closing on January 21st 1946.

the old town with its dainty teahouses, but most of the time they were left to their own devices to annul the boredom.

They had some excitement one day when a German aircraft crash-landed on the beach. They had heard stories about marauding German bombers and fighters randomly dropping bombs or strafing towns along the south and east coasts of England, and Brighton had suffered an attack by a Focke Wulf 190 earlier that year, but seeing a crippled German aircraft stranded on the beach brought them much closer to the reality of the war.

'You chaps will add to that one for us, I dare say,' an elderly lady in the crowd of curious onlookers declared.

Any festive plans they may have made were scarpered when Paddy's posting came through two days before Christmas. Fortunately, this time Jim found the wretchedness of yet another goodbye tempered by Frank's arrival. He had finally graduated his air gunner's course after being laid up for two weeks with a nasal condition.

At Brighton, they were given the opportunity to select which command they would prefer to serve in – Coastal Command, Bomber Command, or the 2nd Tactical Airforce.

'Coastal Command means we'll be looking for bloody U-boats,' Frank said. 'We can do without that nonsense. And Second Tac supports the army. Precision targets. Bugger that. We want to be dishing it out to Jerry where it hurts. Right on his front doorstep. Bomber Command is what we want.'

'We were blissfully unaware of the high casualty rate among Bomber Command crews,' Jim reflected later. 'And we were stupid enough to want some *real* action.'

On 11 January 1944, Jim and Frank were posted to No.11 Operational Training Unit at Westcott, Buckinghamshire. They were excited because 11 OTU meant they'd likely end up with a posting to a front-line squadron in the European theatre of operations, with a good chance of getting on Lancasters. If they survived OTU.

On his first morning at Westcott Jim found himself in a hangar with men of all ranks and aircrew trades. The station commander, a veteran Wingco[14], rattled off a few housekeeping notices before announcing, 'Right, sort yourselves out. Anyone not in a crew by the end of the day will have it done for them.'

This left Jim bemused and baffled. He'd assumed that the air force, being the air force, would assign him to a crew and he'd like it or lump it. Instead, he was left to mill around like a kid on his first day at school. With all the schools he had been shunted around as a child, he didn't find it an unfamiliar situation, but unfortunately, he couldn't go and bunk at the nearest playground this time.

---

[14] Wing Commander.

Like everyone else, he wanted a good crew. But how could he tell a good pilot from one that might nose dive him into the ground the first time up? Or what distinguished a good navigator from one who couldn't find his way out of a paper bag? As Lancaster bomb aimer Miles Tripp said, 'A good flying partner was far more important than a good wife. You couldn't divorce your crew, and you could die if one of them wasn't up to his job at the critical moment.'[15]

There were any number of reasons why blokes got together. It could be as simple as a navigator and a bomb-aimer having met in the mess and deciding to crew up because it just seemed like a good idea. Or perhaps a pair of air gunners had trained together and didn't want to severe their friendship. The mysteries of human nature were unfathomable.

At these giant marriage markets pilots and navigators often teamed up first due to the nature of their jobs, and perhaps because of their loftier status and pay rates, which were higher than other aircrew trades. This irked some of the lesser paid aircrew who considered that regardless of rank or trade they were all taking the same risks and therefore they should all be remunerated equally. Jim remained philosophical on the matter. He wouldn't have wanted the responsibility of getting a fully bombed up aircraft off the ground, or be relied upon to get it to the target on time.

Once a pilot and nav had found each other they selected the rest of the crew, usually starting with the best bomb aimer they could find. Unsurprisingly, gunners often found themselves at the bottom of the pecking order.[16]

Jim, daunted at the prospect of having to approach anyone, was debating how best to go about the business when a tall flight sergeant bearing NZ pilot wings on his chest approached him and stuck out a hand.

'Ian Blance,' he said. 'I'm looking for gunners.'

Ian, twenty-one, hailed from New Plymouth where had attended New Plymouth Boys High and New Plymouth Technical College before going to work as a projectionist at the Mayfair Theatre. He had enlisted in the RNZAF at Rongotai in 1942 as an air observer but had requested re-mustering to pilot training after learning that his half-brother, a pilot, had been killed in a flying accident while instructing on a Liberator conversion unit. After a brief time at Whenuapai he went to ITW, Rotorua and from there to No.2 EFTS[17] in Ashburton before progressing to No.1 SFTS[18] at Wigram where he earned his wings in 1943. After arriving in the UK, he attended No.14 Advanced Flying Unit in Fraserburgh, Aberdeenshire before his posting to Westcott. His had been a typical transition from civvy street to RNZAF pilot.

'Have you got yourself a crew yet?' he asked Jim.

---

[15] Miles Tripp, The Eighth Passenger, p.9.
[16] See Author's notes, Chapter 5 – A Strange Sort of Marriage.
[17] Elementary Flying Training School
[18] Service Flying Training School.

'No,' Jim replied. 'You're the first person I've spoken to.'

'Well, I found myself a nav and bomb aimer in the mess last night. Both Kiwi boys. They're hunting down a wireless op. Would you like to join us?'

'Of course.'

Ian looked around the crowded hangar. 'What about another gunner? Is there anyone you'd like to have with us?'

Jim thought this unusual as he'd been led to believe that only a rear gunner would be required during operational training, because the Wellington bombers that equipped most operational training units had no mid-upper turret for a second gunner. Ian admitted that he'd been under the impression he'd be assigned a second gunner when the crew arrived at a heavy conversion unit where they would be flying a four-engine bomber equipped with a mid-upper.

'But I've been told to select two gunners,' he shrugged. 'So, is there anyone?'

'Frank Jenkins. He's a good bloke. We trained together in Canada.'

'Go grab him before someone else does.'

Frank readily came on board, although he had a more morbid explanation as to why they would be training with two gunners.

'Big loss rate probably. Gunners always get the chop first. Must have prompted the big wigs to push twice as many of us through.' At thirty-years of age Frank would be the old man of the crew.

The navigator and bomb aimer Ian had met in the mess the previous night turned out to be a couple of Maori boys from the North Island of New Zealand - Colin Grieg and Inia Maaka, or Mac as he preferred to be called. They had both entertained ambitions of being pilots but had washed out for different reasons

Colin had attended No.3 EFTS at Harewood in Christchurch, notching up 18 hours of dual instruction under three different instructors but had difficulty getting the hang of it. His first instructor found him heavy handed with very little air sense and no idea at any moment of his proximity to the ground.

His slow progress prompted a change of instructor who found nothing favourable either. He reported that Colin had been unable to do a correct landing, having no idea whether he might overshoot or not. He levelled out far too high above the ground and had a nervous disposition and became very jumpy when close to the ground. The instructor certainly didn't think he would make the grade to fly solo.

The Chief Flying Instructor took Colin up for a final attempt and Colin impressed him enough to earn a reprieve. The CFI ordered some more dual instruction because, in his opinion, Colin could still make the grade if he really tried. Unfortunately, Colin's jitters returned and the axe fell.

'I just couldn't keep the bloody plane from going wobbly during landings,' he confessed. 'Just not cut out for it.'

He took his washout without complaint and requested that he be permitted to remain in aircrew selection.

'If it's any consolation,' Ian told him, 'I force landed during my training ... after a mid-air collision.' He read the speculative faces looking at him. 'Don't worry, I pulled it off perfectly.'

Mac came from Napier and had done his initial training at No.2 EFTS at Tairei where the cold blustery weather hardly made it ideal for open-cockpit flying in a Tiger Moth.

Jim didn't discuss Mac's flying experiences with him much and always thought a surplus of pilots rather than a lack of flying ability accounted for his re-mustering to bomb aimer. Mac's daughter Margaret, however, had a different explanation.

'Mac told me that he initially trained as a pilot, but when he took his final exam, he still had a hangover from partying the night before and landed his plane on the wrong runway (much to the disgust of his examiner). He tried to pretend that he had misunderstood the examiner's instructions, but to no avail.'

Mac had had a girl back home whom he'd asked to wait for him, but she'd turned him down because she didn't want to be known as 'the girl he left behind.' He showed himself to be a gentle giant. A peacemaker. If a raucous ever broke out in the mess and things looked like getting ugly, Mac would just have to put his hand on the shoulder of the instigator and that put an end to any would-be brawl. Everyone respected him and nobody wanted to get a thumping from him.

A further description of him comes from Harry Yates, DFC, in his book, *Luck And A Lancaster.*

'His was a voice full of droll humour, and his sentiments those of a natural team man. He said he had volunteered like most air bombers (their official title) hoping to fight this war as a pilot. He won a place at an Elementary Flying Training course but it wasn't to be. Bombing school followed. But he clearly loved the job and there wasn't a hint of second best.

As he talked, my impressions of him grew ever more favourable. No Englishman I'd met was so sincere and guileless about himself. Mac was simply a stranger to the inner tensions and vanities that make liars of the rest of us. He was mightily proud of his people who, I thought, must be formidable opponents in war if they were like this chap. He had the heart of a lion. I don't think he was afraid of anything or anyone. He had no need to be because he was built like a bunker. I began to see in him a military paragon. I felt his loyalty would be a rich prize, if one deserved it.' [19]

---

[19] Harry Yates, Luck and A Lancaster, Pg. 64-65.

Mac and Colin recruited Fred Climo as their wireless operator. A dark-haired chap possessing dashing good looks, he wore an 'S' brevet,[20]on his chest, a 'fistful of sparks'[21]on his sleeve and New Zealand flashes on his shoulders, but more impressively he displayed a ribbon for the Naafi gong.[22]

Fred came from Timaru and seemed to Jim to be a man of the world. He had left home at seventeen to work as a fisherman on the Timaru wharves before sailing to the UK to join the Merchant Navy where he found more than his fair share of adventure as a gunner on the Russian convoys. After being torpedoed on two occasions and sunk by a mine on another, he decided to join the air force.

After gunnery training at No.10 Air Gunnery School in Barrow-in-Furness, he attended to No. 2 radio school in Yatesbury, followed by a posting to an observer's Advanced Flying Unit in Wigtown, Scotland before being posted to 11 OTU.

There were introductions and handshakes all round. They were about to start the most critical and intensive phase of their training.

---

[20] The 'S' brevet denoted Signals. Because of greater specialization in aircrew trades wireless operators ceased having to do take a gunnery course and were reclassified as signallers.

[21] A cloth insignia depicting a fist holding three lightning bolts which was worn on the upper sleeve by wireless operators.

[22] 1939 - 1943 Star. A man wearing this had already seen active service.

Chapter 6: A Hazardous Environment

The newly assembled crews were in awe of their instructors, even if the instructors didn't necessarily reciprocate those feelings. Most of them would have preferred to be back on ops rather than fostering a bunch of sprogs. Some of them were Late Arrivals, men who had been shot down over occupied territory and had evaded capture to make their way back to the UK, but most were tour-expired veterans, having flown thirty or more operations. The majority had yet to reach the ripe old age of thirty, but they seemed mature beyond their years. Ribbons denoting a DSO[23], a DFC[24] or a DFM[25] were nothing out of the ordinary.

The instructors were dubbed 'screened' which Jim assumed meant they were being screened from operations and the possibility of injury or death. At least at the hands of the Germans. With half the flying at OTU being done at night it could be a hazardous environment.

For the first two weeks Ian trained on the twin-engine Vickers Wellington while the rest of the crew underwent further ground training in their respective trades and endured more lectures, including the military's perennial hobby-horse, venereal disease.

'It must have been someone's idea of a joke to always have these VD lectures and the accompanying slide shows just before lunch,' Jim laughed when he reflected on the horrendous nature of some of the more graphic pictures.

Far less appalling were the escape and evasion lectures where crews were introduced to an amazing assortment of escape aids designed by the boffins at MI9.[26] The Germans had long since discovered the true nature of many of MI9's devices but there were still some useful items in the active inventory. One of the most proven aids was the Pandora Box, a two-piece acetate container measuring about 4 x 5 inches which was designed to fit into a battledress pocket. Crammed with items such as a dried fruit bar, wakey-wakey (Benzedrine) pills, water purification tablets, chewing gum, liver tablets, matches, a fishing line, a rubber bag for collecting water, and a small brass compass, it could be a life-saver for a downed airman during his first 48 hours on the run.

Of course, nobody thought they would get shot down. That happened to the other unfortunate chap.

---

[23] Distinguished Service Order

[24] Distinguished Flying Cross

[25] Distinguished Flying Medal

[26] The branch of military intelligence charged with aiding and abetting downed airmen and prisoners-of-war.

The boffins had dreamed up such an array of compasses that one could be forgiven for thinking they had an unhealthy predilection for them. They came in a variety of disguises, including pocket clips, pencils, fountain pens, battle dress belt buckles and even collar studs. The latter were discontinued early in the war because they were complicated and expensive to manufacture. The most common of the hidden compasses was one that screwed into a standard battledress button.[27]

A cheaper, more simplistic compass used a razor blade marked with an arrow. When the blade was floated in water, the arrow would spin to true north. But unless the user had a puddle or a bucket of water handy, it proved to be of limited effectiveness.

Two other inexpensive compasses were constructed using the flat metal fly buttons from an airman's battledress trousers. The first of these used two buttons. One button had a tiny spike and acted as the base on which the second button, a magnetic one sporting a tiny red dot, balanced on top and spun around with the red dot indicating true north.

The second type of fly compass suspended one button above another by a length of thread with the bottom button spinning to true north, a difficult prospect in any sort of breeze. And, as 75 Squadron bomb aimer Ron Mayhill lamented, 'What we were supposed to do about a gaping fly was not revealed.'[28] Yet another compass had been disguised as a metal collar stiffener. When removed from the collar it hung from a piece of twine to find north.

Other innovations included silk maps which were easy to carry or wear around the neck. There were also flying boots that could be converted into a pair of walking shoes. One of the boots concealed a small knife to cut away the leather and sheepskin uppers to leave ordinary-looking shoes which were a lot less conspicuous than flying boots when wandering around occupied territory. Jim didn't bother with these fancy boots-cum-shoes because if he'd wanted to do a lot of walking, he'd have stayed in the army. Besides, he reckoned the older boots were a lot warmer at 20,000 feet.

Escape and evasion lectures covered basic procedures like burying parachutes and equipment and getting as far away from the site of their crashed aircraft as quickly as possible. Head south for a neutral country they were told, either Spain or Switzerland.

Jim recalled being advised that striking out for a neutral country, while seemingly all very well, might not be the best option. As evaders, aircrew - if they were fortunate enough to reach a neutral country – would most likely end up in an internment camp. However, if they convinced the authorities they were escaped POWs they would most likely be repatriated. To that end they were supposed to concoct a plausible cover story. Jim never discovered why

---

[27] See Author's notes, Chapter 6 – A Hazardous Environment.
[28] Ron Mayhill, Bombs on Target, Pg. 25

neutral countries differentiated between escapees and evaders and he didn't know of anyone who had bothered conjuring up a cover story. He certainly didn't. After all, he had no intention of ever bailing out.

He also recalled them being told that if they were shot down their best chance of avoiding capture lay in making contact with the Resistance, although nobody provided a satisfactory explanation as to how they were meant to achieve this. One bright spark suggested they stroll into a café and let the Resistance find them.

If any of them had to abandon their aircraft the odds of them getting home were negligible. Of the more than 10,000 Bomber Command aircrew forced down over enemy territory during the war only a tiny number, probably no more than a thousand, managed to evade capture. While this reinforced Jim's determination never to bail out, it didn't stop him from going out and purchasing a bone handled knife with a 12-inch blade to keep strapped inside his boot - just in case.

With the possibility of having to ditch in the North Sea or English Channel, dinghy drills were practiced regularly and everyone had a whistle attached to their tunic collar so they could find each other in the dark. They couldn't train by doing an actual ditching at sea so they rehearsed their exit strategy in a static Wellington bomber and used the safe environment of a swimming pool to practice clambering, fully kitted up and soaking wet, into a dinghy. It highlighted how exhausting and difficult the real thing would be, especially in a choppy sea at night.

Even if a crew extracted themselves from their sinking aircraft, that didn't guarantee survival. Nobody knew for sure how many poor beggars had ended up floating around on the ocean for days before dying of starvation, drowning or hypothermia. Many crews simply vanished without a trace.

Following two weeks of ground school, the Blance crew crowded aboard a truck to be taken to Oakley, Westcott's satellite station, where they were introduced to the Vickers Wellington.

Affectionately known as the Wimpy, the Wellington had formed the backbone of Bomber Command at the outbreak of the war. It had the prestige of being the first RAF bomber capable of carrying a 4,000lb Block Buster bomb and thanks to its unique geodetic construction it could absorb an incredible amount of battle damage. They were flown operationally throughout the war, but by January 1944 they had been consigned mainly to training units where they weren't regarded quite so affectionately.

OTUs came under the auspice of Bomber Command, which had more pressing matters at hand than maintaining hand-me-down, battle-weary war horses that were well past their use-by-dates. OTUs would have been better off being run by RAF Training Command.

Clapped out aircraft and inexperienced crews made for a lethal combination. At some OTUs the attrition rate rose as high as 25%. The list of air accidents made for horrendous reading. Flew into high tension wires; crash-landed; crashed in bad weather; crashed on takeoff; fire due to electrical short circuit; wing disintegrated in flight. Consequently, many young men found themselves dealing with the deaths of friends and comrades long before they ever made it onto a squadron. They considered it criminal negligence. No wonder most instructors were so eager to get back on operations.

At least one fatal accident occurred during Jim's time at Westcott. A Wellington bomber (LN660) took off from base at 20.05 hrs for a routine two-and-a-half-hour night cross-country trip involving navigation exercises with a fully operational crew. The Wellington, on finals for landing, collided with a Stirling of 90 Squadron returning from a raid and preparing to land after being diverted. The Stirling struck the Wellington from below and on the starboard side. The crippled Stirling remained airborne for about another 15 minutes before crashing in flames, killing all the crew.

The 11 OTU Wellington lost height rapidly, dropping too low for the crew to bail out before the aircraft erupted in flames and crashed in a field, killing all aboard. An air force investigation report highlighted the Stirling being far from its course for Tuddenham in Suffolk.

To complain or refuse to fly brought with it the risk of being labelled LMF (of low moral fiber) or, to put it more bluntly, to be accused of cowardice. The fact that all aircrew were volunteers apparently didn't count for much if they decided to un-volunteer themselves. Jim had heard stories about men who had completed tours, and had even been decorated for their courage, only to be later labelled LMF by an unbelievably unsympathetic establishment because they simply couldn't continue due to stress, battle fatigue or shattered nerves.

Whether the stories were fact or fiction didn't matter. Nobody wanted their file stamped LMF. It not only meant being stripped of your rank and flying badge and being sent to some far-flung station to scrub latrines or perform some other menial job, but it also meant carrying the ignominy of it well beyond their military service. So, many men hid their fears and got on with the job.

With Ian's recounting of his crash-landing during his pilot training in mind, the crew approached their first flight in the Wellington with a good dollop of nervous anticipation. Needless to say, they breathed a sigh of relief when a flying instructor, Warrant Officer Gustofson, climbed into the pilot's seat to do the first few circuits and landings before letting Ian take over.

Gustofson accompanied them again the next day, but this time instructed from the co-pilot's seat. Allowing for the odd bumpy landing, things went well. When the crew flew again three days later following a suspension of training due to bad weather, a new instructor, Flying Officer Feanihaugh, occupied the co-pilot's seat. After overseeing his charge for an hour, Feanihaugh handed full control over to Ian and instructed him to land the aircraft. Feanihaugh then vacated the aircraft and gave Ian ten minutes to take off, do a couple of circuits, and land.

The next day a more senior instructor, Flight Lieutenant Gunn, joined Ian in the cockpit. After performing a few circuits and landings, Gunn handed over to Ian who flew the crew around for a couple of hours doing circuits and landings until Gunn was satisfied Ian could be trusted with everyone's safety. Thereafter, only specific trade instructors accompanied the crew when skills such as map reading, high level bombing, air firing, or cross-country flights needed to be covered.

On 6 March, the crew made their first night flight which consisted of circuits and landings. Flying at night, with the increased risk of a collision or getting lost, ratcheted up everyone's nerves. All except Frank that is.

'Dear Elva, I started to write this in the Sergeant's lounge but we had to go flying so [I] am using the navigator's table. We are doing take offs and landings. The instructor[29] goes first but now our pilot is going to make his first night landing with a full crew aboard. Our crew. We are lucky to have such a good pilot. In fact, the whole crew is good.

p.s. The vibration seems to have made my writing worse than usual so do your best to read it.'[30]

The two 'washed out' pilots, Mac and Colin, proved excellent in their chosen trades. Colin never got them lost, while on the bombing range, Mac planted a high percentage of hits on or very near the target. Meanwhile Fred sat glued to his wireless set deciphering a jumble of transmissions, QDM bearings and Met reports that often resulted in a recall thanks to bad weather. Flying in England could be frustrating with a large number of training days being lost to inclement weather.

For Jim and Frank, the circuits and cross-country trips were treated as bit of a jaunt but when it came to their gunnery exercises, they had high standards to meet. Their final training reports assessed them in a number of ground and air gunnery tests with both live air firing and the use of cine cameras. Bizarrely, only Ian got to see to the results of their final exam.

Ground work - harmonizing guns, turret component drills, aircraft recognition, tactics, fighter control and turret manipulation - honed the skills Jim and Frank had learned at gunnery school, while the air-to-air work involved shooting at drogues towed 100 - 150 feet behind another aircraft. A gunner's final exam was marked anywhere from Exceptional (90%-100%) to Below Average (anything below 60%). Failure could send them back to gunnery school.

---

[29] Flying Officer Morley.
[30] Letter to Elva Loveridge 6/3/44

They carried out a number of fighter affiliation exercises, with at least one being done at night. Fighter affiliations involved mock attacks by another aircraft and Jim's bouts of air sickness weren't helped by Ian turning the Wellington through a series of dives and climbs. One evasive manoeuvre could be bad enough but half a dozen or more strung together had Jim getting closely acquainted with his new best friend, the standard issue sick bag. As he had done at MacDonald, he tried to alleviate his disposition by making sure he didn't eat or drink anything for two or three hours pre-flight. Vomit could be lethal if it got stuck in his oxygen tube. Worse, being preoccupied with his stomach meant he wouldn't be focused on his job, a job he wanted to carry out to the best of his ability.

Despite the realization that he occupied the most unenviable position in the aircraft, he never considered throwing it in, not even after hearing stories about rear gunners, or what remained of them, being hosed out of their turrets after combat. He didn't consider it misplaced bravado. He just didn't see the point in dwelling on it. OTU was fraught with enough potential dangers without him imposing limiting fears upon himself. Frank Jenkins thought in a similar vein.

'Dear Elva, The Jenks family are able to look after themselves and not take too many unnecessary risks. There seems to be a streak of cunning or good luck about them. Myself, I have plenty of confidence in my ability with a gun and I have an exceptionally clever crew.' [31]

Despite the potential hazards and the life-threatening activities associated with their operational training, Frank's letters made no attempt to disguise the fact that life on an RAF station could also be far from exciting. Sometimes it could be downright tedious, especially when bad weather postponed flying for days on end. If you didn't use your initiative you could go potty, and Frank always showed great initiative. During training in Canada, he had been admonished and forfeited a day's pay and privileges after disappearing for 15 hours without leave. This behaviour didn't stop once they reached England and Jim found himself forever making excuses for him.

'Dear Elva ...My bike ride to the village was very pleasant for I met several locals and spoke to them. I didn't have leave to go but just went and didn't tell anyone and little Winkie has just been telling me about all the lies he had to tell on my account. I had to laugh. This is the first of spring in England and it looks promising and needs to be after the cold we have been suffering. Everyone's lounging around after their dinner but it will soon be time to go

[31] Ibid, 7/3/44

again. There is a dance I would like to go to tonight but am afraid I will be disappointed for I think we are going flying.' [32]

Compared to some of the more complicated crew positions, like pilot or navigator, an air gunner's job might have seemed a doddle, requiring nothing more than a good eye and an ability to squeeze a trigger, but in reality, the Fraser Nash turrets used in the Wellington were sophisticated pieces of equipment requiring constant practice to operate proficiently.

Every time Jim and Frank climbed into their turrets, they had a strict ritual to go through which by the end of training had become second nature. The following narrative of a wartime RAF gun turret training film gives a good idea of that ritual:

* *Open turret doors.*
* *Fold the safety harness upwards and backwards over the ammunition tanks so you don't sit on the harness when getting in.*
* *Swing into the turret feet first, using the hand rail on the roof of the fuselage.*
* *Plug in intercom.*
* *Close turret doors. Left first and then right. Bolt the doors. Lean back and make certain they are locked.*
* *Do up Safety belt.*
* *Test reflector sight, setting it for the correct strength.*
* *Check ammunition by removing the lids from the tanks, inspecting the base of the rounds to make quite certain the ammunition in both tanks is joined and is being fed from the rear tanks.*
* *Replace lids.*
* *Remove arming cable and loading toggle. Check them and return to stowage.*
* *Adjust the seat by winding handles on both sides to suit your height and then return handles to their stowed positions.*
* *Unlock turret and test for rotation, depression and elevation, and check operation of firing gear.*
* *Load guns by putting the rounds up into the feed opening with the arming cable.*
* *Detach the arming cable and push down the last link.*
* *Close the breech cover and return the arming cable to the proper stowage.*
* *Cock guns twice by inserting the toggle over the cocking stud and pulling back.*
* *Return the loading toggle to its proper stowage.*
* *Move the fire and safety unit to 'fire'.*

---

[32] Frank Jenkins, letter to Elva, 25/3/44

Fire a tester burst. If airborne, over the sea. If on the ground, and station orders permit, into the ground.
Ensure that hand rotation is disengaged.
Report guns ok to captain.

General hints for air gunners included:

Search the sky before takeoff and landing because this is when the aircraft is most vulnerable.
If gun fire is observed, search for the fighter and take evasive action.
Patrol across the sun, never into it or away from it.
If using tracer at night, remember it tends to momentarily destroy your night vision; hold your fire if necessary. The aim of an enemy fighter is to destroy; the aim of a bomber's air gunner is to get safely to target and back to base.
Never fire until fired upon.
Always watch your tail.
Conserve your ammo; if you are fired upon from long range instruct the pilot to take evasive action.
Never fly straight or dive when under attack; never turn away from an attack, always toward.
Use good team work with the rest of the crew.
If on a reconnaissance aircraft, your job is to return with information; not seek combat with enemy aircraft.
All aircraft approaching are considered to be enemy until identified positively.

As they clocked up their flying hours Jim showed a preference for the rear turret, and he got no argument from Frank who couldn't wait until they got to a heavy conversion unit where the four engine bombers they would be flying were equipped with mid-upper turrets. In the meantime, because the Wellington did not have a mid-upper position, he and Jim alternated between the rear and front turrets.

Strictly speaking, the front turret, accessed from the bomb aimer's compartment, should have been Mac's responsibility. However, as their instructors had pointed out, the forward turret had been shown to be of limited usefulness on operations so Mac only got familiar enough with it to cope in an emergency. For training purposes, it belonged to Jim or Frank.

On bombing practice flights, with Mac in the bomb aimer's compartment, the front gunner became redundant so the toss of a coin decided whether Frank or Jim would fly as the rear gunner. The loser had to report to the gunnery flight for cine-camera work or combat manoeuvres. The latter meant going up in a Wellington with an instructor and half a dozen other trainees. It invariably involved a fighter affiliation exercise which was always met with a collective groan, and upon returning to base there would always be one or two young gunners stumble out of the aircraft reeking from the unpleasant side effects of some stomach-churning flying manoeuvres. Don't worry, they were told, it won't affect you when the shooting starts. You'll be too busy trying to stay alive to be sick.

After eleven days training the Blance crew jumped on a train to London to enjoy their first leave. The trains were often standing room only. Not that it bothered Jim. Being small enough to squeeze into the rear turret of a Wellington, he had no difficulty climbing into a British Rail overhead luggage rack.

Everyone they met on the train appreciated what they were doing, and the children were especially taken by the young men in their uniforms. One little chap sitting with his mother spent an age silently shifting his gaze around before pointing at Ian's pilot wings.

'Why has that man got two wings and all the rest of them have only got one?' he demanded.

His mother breathed an exasperated tut. 'Silly boy,' she said. 'That's because those men are only half trained.'

The boy then pointed at Freddie. 'Why have you got an S on your badge?'

'Because I'm the stoker,' he replied with a deadpan face.

If Jim thought the trains were packed then London's underground stations at night were organized chaos. People slept on the ground, or in makeshift cots and bunks (usually reserved for people with special vouchers) while babies wailed, men shaved, and people had sing-a-longs and indulged in George Formby impressions. The stations may have been tumultuous but they saved thousands of lives as V-1 (Doodle Bug) and V-2 rockets rained down on the capital.

'The V-2s were hard to detect because they arrived at supersonic speed,' Jim recalled. 'But the V1s were instantly recognizable by the sound of their motor as they chugged across the sky. As long as you could hear them you were safe, but the moment they spluttered and conked out you had to worry.'

A few seconds of haunting silence descended over the capital before a huge explosion would rock an unfortunate neighbourhood. The Doddle Bugs more than lived up to their status as terror weapons.

Still, London had everything for adventurous young men on leave and the Blance crew quickly discovered all the best pubs and hotels and their opening hours, which varied from place to place.

'Some of the lads knew the opening and closing times of just about every establishment, which allowed us to leave one pub at closing time and get to the next right on opening,' Jim recalled.

Jim celebrated his twenty-first birthday mid-way through operational training. Until then he hadn't been a drinker at all and the rest of the crew had amused themselves with some genial ribbing at his expense. Once he'd 'come of age' they made sure his tee-totalling ways were over for good and Jim greeted the prospect of a pub crawl with a new enthusiasm.

Some of the plush hotels were reserved for officers, which the boisterous young men from New Zealand found boorish and snobby, while lower rated establishments catered for the less refined 'other' ranks'. The New Zealand Forces Club, however, welcomed officers and NCOs alike.

The Blance crew always stuck together on leave. This worked well until Ian received a commission. As a newly promoted Pilot Officer, fraternizing with his crew of lowly sergeants would have been frowned upon so he always went on leave with his old Flight Sergeant's tunic in his kit.

'He would have been for the high jump if he'd been caught impersonating a Flight Sergeant,' Jim said. 'But he didn't care, and the of us rest greatly appreciated his gesture.'

While the crew always started their leave together it didn't always finish that way.

'Freddie had got himself engaged to a Wren[33] and Frank always had some girl or other on his arm,' Jim said. 'They would disappear after a few drinks and we wouldn't see them again until we got back to base.'

Spending every leave in London would have been an expensive business and a man could easily fritter away a month's pay, but fortunately, there were other avenues open to them, and many families took in the far-from-home antipodean airmen. Jim often spent his leave in Aberdeen with a lady named Ma Jamison and her daughter Anne.[34]

Back on base, to complete OTU crews were required to fly at least one night-time training operation. This could have been a Nickel (a leaflet drop over enemy occupied territory) a Diversion (a feint to distract German radar and night fighter forces away from the main force during an actual bombing raid) or a Bull's-eye (a sortie to 'bomb' a home target). Perversely, Nickels and Diversions didn't count toward a crew's tour of 30 operations because they were still not officially operational.

It hadn't been unknown for crews flying Nickels or Diversions to be posted FTR (Failed to Return) so needless to say the Blance crew were pleased when they were detailed to fly a far less hazardous Bull's Eye over London with two other crews. The main objective was to take an infrared photo of their 'target' – London, but a secondary purpose was to give the capital's anti-aircraft defenses valuable searchlight practice.

Everything went all right on the night until the Blance crew found themselves trapped by a powerful master beam searchlight. A huge bright blue devil of a thing, as Jim described it. More intense than a normal searchlight.

---

[33] Women's Royal Naval Service

[34] Jim never said how he met these wonderful people, but he certainly enjoyed his time with them.

'We were blinded. Within seconds, dozens of other lights had joined the master beam and we were coned. The skipper tried every avenue he could think of to escape. He threw the aircraft this way and that. He dived and climbed, but all to no avail. The searchlight operators had done a decent job on us. Freddie finally had to signal them to kill the lights. Over Germany we couldn't ask them to put the lights out!'

Following the Bull's Eye, the crew were granted a few days leave before going to their new posting, a heavy conversion unit (HCU) where they would be operating the Stirling or Halifax in preparation for a front-line squadron.

They were all ready to go and enjoy themselves in London when they received the startling news that when they returned, they weren't going to have to worry about German searchlights, or German anything for that matter. They were being posted to India. They were flabbergasted. All their training had pointed toward the European theatre. Worse, in India they wouldn't be needing a bomb aimer (they were never told why not) so Mac wouldn't be going with them. He'd be staying on for another bout of operational training with a new crew. They went on leave, dispirited at having to say goodbye to him.

Freddie found a silver lining in this dark cloud by taking the opportunity to marry his fiancée, Margaret. Had he been going to the European Theatre of Operations he would have waited longer, but India, he argued, didn't hold the same dangers as the flak and fighter infested skies of Europe.

It turned out to be a premature decision, because when they returned from leave, they were told that their India posting had been scrubbed and they were being sent to a heavy conversion unit in preparation for a posting to Bomber Command after all.

This annoyed them no end because they had lost a competent bomb aimer in Mac, who had already crewed up again. Not to worry, they were told, another bomb aimer would be assigned to them when they arrived at their heavy conversion unit.

At the conclusion of the crew's operational training, Ian actually received a posting to 11 OTU as a general duties pilot only for it to rescinded the next day without explanation.

The crew were generously given another 4 days leave, so to London they returned where a journalist named Keith Hooper came across Ian in the NZ Forces Club. He wrote:

Two New Zealand airmen in the Forces Club were sitting in an attitude of boredom. Wandering over I introduced myself. One of them lifted a listless hand and muttered a tired, 'Hiya, fella. Sit down and pour yourself a drink. I am Doug Lee, Flight-Sergeant, of Auckland - and this,' indicating his cobber, 'is Pilot Officer Ian Blance.' 'Of New Plymouth,' put in Blance as I produced pencil and paper.

Lee had no story but he certainly had plenty of bellyaches, the main one being the same old one: 'I came over here to fight so they made me an instructor - why? Twelve months spent showing ham-fisted sprogs just out of the cradle how to put an Oxford trainer on the deck in one piece!

Lee's cobber, Ian Blance, having finished his O.T.U., is off to a course at a battle school preparatory to a posting to a four-engine conversion unit.

Just to keep this record straight for posterity, Blance gave me the names of others who will be similarly bashing the Boche. They are Flight Sergeants Colin Greig, navigator, of Hamilton, Aubrey Kirk, rear gunner, of Christchurch, Fred Climo, wireless operator, of Timaru (Fred by the way got married last week), and Sergeant Frank Jenkins, air gunner, of Taranaki.

Jim did not recall attending a battle school, which he supposed might have been reserved for officers, but he did reminisce about an escape and evasion exercise the crew were subjected to near the end of their operational training.

They were dumped off the back of a truck in the middle of the night with instructions to get themselves back to camp without being picked up by the home guard or any overzealous police bobbies who would be looking out for them. After a brief assessment of their situation they concluded that the best course of action would be to find a pub and down a few pints. But finding a pub proved unexpectedly difficult, so they ditched the plan and thumbed a ride back to base with a local farmer in his rattletrap of a truck. He dropped them a mile from base and they traipsed back in pairs at appropriate intervals so as not arouse suspicion. No questions were asked and the exercise, to which Jim would later be able to attest, proved next to useless as a simulation of a genuine evasion.

Chapter 7: Onto the Heavies

The Blance crew were posted to 1651 Heavy Conversion Unit[35] at Wratting Common in Cambridgeshire for training on the four engine Stirling, a massive step up from the Wellington.

Situated mainly in West Colville parish, the airfield at Wratting Common also extended into neighbouring West Wratting, West Wickham and Witherfield parishes. With small picturesque villages dotting the surrounding fens and farmland, and with spring in the air, it looked like an ideal place for the next phase of their training. First, Jim and the others had to meet their new crewmates.

Mac's replacement turned out to be a veteran, at least in the eyes of the rest of the crew. At the age of twenty-five, Flight Sergeant Ronald Howard Spencer, RAFVR[36] from Walsall in Staffordshire wore the NAAFI ribbon and had already flown 14 ops with 90 Squadron, which incidentally had operated from Wratting Common before being moved out to make way for 1651 HCU.

He was known as Oscar, a nickname popularly given to bomb aimers who wore the old fashioned 'O' observer wing. In the early days of the bomber offensive, observers were responsible for both navigation and bombing, but as navigation grew more complicated, especially with the introduction of sophisticated aids like Oboe, Gee and H2S, it became too much for one man, so a separate bomb aimer (more correctly called air bomber) role was created. Old observers were given the option of training as navigators or continuing as bomb aimers. New 'N' (navigator) and 'BA' (bomb aimer) brevets were issued but many observers preferred to keep the original 'O' (observer) badge.

More recently, Oscar had done a stint as an instructor at 12 OTU, so his new crewmates greeted him with the sort of awe rightly reserved for someone of his experience. Not that such reverence affected him. He came across as very unassuming and without fuss. The crew liked him immediately.

Flying a heavy four engine aircraft like the Stirling required a flight engineer to assist with take offs and landings, attend to in-flight mechanical repairs, and, most importantly, to watch the engines (four massive Bristol Hercules XVI engines, each producing 1,650 hp) and keep a particular vigil on fuel consumption. Going to distant targets might involve unexpected detours or cork screwing which used up extra fuel, so the lives of the entire crew rested on calculating mixtures accurately and getting flying times exactly right.

Sergeant Bill Hyde took on the responsibility for the Blance crew.

---

[35] See Author's notes, Chapter 7 – Onto the heavies.
[36] Ronald Howard Spencer, 1575186, 75 Squadron, Royal Air Force Volunteer Reserve. Son of William and Elsie Spencer, of Bescot, Staffordshire. Enlisted 13.6.41; 26 Operational Training Unit 20.9.42; Joined 90 Squadron on 31.3.43; 7.9.43. 12 Operational Training Unit. Joined 75 on Squadron 10.7.44.

Bill had left his job with the Manchester Fire Brigade to sign up. Like many flight engineers he'd started life as a member of the ground crew before volunteering for flying duties. He did his initial training at St. Athan in South Wales, the only place to hold the flight engineer course. At thirty years of age he might have been old for aircrew but he fitted in perfectly.

Jim remembered Bill as a real gentleman. Never a cross word. Never swore. He wasn't married either, and before joining up he'd stayed at home to look after his mother. Jim found him quiet, courteous and reliable, and took a liking to him right off the bat. Bill didn't get a lot of mail, and as he didn't have a girl, Jim asked his sister Pat if she wouldn't mind writing to him, which she graciously agreed to do.

Soon, Jim and the rest of the crew were out at dispersal getting a close up look at the Short Stirling, 'The most expensive contraption ever invented for the purpose of lifting an undercarriage into the air.'[37] Rather than having anything to do with the size of the aircraft, the name Short belonged to the brothers who had started the company that manufactured these four-engine behemoths which were a far cry from the Wellington and a universe away from the Fairey Battle. The crew didn't so much face a conversion as an initiation.

The Short Stirling had one major flaw - its short wingspan of 99 feet and 1 inch. This was the result of an Air Ministry stipulation that it had to be less than 100 feet because the doors on the RAF hangars at the time were only 100 feet wide. Unfortunately, for the aircrews operating the Stirling the shorter wing span meant they couldn't reach the same heights as the Lancaster or Halifax, which made them easier prey for fighters and flak. The reduced wingspan also meant having to employ a longer undercarriage to raise the wings into a better angle of attack for take-off. This resulted in the cockpit being more than 22 feet off the ground.

The addition of a mid-upper turret made Frank very happy. He felt much more at home, even though he held steadfast to the nonsensical belief that if he turned the turret through more than 360 degrees it might unscrew itself!

A lot had to be learnt in a short space of time, especially for Ian and Bill who had the task of getting the monster into the air. At just over 87 feet long and weighing 44,000 pounds, it couldn't plod along any faster than 260 mph, making it the heaviest, and slowest, four engine bomber of the war. Bill also had the responsibility of flying the aircraft if Ian became incapacitated, although this would hopefully involve nothing more strenuous than keeping it straight and level. Fortunately, for an aircraft that appeared untameable on the ground, the Stirling exhibited fine handling qualities in the air. If it stayed in the air.

---

[37] Chaz Bowyer, Royal Air Force - The aircraft in service since 1918, pg.136, quoting an anonymous operational captain.

The Stirlings at many HCUs were no better than the hand-me-down Wellingtons found at OTUs. Many had poor serviceability records. In combination with inexperienced crews it wrote another recipe for disaster. Kites crashed or suffered any number of complaints from oil leakages and faulty hydraulic systems to engines cutting out. It left Jim wondering how they would get through the conversion course in one piece.

As it turned out the only casualties were Jim and Bill, both of whom had to utilize the regulation sick bags so thoughtfully provided by the Air Ministry.

'We had a big day flying. The rear gunner and the engineer both got very sick. We didn't go very high so I am not feeling tired. I would like to tell you where we went and what we did but the censor would just cut it out. The bomber stream is going over again now and has been for over an hour. Jerry must be really getting a pounding.

'I am in good spirit though this training of ours in inclined to get a bit trying at times but the long period of time we have been at this racket is proving itself every day for it is experience that counts a lot. I would like to have been in on the second front though I am not complaining for I know when I am well off. I will send you a crew photo as soon as we can take one. We have one but everyone is not in flying gear. I haven't been to London lately and don't know when we will get leave again as all is stopped at the moment.'[38]

When the crew did get some leave, they went to Cambridge or one of the local villages.

'England still looks pretty and green though the land doesn't seem to carry much stock. I like the lanes and roads which wind and twist and are quite often overhanging with pretty green trees. We have been to several small towns around about and their quaintness is very interesting. I went to Cambridge last week and thoroughly enjoyed myself for our crew and myself met lots of interesting people. The undergraduates particularly for they were all nationalities.

In every village, there are one or two inns and they are very comfortable and quiet places. They open about 7pm and close at 10pm so you can enjoy a pint or two in comfort and sometimes sing a song. A dart board is standard equipment in every bar room. The proprietor and his wife and daughter serve the beer. You see the same old farmers in the hotel every night you like to go there. They wander down to the inn every night without fail, rain, hail or snow. There are some houses in this district over two hundred years old. One near our camp has 1683 on the door. Most of the houses have thatched roofs and the windows are very small and the doors are not high enough for me to go

---

[38] Frank Jenkins, letter to his sister Elva, June 1944.

through without stooping. The houses haven't got water laid on for there may be one tap out on the road which supply [sic] 3 or 4 houses and the people get water from these taps on the road all their lives, generation after generation. You never see much livestock and there are very few cats and dogs. I take my laundry to one of these old houses.

What girls there are about are good looking and have a very good complexion which is due to the damp climate, I guess, but they all have girlfriends it seems. English girls are very modest and prim and proper for you never see a girl's under clothes from one month's end to another. It's the way they conduct themselves, for in Canada and NZ it wasn't uncommon to see a girl fall or be off her guard in some way but English girls never. They are mostly hard to get along with.'

After surviving approximately 50 hours flying time in the clapped out Stirlings during their ten-weeks at Wratting Common the Blance crew were deemed fit to progress to their next posting, which would be … 'Feltwell!' Ian beamed. 'We're going to No. 3 Lancaster Finishing School.'

Chapter 8: Lancaster Finishing School, Feltwell

They were thrilled to know they would be flying the Avro Lancaster, the jewel in Bomber Command's arsenal. Its 'shining sword'.[39]

Like 1651 HCU, No. 3 Lancaster Finishing School (LFS), located near the quiet, discreet Norfolk village of Feltwell[40] came under the sphere of 31 Base, supplying crews to the squadrons of 3 Group.

Surrounded by flat fens and farmland, Feltwell provided an ideal setting for flying. From 1940 until 1942 it had actually been the base for 75 (NZ) Squadron. Back then there hadn't been a Lancaster in sight, with the squadron flying the Vickers Wellington I.

Being posted to a Lancaster Finishing School suggested the Blance crew knew something about the Lancaster before they arrived, when in fact they knew nothing. Considering the course lasted a mere ten days they wondered how much they could learn before going operational.

They fell in love with the Lancaster the moment they set eyes on it. It looked good, and it felt good when they undertook an orientation exercise with a seasoned instructor showing Ian the ropes. Before long the skipper took over the controls, marveling at the power of the four Merlin Engines and the outstanding qualities of the aircraft's handling.

In the back of the aircraft, Jim and Frank had to get familiar with both the rear and mid-upper turrets. As usual, Franks wanted nothing to do with sitting in the rear.

'You're welcome to it, Winkie. Up top I get to see where we're going.'

Colin and Oscar went back for a 'play' in the rear turret.

'Bugger that,' Colin said.

'Just make sure you keep yourself out of trouble,' Freddie said. 'I don't fancy having to take over if you get yourself killed, Winkie.'

Despite its many praiseworthy qualities, the Lancaster could be a difficult aircraft to escape in an emergency. The Germans had christened it The Flying Coffin. More aircrew had died in Lancs than either the Halifax or Stirling.

Rear gunners - lucky fellows - were instructed by those with supposedly more nonce that they should use the official emergency exit at the front of the aircraft as their first escape option. Jim considered it ludicrous to think he could get to the front of the aircraft in an emergency. The Lancaster's cramped fuselage proved difficult enough to negotiate with the aircraft stationary on the ground never mind when bumping around in flight. The dreaded main wing spar which barricaded the fuselage just behind the wireless operator's position

---

[39] See Author's notes, Chapter 8 – Lancaster Finishing School, Feltwell. Note 1.

[40] See Author's notes, Chapter 8 - Lancaster Finishing School, Feltwell. Note 2.

provided a difficult obstacle to negotiate at the best of times, let alone with the aircraft on fire and out of control.

Even if by some miracle Jim and Frank managed to fight their way down the dark tunnel of the aircraft and clamber over the main spar, they would still have to squeeze down into the bomb aimer's compartment and get out through the small escape hatch before the aircraft plummeted into the ground.

Fortunately, they had other options, including the entrance door near the mid-upper's position. However, this could be tricky, with a high probability of getting clobbered by the tail section on the way out if you didn't get it right. The know-it-alls decided this escape exit should only to be used in an extreme emergency. Jim considered any situation requiring a parachute must surely constitute extreme.

There were in fact two Lancaster parachute drills; a normal drill and an emergency drill.

NORMAL DRILL

Pilot AT CONTROLS
Warn crew "Strap on parachutes." Flash PPP On Call light. Engage George (auto pilot) if possible. Order "Jump". Keep aircraft on even keel. Follow last man out via forward hatch.

Flight Engineer BESIDE PILOT
Acknowledge. Strap on pack. Assist pilot. Stand by.

Navigator AT TABLE
Acknowledge. Strap on pack. Move forward. Stand by.

Wireless Operator.
Acknowledge. Jettisons aerial. Strap on pack. Move forward. Stand by.

Air Bomber (Bomb Aimer) IN NOSE
Acknowledge. Strap on pack. Stand by.

Mid Upper
Acknowledge. Vacate turret. Strap on pack. Move forward. Standby.

Rear Gunner.
Acknowledge. Vacate turret. Strap on pack. Move forward. Stand by.

All wait for the second order "Jump Jump". Jettison helmets. Air Bomber jettisons parachute escape hatch. All crew members leave aircraft via forward escape hatch, kneeling facing forward, leaving aircraft head first. Order of leaving, A/B, F/E, Nav, W/Op, M/U, R/G, Pilot. Order of acknowledgement being the same.

EMERGENCY DRILL

Pilot
Warns crew Abandon aircraft by parachute, Jump Jump. Flash PPP On Call Light, check that all of crew are out of aircraft. Leave via forward hatch.

Flight Engineer
Strap on pack. Move forward. Leave via forward hatch.

Navigator
Strap on pack. Move forward. Leave via forward hatch.

Wireless Operator
Jettisons aerial. Strap on pack. Move forward. Leave via forward hatch.

Air Bomber
Strap on pack. Move forward. Leave via forward hatch.

Mid Upper
Acknowledges. Vacates turret. Straps on pack. Leaves Via the entrance door.

Rear Gunner
Acknowledges. Vacates turret. Straps on pack. Leaves Via the entrance door.

If circumstances make it advisable for the W/OP to leave via the rear entrance door he should acknowledge the order.

Method of leaving via the rear entrance door is to sit on the step facing aft and fall over to the left. This minimises the danger of striking the tail-plane. In each drill, it is the responsibility of the flight engineer to ensure the pilot has his pack strapped on. Helmets must be jettisoned before leaving the aircraft in both procedures.

It's interesting to note that neither the normal drill or the emergency drill mentions the rear gunner having the option of abandoning the aircraft via his turret.

Despite the edict about using the nose hatch or entrance door, most rear gunners jumped from their burning Lancasters directly from their turrets. After rotating the turret to port or starboard they simply had to open the doors and

69

tumble out backwards. At least in theory. As Jim later discovered, theory didn't always count for much.

Being so cramped, the Frazer-Nash turret didn't allow the gunners to wear their parachutes, which had to be stowed in the fuselage. This could be an issue if they had to get out quickly. In fact, the claustrophobic nature of the rear turret meant some rear gunners had to throw their boots in first then clamber in after them.

There were a few other deficiencies with the turret, not least the Perspex panels frosting up at high altitude and severely impairing vision. To combat the problem, rear gunners usually removed the front Perspex panel. This exposed them to the elements but gave them a much better chance of spotting night fighters. One of Jim's gunnery instructors told him about a rear gunner who'd opened fire on a 'fighter' only to realize to his horror that he had fired at a black speak on the centre Perspex panel. Reason enough to remove it.

The rear gunner also discovered he had to rely on the Lancaster's port outer engine to power his turret. If the engine quit then so did his turret. At the HCU Jim and his fellow gunners had been told stories about an alternative power source being supplied by the Lancaster's starboard inner engine.

'Unsuspecting twits that we were, we held firm to this belief until our LFS instructors happily exposed the notion as a cruel hoax,' he recalled. 'The only alternative power turned out to be elbow grease. We had to elevate and depress the guns by hand, and rotate the turret using a small crank handle situated beside the seat.'

As well as familiarising themselves with their respective positions, Ian gave everyone some basic flying instruction in case one of them should have to take over in an emergency. As Ian's right-hand man in the cockpit, Bill received the majority of instruction, with Colin next in line thanks to his brief pilot training background. Jim felt the crew should have all jumped well before it got to the stage where he had to take the controls.

They totalled about 20 hours of daylight and night flying, including cross-country trips and fighter affiliation. Veteran Lancaster pilots often applaud the aircraft as a dream to fly, but cork screwing – the most effective manoeuvre for eluding night fighters – drew on every ounce of a pilot's skill and physical strength. The rest of the crew could do nothing but grab hold of whatever they could as the skipper threw his aircraft into a turning dive and then hauled back on the column to go into a steep climb. In the back of the aircraft, with the G-forces pressing his chin into his chest, Jim could only pray it would be over as quickly as possible.

After a long day of flying the crew enjoyed nothing more than a bicycle trip to the nearest village pub to unwind over a pint of beer. The public received them enthusiastically, encouraging them with plenty of bluster. Cries of 'Give Jerry one for us' or 'Clobber the buggers' strengthened their resolve, and it mattered little that they hadn't actually been on ops. The bomber boys were basking in the sort of public adulation that had once been the preserve of the fighter pilots.

Their time at Feltwell hardly seemed to have started before it came to an end with a posting to an operational squadron looming. They knew where they wanted to go - 75 New Zealand Squadron. What could be better than a bunch of callow Kiwis not only going to a famous New Zealand squadron, but a New Zealand Squadron operating Lancasters?

They had already experienced a brief taste of 75 Squadron during their heavy conversion training, as referenced in a letter Frank Jenkins wrote to his sister at the time. Although he didn't elaborate, they most likely visited the squadron as part of a cross-country or navigation exercise.

'This is only going to be a few lines before lights out as I want to send this photo [crew photo] before I give it to someone else or lose it. We have been up to the village where we had fish and chips and lots of strawberries. Two of our crew are at the foot of my bed right now trying to force chips and strawberries on me but I can't go any more. We have had a big day flying in which time we went to see a famous NZ squadron. One of our tyres blew out when we landed so we had dinner there while the ground staff changed the wheel. All for now. Bags of love to all, Frank.[41]

A couple of days later they were thrilled to be posted to 75 Squadron at Mepal. They might not have been quite so keen had they been aware of the Squadron's high attrition rate. With a reputation as a highly disciplined 'press-on regardless' outfit, many considered 75 a 'chop' squadron. It carried the dubious distinction of having the second highest casualty rate within 3 Group, second only to 115 Squadron stationed at nearby Witchford. In fact, the landing circuits for both airfields overlapped and both squadrons mingled at the same pubs, enjoying a friendly rivalry.

For Jim, the posting brought two years of training to a climax. Burnham, Ohakea, Rotorua, and the clear blue skies of Manitoba seemed like a lifetime ago.

---

[41] Frank Jenkins, letter to his sister Elva, 5/6/44.

Chapter 9: Mepal

When the Blance crew arrived at Mepal on 10 July 1944, the squadron adjutant made a brief note about the momentous event in the operational record book. 'P/O Blance & crew arrived on posting from 31 Base.' No trumpets, no drums.[42]

They were allocated a Nissan hut some distance from the operation huts and mess, making the acquisition of a bicycle a priority. If there were none readily available a chap didn't have to wait long, because when a crew went missing their bikes were returned to the bicycle pool - unless they were pinched first or, if privately owned, sold, with the proceeds going to the man's next of kin. Ian Blance bought himself a Raleigh and Frank, who had roared around on an Indian motorcycle back home, purchased a Raleigh Roadster off a Yank for £3.10.

The Nissan huts were similar to the accommodation Jim had experienced in Canada, warmed by a crude heater/stove, and with beds lining each wall. He tried to keep his space as tidy as possible but some of the chaps had their gear strewn from one end to the other.

Jim couldn't believe his luck when he discovered Paddy and Jock, who had crewed up with Pilot Officer Wilson Hadley at 26 OTU, were joining the squadron on the same day. They shared an ebullient reunion and that night they were given a wonderful introduction to squadron life with a boisterous night at *The Chequers* in the nearby village of Sutton.

The next day they made visits to the numerous sections where they gathered firsthand knowledge from seasoned section leaders who did their best to make them feel at home. But Jim and his crew definitely felt like the new boys at school. Here lessons had to be learnt quickly.

At the photographic section they were photographed and supplied with passport sized escape photos. If they were shot down over occupied territory the photographs would be of enormous help to the Resistance in creating false identity papers for them Because the Germans often changed the pose required for civilian documents, the airmen were photographed full face, side profile, and three-quarter profile.

'The trouble was,' Jim said, 'we all wore the same jacket, and the lighting, background and poses were alarmingly similar. We didn't imagine the Germans were idiots.'

Not that Jim had anything to worry about as he sewed his escape photographs into the belt of his battledress tunic. Fake papers were for the unfortunate blokes who had to bail out.

---

[42] See Author's notes, Chapter 9 – Mepal.

The next day, twenty-five crews selected for that night's operation against the marshalling Yards near Varies in Paris, conducted air tests. The Blance crew were not on the battle order. Instead, they were briefed on a cross-country flight to orientate ourselves with the area and terrain, a necessary undertaking for any crew when posted to a new station. While it provided an ideal opportunity to discover their new surroundings and get a bird's-eye view of Ely and the many tiny villages that dotted the green landscape, they were itching to start on ops.

Blance crew, June 1944. Back row L-R: Ronald Spencer, Bill Hyde, Colin Greig, Frank Jenkins. Front row L-R: Jim Kirk, Ian Blance, Fred Climo. (Kirk Collection).

Course 72. B, Heavy Conversion Unit 1651, Wratting Common, 12 June 1944.Blance crew:
Middle Row from 5ᵗʰ on the left: Bill Hyde, Fred Climo, Oscar Spencer, Colin Greig, Frank
Jenkins, Jim Kirk. Ian Blance is front row, 4ᵗʰ from the right. (Kirk Collection).

Jim 'Winkie' Kirk (right) and Jock Biggar in England, 1944(Kirk Collection).

Sergeant Bill Hyde, RAF. Photo Courtesy of John Thorpe

75 Squadron Control tower the day before its demolition in 1988. (Kirk Collection).

The author at Mepal, 2014. Photo: Daphne Hobson

The author at The Chequers pub in the village of Sutton. Photo: Daphne Hobson

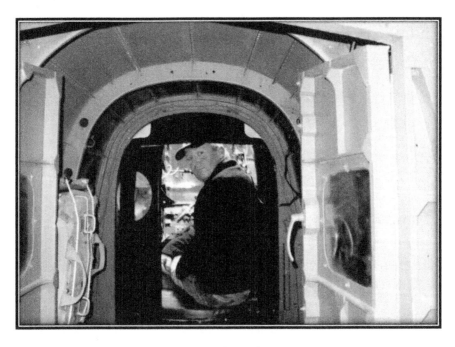

Showing position of the stowed parachute. Photo: Daphne Hobson

Peter Wheeler, Q.S.M discusses the finer aspects of the Lancaster's cramped interior.

The Avro Lancaster's well laid out cockpit. Photos: Zane Kirk

The Rose turret gun control column. Photo: Zane Kirk

AA-M (Mike) Mepal, 1944. (Kirk Collection).

AA-M (Mike) Mepal, 1944. (Kirk Collection).

Chapter 10: Ake Ake Kia Kaha

The twenty-five Lancaster crews detailed for the raid on the marshalling yards at Vaires on the night 11/12 July didn't even get to start their engines. Inclement weather postponed the operation until daylight. The battle order for the rescheduled daylight raid now included the Blance crew.

Disconcertingly, however, the crew was listed as Sqd. Ldr. Berney (Pilot), C. Grieg (Nav), W. Hyde (F/E), R. Spencer (A/B), F. Climo (W/O), F. Jenkins (M/U), and Flt. Lt. McAlpine (Gunnery Leader) (RG). Neither Ian Blance nor Jim appeared on the battle order.

This contradicts Ian's RNZAF file which clearly states he flew one raid against Varies. 75 Squadron participated in a number of raids against the marshalling yards at Varies, but only one (the 12 July daylight raid) occurred during Ian's time on the squadron, so it's most likely Ian either flew the operation as second dickey[43] with another crew or went with his own crew as second pilot to Squadron Leader Berney.

While it doesn't appear to have been standard policy within Bomber Command for a new skipper to fly second dickey with his own crew, a perusal of squadron records suggests it wasn't an unusual practice for 75 Squadron.

For example, the crew of Pilot Officer May, who joined the squadron three days after the Blance crew, flew their first operation to Cagny, France on 18 July with Wing Commander Leslie at the helm and their skipper flying second dickey to him. That same night May and his crew were back on the battle order flying to Aulnoye, this time with May in command.

Likewise, Flight Sergeant Mulchay's crew, having originally been detailed to fly an aborted operation against Varies on 17 July, flew their first trip to Cagny on July 18 with their skipper as second dickey to Squadron Leader Berney. That night Mulchay captained his crew on the raid against Aulnoye.

While Ian's omission from the battle order seemed to be an administrative oversight, the same cannot be said for Jim, who flew on the Varies raid despite not being named on the battle order.

The anomaly arose due to the squadron's gunnery leader, Flight Lieutenant McAlpine, wanting to fly with the crew, much to Jim and Frank's chagrin. It meant one of them would have to stay behind. They tossed a coin and Frank lost. In hindsight, Jim wished he hadn't won, because Flight Lieutenant McAlpine wanted the rear turret, which pushed him into the less familiar mid-upper turret where he felt more exposed and insecure. Not even on training flights had he felt much empathy for the mid-upper position. He found it

---

[43] Second pilot (or co-pilot)

difficult to get in and out of the turret and he didn't find the canvas sling seat at all comfortable.[44]

'Sure, it had a fantastic outlook,' he said. 'But I wasn't there to admire the view, and I felt extremely vulnerable with a huge roundel painted on the fuselage right beneath me.'

Jim might not have relished the idea of a German fighter pilot trying to score a bulls-eye on the roundel painted beneath the turret, but it's peculiar that he should prefer the more dangerous rear turret position.

While most chaps could vividly recall their first op, Jim didn't remember much about his at all. Perhaps in his mind it had been overshadowed by later events. He really couldn't explain his dearth of recollection.

Squadron records show that the twenty-five-aircraft detailed to attack the Marshalling Yards at Varies took off in daylight and all reached the target area, but only two identified the Marshalling Yards and bombed as ordered. Owing to 10/10ths cloud obscuring the target the remaining crews abandoned their mission as instructed by the Master Bomber and brought their bombs back to base. They encountered considerably heavy A.A. fire but all aircraft returned safely.

The Blance crew were flying Lancaster ND752[45] on this operation. They were one of the first crews airborne, being up at 18.05 hrs, and landed at 22.00 hrs. This would be Jim's only daylight trip, but not be his last as a mid-upper gunner, as he had the unnerving experience of flying a night op in that position with another crew.

Unlike the rear turret, where Jim happily didn't see anything of the target until he had passed over it, the mid-upper turret left him exposed to the whole shooting match. Approaching the target, with batteries of search lights combined with a seemingly impenetrable gauntlet of flak and coloured tracer, he thought, 'Crikey Frank, you're welcome to this.'

Having given up all hope of getting through the barrage unscathed, he suddenly had cause for optimism as a clear path began to open up like the parting of the Red Sea, and miraculously they enjoyed an unobstructed run the rest of the way to the target. Jim's respect for Frank, not to mention the fellas up the front of the aircraft, grew immensely after that experience.

Jim lost his logbook after the war so it's difficult to ascertain which crew he flew with, or what the target was on his night op as a mid-upper gunner. During his time on the squadron it could have been an operation against the construction works at Bois des Jardine on July 15/16, the oil refinery at Homberg on 20/21 July, laying mines in the Kattegat area on 22/23 July, against Kiel on 23/24 July or against Stuttgart on either 24/25 July or 25/26 July.

---

[44] See Author's notes, Chapter 10 – Ake Ake Kia Kaha.
[45] ND752 was lost on the Homberg raid 20/21 July 1944.

83

One of the Stuttgart raids is most likely because he said he flew two raids against Stuttgart. Although his name doesn't appear on the battle order for either of the two Stuttgart raids mentioned, that doesn't exclude his participation. Squadron records can be notoriously unreliable. That was especially true when there were last minute changes for sick or injured aircrew, with many such changes escaping amendment by the squadron adjutant.

The unreliability of some records can be highlighted by Jim's request to the Ministry of Defense in Wellington many years later for his service record. They sent him his file along with a slip of paper noting that he'd joined 75 Squadron on 10 July 1944 and had flown his first operation to Hamburg on 18/19 July. That is incorrect.

On the night of 18/19 July 1944, the Squadron operated against Aulnoye. 75 Squadron hadn't raided Hamburg since the night of 2/3 August the previous year, the last time they did so for the rest of the war.

The squadron operational record book, from which official accounts are undoubtedly taken, shows Jim flying his first operation on the night of 18/19 July 1944, albeit to Aulnoye, not Hamburg. However, what the operations record book doesn't reveal is Jim going to Varies on the toss of a coin on 12 July.

Squadron records don't show a battle order for the next operation, a daylight trip to Vinneneuve St. George, but it's of little consequence as a cold front moving across Britain scrubbed the operation. In the wake of constant delays and postponements, a return to Varies on 14 July also had to be scrubbed.

Jim recalled the crews being given permission to leave the station when an op had to be cancelled or postponed. 'As long as we were in bed by midnight.'

Dozens of them would cycle along the narrow country lanes to Mepal or the little village of Sutton sitting on the southern edge of the perimeter track.

The locals couldn't do enough for them and were very forgiving of their boisterous ways and singing and horse play. Chaps who were thoroughly professional in the air could be mad as hatters in the pub. Officers, who had a separate mess on base and had little to do with the other ranks outside of their sections, mingled freely with them at the pub.

The Blance crew had joined 75 squadron at a time when the Allied high command was focusing their attention on knocking out German rail and communication networks in France, rather than hitting targets like Berlin or the heavily fortified industrial cities of the Ruhr Valley. Bomber Command's chief, Arthur Harris, didn't like having to divert his crews from punishing German cities to concentrate on what he described as 'panacea' targets. He wanted them wrecking cities from one end of Germany to the other, because an all-out assault, he argued, would cost Germany the war. But he begrudgingly followed orders.

On 15 July, the squadron split in two for separate attacks against the marshalling yards at Charlons-sur-Marne and a V1 rocket site at Bois de

Jardine. Ten aircraft were detailed to bomb Charlons-sur-Marne where a strategic transportation network of railways, highways and a major canal congregated. The Blance crew were not on the battle order for either raid. Nor did they fly two days later on 17 July when twenty-seven Lancasters were detailed for a return to the marshalling yards at Varies. They didn't miss much, because shortly after takeoff bad weather scrubbed the op. Landing with full petrol tanks could be fraught with danger so the crews milled around dumping their precious fuel before landing. They were refuelled and put on standby to attack a tactical target, but once again the weather conspired to scrub the planned operation.

The next day, 18 July, twenty-eight Lancasters were detailed for a dawn attack on the French village of Cagny where heavy concentrations of German armour and troops were situated. It would be the first time 75 Squadron had flown in direct support of land operations, and to date it would be the largest number of Lancasters the squadron had assembled for a single operation.

The raid produced exceptionally accurate bombing results and history would later prove it to be 75 Squadron's most important operation in support of the army. It also resulted in the awarding of the Conspicuous Gallantry Medal to Flight Sergeant Dave Moriarty.

A Perspex splinter penetrated Moriarty's head close to his left eye and exited behind his left ear. Not wishing to alarm his crew, and with blood in his eyes, he continued to fly his aircraft with his bomb aimer and flight engineer reading the instruments for him. As they neared Mepal, he calmly called the control tower and told them to have an ambulance waiting because one of the crew had been injured. Barely able to see, he brought his aircraft in for a perfect landing.

That night the squadron returned to ops, with a raid on the German aircraft works at Aulnoye in northern France. The Blance crew, this time with Jim listed as rear gunner, were back on the battle order.

Chapter 11: Prepped for Flight

Jim clearly recalled his first night raid, although he couldn't remember the name of the target - Aulnoye in Northern France. In preparation for the raid, the crew did a twenty-minute test flight in the afternoon, after which Ian signed the form 700 confirming the aircraft fit to fly. As every aircraft handled differently the test flight helped identify any intricacies or idiosyncrasies as well as potential problems. Nobody wanted to turn back on an op because of a technical or mechanical difficulty. Not only was it a bad look but, more importantly, the op might not count toward the crew's tour.

Some Lancs were a dream to fly while others were plagued by gremlins – nasty, mythical creatures that fouled up the fuel lines, wireless sets, compasses and a myriad of other things. Other unfortunate Lancs seemed jinxed, attracting night fighters, searchlights and flak. Yet they seemed to be the ones that always came back, to haunt another crew on another night.

Being new boys, the Blance crew were not immediately allocated a regular aircraft but flew whatever they were assigned. For the Aulnoye raid they flew in ME 691[46] (AA-R), a Mk1 Lancaster with 214 operational hours behind her. In the face of the squadron's steady losses she could have been considered a veteran.

According to Jim, there were two schools of thought concerning such veteran aircraft. On one hand, they were considered lucky because they always came back. On the other hand, with so many ops in the bag, its luck, and that of its crew must surely be ready to expire.

Similar discussions occasionally cropped up among the crew concerning their own mortality. Some of the chaps were convinced the more ops they flew the better their chances of surviving. After all, the more a crew flew together the more proficient they should become. The first five trips were considered the toughest, although Jim considered the old adage, 'Do five you'll stay alive' to be a ridiculous, because disaster could strike at any time from any quarter. Most crews would admit that a dollop of luck played an essential part in whether or not they survived.

Crews usually operated at their best during the middle stages of their tour. They were past the novice stage and fatigue hadn't set in the way it often did with seasoned crews who, nearing the end of their tours, risked complacency or excessive nerves.

Jim thought that nearing the end of a tour must have been a bit like a batsman sitting on ninety-nine during a cricket match. Deliveries he would normally smack to the boundary with ease are prodded and poked at rather than being played at with the confidence that got him to ninety-nine in the first place

---

[46] Lancaster ME691 lost on Homburg raid 20/21 July 1944.

because he's more concerned with survival than getting on with the job. Making that mistake on an op didn't send you packing to the pavilion on ninety-nine, it got you killed, and your crew along with you.

Jim talked to a gunner who had flown as a spare bod with a crew who were on their last trip. The veteran crew spent the entire time on a razor's edge, calling out non-existent fighters and jumping at the slightest thing. The gunner vowed never to fly with such a crew again. Ian didn't let his crew waste their energy debating the chances of survival. If they concentrated on doing their jobs the rest could be left in the lap of the gods.

As far as Jim and Frank were concerned, part of their job involved harmonising their guns to achieve maximum hitting power. While the armourers on 75 Squadron did most of the work, Jim and Frank liked to help. 'It made us feel better knowing for ourselves that we were free of gremlins.'

With preparation of the aircraft complete, the crews didn't have much to do except wait around for the briefing. Pilots, navigators and bomb aimers had a separate briefing concerning the aiming points, the routes to the target and other gen that the 'unsophisticated oily rags', as Jim referred to himself and his fellow air gunners, didn't have the intellect to fathom. Then came the main briefing attended by all aircrew crammed into a hut filled with cigarette smoke and nervous chatter.

The Blance crew took a position on a long wooden bench at the back of the room. The more experienced crews sat up the front. For some, this would be their last briefing. At the front of the hut a low stage had been set with a table and chairs where the section leaders sat with their charts and maps, and on the wall hung a large curtain.

A roll call of the skippers confirmed all crews were complete and present and then came a crash of feet on the floor as the men reacted to the appearance of their C.O. Wing Commander Jack Leslie.

Leslie didn't stand too much on ceremony and immediately invited everyone to resume their seats and light their pipes and cigarettes. Following that, came the worst part of any briefing as Leslie announced, 'Gentleman, your target for tonight is …' The curtain went back to reveal a map of Europe with a length of red tape stretching from Mepal to their target. Everyone wanted to see a short piece of tape directing them to Paris or the French coast. Nice milk runs. They never appreciated a strip of tape extending to a place like the big city, Berlin, or to one of the heavily fortified industrial targets in the Ruhr Valley. Such targets were often greeted with groans and disgruntled, ribald comments about the top brass.

Following the C.O., the Intelligence officer offered the latest gen about the target and how knocking it out would help shorten the war. Next came the section leaders. The crews listened to them intently, making notes and nodding knowingly as they were shown the proximity of the German night fighter bases and flak batteries en route to the target. To avoid them, the flight plan made numerous diversions, adding time to the flight and burning up extra fuel. The operation planners attempted to plant uncertainty in the minds of the German night fighter controllers by creating feints toward different cities, so by the time they identified the real target it would be too late for them to respond with sufficient numbers of fighters. Finally, the Wingco delivered a few final words of encouragement. Well known for his vitriolic distain of the enemy, his rousing addresses usually finished with a hearty 'See you in the smoke!'

After briefing, a flying meal of bacon, eggs and chips waited for them in the mess. At a time when rationing meant most people might manage one egg a week if they were lucky, the air crews were extremely privileged. After the meal, they collected their escape kits, sweets, coffee flasks and Mae West life preservers. Pockets were emptied. Not so much as a movie ticket stub could be left to aid the enemy. Then there were last letters and wills to deposit, a practice Jim viewed rather darkly, as though it were akin to signing a death warrant.

'I didn't want to tempt fate by leaving a will,' he reflected. 'Some of the other chaps thought the same way.'

At their next stop, the connecting crew huts, flying gear could be found strewn from one end to the other. Some blokes found it amusing, others looked ready to explode as they hunted for their equipment. Some became quiet and reticent. Others talked non-stop. The tension could get quite palpable.

Lucky charms abounded. Young men flew with everything from rabbit's feet to lucky scarves. A pilot that Jim met after the war said he always waited an extra ten seconds after receiving the green light for take-off.

'He thought it might save his life,' Jim explained, somewhat matter-of-fact. 'He'd come to this conclusion after one of his early ops when flak had exploded in front of his aircraft. He argued that if he had arrived ten seconds earlier the flak would have got him in the bomb bay.'

Superstitions proliferated through all areas of the young airmen's lives, even as far as affecting who they dated. They had to be mindful of which girls they associated with because nobody wanted to get involved with a 'chop girl', so-called because every man the poor girl dated got the 'chop' soon afterwards.

Back in the crew hut the poor gunners took the longest to get sorted, especially the lucky rear gunners who needed extra layers of everything. Being in the coldest part of the aircraft, Jim started by pulling on thick woollen long johns. Next, came his standard uniform and battle dress. Over the top of his blouse he wore a cream-coloured polo-necked jersey called a white frock, which was neither white nor like a frock.

'Mind you, compared to the colour of those worn by the old lags, it looked pure white,' Jim said.

Next, he donned two or three pairs of socks, the last pair being thick stockings known as 'sea boot' socks. Then came his full length electrically heated suit and electric booties, essential for keeping him alive in sub-zero temperatures at high altitude. Over the electric suit, he wore an inner suit for extra insulation, and then either a Sidcot suit, or a two-piece Irvin suit. His boots were the older zip-up suede 1941 pattern with fleece lining.

Some gunners wore the Taylor buoyancy suit, a bulky one-piece ensemble made of the same canary yellow fabric as the Mae Westlife jacket, and were so heavy they were fitted with integral braces. Reserved for gunners, Jim considered the Taylorsuit cumbersome. It was not very popular, but an advert of the time by the manufacturer, Baxter, Woodhouse & Taylor Ltd, described the Taylorsuit as *'the latest and most comprehensive flying suit yet evolved – as near perfection as we can get. The Taylorsuit is a "safety suit" and an essential part of equipment. It has been designed for comfort, freedom of movement, warmth, electric heating, buoyancy, fire resistance, quickness of removal.'*

Jim also described having to wear five pairs of gloves.

'A silk pair to retain a sense of touch, a cotton pair, a pair of chamois, an electric pair, and finally sheepskin-lined gauntlets.'

There were a couple of problems with the electrically heated gear. First, every piece had to be produced in both 12 and 24-volt versions because of the two currents available in the aircraft the RAF operated at the time. Second, they had no thermostat control, only an on/off switch. If a gunner got too hot, he could easily fall asleep. If he got too cold, he could have trouble moving. The suits also had a nasty habit of sparking when they got damp, made worse if the internal wiring snapped. This alarmed Jim at first, but once he realized he wasn't going to fry he took comfort in knowing he must be alive if he could feel a zap.

The last pieces of equipment to be put on were the Mae West life preserver and the parachute harness. With the harness worn correctly, Jim found it almost impossible to walk upright. Fortunately, it felt a lot more comfortable when sitting down. Rear gunners who had removed the central Perspex panel from the turret to provide better vision had the option of spreading anti-freeze lanolin ointment on their cheeks to ward off frostbite, but Jim never bothered.

Finally, they collected their parachutes, which the Waafs always handed over with a cheery, 'If it doesn't work bring it back.'

One chap had to do just that. He snagged his parachute when climbing into his aircraft and it popped open. Normally this would have been viewed as an offence worthy of a one pound fine, but not on this occasion. When his chute opened, instead of a pile of silk, a couple of old blankets spilled out. The op was scrubbed. All parachutes were returned for inspection and an investigation was launched.[47]

---

[47] See Author's notes, Chapter 11 – Prepped for Flight.

By the time the transport arrived to take the crews to dispersal, Jim, in his multiple layers, found himself 'perspiring like the dickens.' At times like that, he envied the lads sitting in the front office of the Lanc where they could get away with minimal layers of clothing, especially Freddie who sat right next to the hot air duct.

Nobody admitted it but they were all apprehensive about their first night op. Crews often released the tension with superstitious rituals like 'wetting the wheel' (urinating on the main undercarriage or tail wheel), a practice the ground crews frowned upon because they said it rotted the tyres.

Jim never partook. For one thing, he would have been too embarrassed, and for another, he had too much clothing to undo. In flight, when the others could use the Elsan, a rarely used small rudimentary porta loo, he and Frank had to either hold on, or wet themselves, because they couldn't abandon their positions.

The crew settled in and started their pre-flight checks an hour before takeoff. With everything in readiness, Ian and Bill started the engines; the port outer first, followed by the starboard outer, port inner and starboard inner.

With the port inner engine running, Jim could operate his turret. He traversed it through 180 degrees and tested the depression and elevation of the guns. He cocked the guns, fired with them set on 'safe', then re-cocked them to set a live round in each breech. He would test fire them once they were over the sea.

Ian's voice came over the intercom. 'Pilot to rear gunner, test your intercom?'

'Rear gunner to pilot, ready, skipper. Testing, one, two three …'

When communicating, the crew always used their trade names, i.e. pilot, rear gunner, navigator etc. to avoid being mistaken for another member of the crew. In the Blance crew, an exception to the rule allowed Frank or Jim to call for a corkscrew without the formality if they sighted a German fighter already on an attack course.

'And if we had no time to shout 'fighter, fighter, corkscrew port,' Jim said, 'we had our own code-word - 'jenks'- which told Ian to throw us into a steep port dive. After that we could call out evasive manoeuvres as required.'

Ian ran through the intercom drill with the rest of the crew and then taxied the Lancaster onto the perimeter track using a combination of braking and engine power. Getting a bombed up Lanc around the track without running off onto the grass or colliding with another aircraft required a good measure of skill. Any miscalculation could put an entire operation in jeopardy. Ian kept in close contact with Jim, checking to make sure any following Lancasters weren't too close.

They paused at the top of the runway and waited for the green light. The noise inside the aircraft, as Bill and Ian held the engines at three quarter power with the brakes jammed hard on, made it almost impossible for Jim to keep a clear thought in his head.

'It felt like the old girl would shake herself to bits,' he reflected.

Ian's voice came over the intercom. 'Pilot to crew, ready for takeoff. Rear gunner, all clear behind?'

'All clear, skipper.'

The green light flashed.

'Full power please, Bill.'

Now the Merlins erupted into a deafening symphony of raw horsepower and the Lancaster strained against the brakes, the entire airframe rattling and vibrating. Finally released, it started to roll forward, heavy and reluctant at first, then gathering speed, leaving one to wonder how such a beast could lift itself into the air.

Roaring down the runway in an opera of grace, beauty and primal omnipotence, with the wind flowing over the Lanc's giant wings and Bill calling out the ground speed, Jim kept his turret facing dead astern. Any shift left or right would disturb the airflow making the aircraft yaw, compounding Ian's already difficult job. Sitting over top of the tail wheel, Jim suffered an uncomfortable ride as the aircraft snaked and everything strained, creaked, groaned, rattled and banged. The tail wheel might as well have been made of concrete. Then the tail came up, suspending him in mid-air. He used to chuckle, 'Lucky me, always the first to leave the ground, and the last to land.'

The Lancaster rapidly increased speed; eighty miles per hour ... eighty-five ... ninety ... ninety-five ... one hundred ... the Lancaster demanded to be let off the ground. At one hundred and ten miles per hour Ian pulled back on the column.

Someone once calculated that there were about a thousand things that could go wrong with a Lancaster on take-off, with most of them resulting in an instant funeral pyre. Engine failure often meant certain calamity but once a pilot had exceeded stalling speed, he might, with skill, have a slim chance of being able to climb out of trouble, although it would take an exceptional effort. No wonder Jim found take-off the most terrifying moment of any op.

Chapter 12: Night Flight

The crew took off at 23.00hrs. As the runway dropped away and they climbed into the inky blackness of the Cambridgeshire night, Bill retracted the undercarriage.

'Undercarriage up, Skipper.'

'Ok,' Ian said.

'And locked,' Bill said. 'Flaps up.'

'Flaps up,' Ian concurred.

Once clear of the airfield their navigation lights were switched off. Jim had the responsibility of extinguishing the rear light. If a rear gunner forgot to do this, he courted potential disaster, giving night fighters a free invitation to shoot up his aircraft.

Colin gave Ian a heading and an estimated time of arrival (ETA) at the rallying point where they would merge with four engine heavies from many other squadrons to form a huge bomber stream.

They clawed through the darkness, alert for any shadows or movement that might betray another Lanc getting too close. With so many aircraft milling about, collisions were an ever-present danger. In fog and rain, they were almost inevitable. If take-off and assembly were bad enough for collisions, turning back mid-flight could be just as dangerous. So much so that many pilots who found their aircraft in trouble continued on to the target rather than risk a collision by turning back against the bomber stream.

Bombing at night posed many problems, one of the biggest being able to find the target. Early navigation aids like Gee, which came into use by the RAF in 1942, had a limited range and couldn't be employed against distant targets like Berlin or Stuttgart, and by 1944 German scientists had figured out how to jam it. Over friendly country, however, it still worked remarkably well and saved many a navigator from getting lost in the treacherous fogs that regularly enveloped Britain.

The development of H2S was a giant leap forward. This ground mapping aid let the navigator see an outlined image of the ground on a screen. Dark areas represented water (lakes and sea) and bright areas highlighted built-up areas. Although introduced as a navigational aid, H2S could also be used effectively to drop bombs blind through heavy cloud and smoke. Initially it had been limited to the Pathfinder Force, but by 1944 many aircraft in the main force were equipped with the device. Colin didn't like it. He preferred a pencil and slide rule and left the intricacies of modern technology to Oscar.

Night bombing also brought the risk of being clobbered by friendly bombs from aircraft operating at higher altitudes. Until its withdrawal, the Stirling copped it the worst in that regard. With its short wingspan, it was limited to a maximum height of about 12,000 feet while the Lancaster and Halifax could operate much higher.

Not that the Lancaster was immune. Colin had a conversation with another navigator whose Lancaster had been hit by a bomb from an aircraft directly overhead. The bomb came through the top of the fuselage, destroyed his table, and carried on through the floor. Thankfully, he had not been at his table at the time.

Night raids were frightening, dazzling pyrotechnic displays with flares and sky markers from the Pathfinders drifting gracefully earthward while on the ground hundreds of fires burnt and bright explosions of detonating bombs flickered across the target area. Occasionally, a bomber went down in flames.

From his isolated cocoon in the tail, Jim watched the green and orange tracer coming up from the anti-aircraft guns. It seemed to come up so slowly at first that he didn't think it could hurt them and then it rapidly increased speed and streaked past terrifyingly close. Combined with dozens of crisscrossing searchlights and German night fighters dropping flares from above to aid the flak gunners, he began to wondered how he would survive one night op let alone an entire tour.

During his training, he had been instructed never to look down at the target because the explosions and fires would ruin his night vision. It took about forty minutes to obtain really good night vision, so if he ever did look, he did so with one eye while keeping the other tightly closed. According to Jim, crews were encouraged to keep up a high dosage of vitamin A, so to that effect there was always a good supply of carrots to be found in the mess. He doubted they did any good and reckoned there were plenty of men who never touched another carrot for as long as they lived.

Once Colin had directed Ian to the initial aiming point, Oscar took over for the bomb run. They were lucky to have someone of his experience because it usually took bomb aimers four or five trips before they felt confident in what they were doing. Unfortunately, many of them didn't last that long.

Approaching the target on the bomb run, things got even more nerve-racking. Committed to flying straight and level, they were helpless to avoid flak or night fighters. The slightest deviation from their course could see their bombs fall miles from the target.[48] Without question, the introduction of H2S significantly improved bombing accuracy, but the aircraft still had to be held straight and steady to drop the bombs. Results were sometimes scattered and remained a far cry from the kind of pin point accuracy the Americans were boasting with the use of their revolutionary, and highly secret, Norton bombsight. To some critics the boast had no merit because the amazing bombing accuracy the Americans were claiming had been achieved over the clean, clear skies of the southern United States, which were a far cry from the

---

[48] See Author's notes, Chapter 12 – Night Flight.

hostile, often inclement conditions found over Europe where the American boast fell somewhat flat. When comparing the British and American bombing strategies, one clever wit once remarked, 'The British precision bomb area targets, while the Americans area bomb precision targets.'

Everyone had heard stories about bomb aimers who had refused to drop their bombs due to cloud cover, wind, or a pilot not keeping them straight and level, and those bomb aimers, while doing their job, were not popular. Nobody wanted to 'go around' again on a bomb run. Those few minutes of having to fly straight and level through a barrage of flak and groping searchlights with the bomb bay doors agape were the most terrifying of Jim's young life.

Freezing in the rear turret, exposed to the elements with the central Perspex panel removed, he watched thick puffs of smoke billow from bursts of flak. The Lancaster vibrated from the concussion of the explosions and the stench of cordite filled the air as shards of flak clattered against the fuselage. If the bursts of flak produced black or white smoke, they were out of harms reach. If they burst out yellow it meant they were getting uncomfortably close. It would only take one splinter to pierce the thin casing of the 4,000- pound Cookie and their lives would be extinguished in a blinding instant. He tried not to think about it.

Oscar gave Ian the bombing instructions. 'Right …right …left, left …steady …right …left, left …right …steady …bombs gone!'

With the Lancaster released of its lethal cargo the engines rose to a higher pitch and the aircraft lifted about a hundred feet in an instant. Jim just wanted them to get the heck out of there, but they couldn't. They still had to get a photograph. That meant flying level for another twenty to thirty seconds until their photoflash burst, thereby automatically triggering the onboard camera. Only then could Ian pull them away from the target.

They had avoided the searchlights on the way in, but coming out of the target area Jim vividly recalled getting hit by a massive blue master beam.

'It lit my turret up like daylight. Hell, I thought, this is it! And only our second op!'

With quick thinking and the correct evasive manoeuvre, a good pilot might escape an ordinary searchlight, but master beams were radio controlled and almost impossible to elude. Once they latched onto a victim, other searchlights would join the party and like a hapless dancer trapped in the middle of a black stage with every spotlight in the room directed upon them, the trapped bomber would be left to dart and twist and turn in a desperate search for a cloak of darkness. Getting coned usually meant you weren't going home.

Before Jim had time to consider how unfair his early demise would be, the tail of the aircraft flung up with such force it slammed him back against the turret doors and tore the ammunition through the servo feeds, dumping the lot in his lap. He grappled for something to hold onto as the Lancaster launched into a steep dive with the G-forces pinning him to the doors as the aircraft pitched nose-down through the blue daylight. With the horrendous hail of the wind and the high-pitched screaming of the engines, Jim thought the wings were going to rip off. Then suddenly the screaming Lancaster, still in its dive, went hard over to port, rattling him around like a ragdoll before plunging abruptly into merciful darkness. The dive lasted several more seconds before the Lancaster pulled up and returned to level flight, the screaming engines regaining a sliver of normality.

Ian's voice gasped over the intercom. 'Everyone ok? Rear gunner, report.'

Jim scrambled to fix up his guns, terrified a night fighter would pick that moment to pounce.

'Rear gunner to pilot, I'm OK, skipper.'

'Pilot to Mid-upper, report.'

'Mid-upper to pilot. Crikey Skipper, I think I just left my dinner on the floor.'

'Sorry about that chaps. Keep an eye out for fighters.'

Ian gently banked left and right to allow a for a better view beneath the aircraft, the favourite position for night fighters to attack. Pilots never flew straight and level except on the bomb run, but even with the constant weaving and waggling, night fighters could still be difficult to spot, especially when flying in cloud.

Some aircrew considered keeping a look out for night fighters solely the gunners' responsibility but the Blance crew thought the more eyes the better. When Oscar and Bill weren't busy with other duties, they helped keep an eye out from the astrodome. Oscar also had the job of chucking out the 'window', an uncomplicated counter measure against the German radar defenses. Absurd in its simplicity, window consisted of bundles of aluminium foil pushed out through the flare chute to scatter across the night sky. It subjected German radar screens to a snow storm of false readings and night fighter pilots, vectoring in on co-ordinates from their controllers, often ended up searching a frustratingly empty sky.

Window met with great success on the Nuremburg raid of 1942 but by 1944 experienced Nachtjagd pilots were easily distinguishing the difference between fast moving signals (aircraft) running ahead of the hailstorm of slower signals produced by window.

A bomber crew's best defense remained the gunners' vigilance. Easier said than practiced. Operating at temperatures as low as minus forty degrees it could be a mentally and physically enervating task. Isolated in the back of the aircraft, Jim had the worst time of it. Despite being wrapped up in sheepskin, kapok and electrically heated clothing he found it impossible to keep warm.

'Just to rub it in,' he recalled, 'I heard Freddie, who sat next to the heating duct outlet, asking Bill to turn the heat down!'

Throughout their training, Jim and Frank had been constantly reminded that first and foremost a good gunner always protected his aircraft. He didn't look to get into a scrap with an enemy fighter and he never opened fire on one unless being attacked. One of Jim's gunnery instructors at OTU had completed a tour of thirty ops, some to Berlin, without ever firing his guns. 'Seeing a fighter doesn't necessarily mean it's seen you,' said the instructor. 'By sending out a spurt of tracer, you'll give away your position.'

Contrary to the instructor's claim, tracer very rarely gave away a bomber's position according to German night fighter ace Major Wolfgang Schnaufer who was credited with destroying an incredible 121 enemy aircraft. He found it remarkable that RAF gunners didn't use their guns in an offensive role more often.

'The bomber's tracer or gun flash did not give away the bomber's position,' he claimed. '…and there were only two or three cases when bombers were shot down due to this.'[49]

Schnaufer held the opinion that RAF gunners didn't fire often enough or soon enough, and he remained convinced that if they had done so, and used brighter tracer, many of the German pilots would not have attacked. On two occasions Schnaufer had been surprised by fire from a bomber which he had not seen. In both cases accurate fire deterred him from attacking.

Later during the homeward flight Freddie reported a blip on the Monica.[50] High alert for the gunners. The blip turned out to be another Lancaster. Being too dark to make out its recognition markings, and because the Germans had been known to stack captured British bombers with machine guns and infiltrate the bomber streams, Ian had established a firm rule that if an aircraft followed them through more than two turns, they would get a warning shot.

Ian made a turn to port. The trailing Lancaster followed suit. He then made a turn back to starboard. The shadowing Lancaster hung on. He advised Jim and Frank that if they were followed through the next turn they were to fire. Jim didn't want to attract the attention from any night fighters that might be lurking in the area by loosening off a few rounds so it came as a relief when the pilot of the following Lancaster didn't trail them through the next turn but slipped away into the darkness.

The remainder of the trip settled into a quiet, uneventful rhythm with only the constant heavy drone of the engines and snippets of conversation over the intercom to keep Jim company as he endlessly traversed his turret and elevated and depressed his guns with tiring eyes searching the blackness beyond the solitude of his cramped station.

As they approached base he couldn't afford to relax. Incursions by German intruders were a rarity in mid-1944, but he'd still heard about bombers being shot up by night fighters while in their landing circuits and he wasn't about to let his guard down. They landed safely at 02.35 hours.

---

[49] Leo McKinstry, Lancaster, The Second World War's Greatest Bomber, pg 166.
[50] Rearward facing radar fitted in the tail of the Lancaster.

After returning to dispersal, and with the engines shutting down, Jim disconnected himself from the array of tubes and wires that had kept him alive for the past few hours. Now he faced the excruciating aftermath of the flight. All the electric gloves in the world couldn't prevent frozen fingers, and nothing could avert the inevitable agony that came with them thawing out. While the other chaps sat in the back of the truck talking merrily about bacon and eggs, Jim was holding back tears of abject misery as the blood slowly returned to his fingertips.

Possible chilblains were just one of the problems rear gunners had to put up with. Later in life, many suffered hearing problems thanks to the noise of Merlin engines rumbling in their ears for hours on end (something suffered by all aircrew) and there was also a high number who suffered from testicular cancer, thanks to long hours sitting in cramped turrets. Tail End Charlies seemed to get the worst of it in every way.

On the way to debriefing, Jim quizzed Ian about the searchlight. 'Oh,' Ian said rather matter-of-fact. 'I'd been thinking about what to do in that situation ever since our Bulls-eye over London. As soon as that master beam hit us, I just threw us into the steepest dive I could and then yanked hard over to port to get under it.' Had it not been for their London experience they wouldn't have been home for breakfast. Nobody enjoyed the bind of a debriefing when there were comfortable beds awaiting them, but it had to be endured. Not even the rum-laced tea on offer helped because Colin was the only one who could stomach it. Officers and Waafs from the intelligence section grilled them about the trip. 'What was the cloud like?' 'Was the target visible?' 'Did you bomb on the markers?' 'Were there fighters?' 'Did you see any aircraft go down?' 'Were the navigational aids working properly?' 'Did you have any combats?' If so, a separate combat report needed to be filled out. Jim never doubted the intelligence bods' thoroughness. Afterwards, he and the rest of the boys were happy to go to bed and sleep through until mid-morning.

Only one of 75 Squadron's Lancasters, LL921 captained by Flt.Lt. John 'Snow' Myers, failed to return from Aulnoye. A night fighter flown by either Ofhr. Rinker, who operated with 1. /NJG4, or by Hptm. Josef Krahforst of 2. /NJG 4, attacked Meyers over Belgium west of Mons-Maubeuge. Rinker claimed the victory at 1.04 hrs and Krahforst claimed it at 01.06 hrs. Confusion arises because Lancaster LL493 of 115 Sqn. succumbed to a fighter at the same time within close proximity. Neither Nachtjagd pilot could claim with absolute certainty which Lancaster he had shot down.

Jim had not known any of the Myers crew but their failure to return provided a sobering shot of reality. Myers, on his twenty-second operation, had been an experienced pilot with a seasoned crew well on their way to completing their tour. Like many other captains, he had managed to get his crew out safely at the cost of his own life.

'It hit hard when chaps went missing, especially old hands,' Jim recalled in a rare moment of somber reflection. 'A few hours earlier you had seen them in the mess or the crew hut, perhaps envying them for being only a handful of ops away from finishing their tours. The next thing you knew, the RAF police and station adjutant were clearing out their lockers.'

Sometimes there might be a witness to what had happened to the ill-fated crew, but on night raids that was a rarity and the fates of many crews remained unsolved mysteries. There were occasions when crews reported unexplained explosions or bursts of flames, and rumours circulated about 'scarecrows' - shell blasts that mimicked exploding bombers. Jim thought 'scarecrows' were Air Ministry propaganda designed to calm their fears about the mysterious explosions and the unexplained losses. Only later in the war did crews became aware of Schrage Music (Jazz Music), the upward firing canon equipping many German night fighters.

These fighters, guided to their target by a ground controller and their own onboard radar, slipped undetected beneath a bomber before unleashing a devastating barrage from two 20 mm canons. Even with weaving tactics and vigilant gunners, spotting a night fighter in the Lancaster's huge blind spot in the dark, especially in cloud, relied more on luck than skill and a crew only became aware of the presence of a night fighter when their aircraft suddenly erupted in flames. Many German pilots insisted they aimed for the petrol tanks located in the Lancaster's wings in order to give the bomber crew time to escape, but it was far from a convincing plea. A Lancaster or Halifax hit in the petrol tanks would ignite almost instantly, going out of control and giving the crew little hope of survival. A more plausible explanation is that night fighter pilots aimed for the wings because it proved inherently safer than attacking the fuselage where they ran the potential risk of igniting a full bomb load and destroying themselves along with their victim.

Chapter 13: Into the Reich

On 20 July, twenty-six of 75 Squadron's Lancasters were part of a force comprising 147 Lancasters and 11 Mosquitoes detailed to attack Homberg, site of a large refinery producing vast quantities of oil and aviation fuel. Homberg lay in the Ruhr Valley, a place sardonically coined 'Happy Valley' by the crews.

The towns of the Ruhr - places like Essen, Dortmund, Duisburg, Hagen and Homberg - were ringed with thousands of searchlights and massive flak batteries. Happy Valley had a reputation for being a far from happy place for Bomber Command, and of all the Ruhr's industrial towns, Homberg had become 75 Squadron's particular bogey. After the night of 20/21 July it became doubly so.

Jim fought a peculiar internal battle when it came to ops, always envious of those not on the battle order when his crew were flying, and then grappling with a perverse resentment, like he might be missing out on something, when they weren't flying. In the tightknit world of a bomber command squadron being left behind while others faced potentially fatal hazards could leave a man with the impression that he'd let the side down. Homberg turned out to be one op he later counted his blessings at having missed.

1, 3, and 8 Groups lost a combined total of twenty Lancasters - 140 aircrew - with 75 Squadron being particularly hard hit, losing seven of its twenty-six aircraft. Among the casualties were P/O Edward Howell and his crew who were all killed,[51] P/O Kenneth Mackay and his crew who were lost without trace,[52] and P/O Harold Whittington and his crew who were shot down over the Netherlands. Only their flight engineer, Sgt. Gore (RAF) survived to become a POW.[53]

Also, posted FTR were the crew of F/S Davidson who were shot down over the Netherlands and crashed into the River Maas near Kassel. Again, only one crew member, the RAF bomb-aimer, survived to become a POW.[54]

From the crew of P/O Henry 'Hank' Burtt the navigator and bomb-aimer escaped the crash of their Lancaster and were taken prisoner. Their five

---

[51] Lancaster PA976 claimed by Ofhr. Gerhard Warenbarger, 4. /NJG3, S.W. Eindhoven at approx 17,000 ft. 01.09 hrs. Warenbarger's first Nachtjagd claim.

[52] Lancaster ND800 lost at sea. Three possible Nachtjagd claims for this particular aircraft: (1) Oblt. Fredrich Berger, 3. /NJGr10, N. Rotterdam at approx 11,500 ft. 01.05 hrs. Berger's seventh Nachtjagd claim. (2) Lt. Josef Forster, 8. /NJG2, S.W. Rotterdam at approx 3,000ft. 02.09 hrs Forster's fourth Nachtjagd claim. (3) Uffz. Gustav Sarzio, 6. /NJG1, Sea 20 km W. Katwijkaan Zee at approx 10,500ft. 02.16 hrs. Sarzio's fourth Nachtjagd claim.

[53] Lancaster ME691 claimed by Lt Walter Briegleb, 10. /NJG3, Vught, 20 km NE Tilburg at approx 17,000 ft. 01.33 hrs. Breigleb's thirteenth Nachtjagd claim.

[54]Lancaster HK569 claimed by Oblt. Dietrich Schmidt, 8. /NJG1, Kessel near Venio at approx 20,000 ft. 01.16 hrs. Schmidt's twenty-ninth Nachtjagd claim.

comrades were killed.[55] Likewise, the navigator and mid-upper gunner of the Lancaster captained by W/O Gilmour (RAAF) survived the crash of their aircraft and went into captivity.[56] From the crew of F/S Brian Roche, only the New Zealand bomb-aimer, F/S Burgess (POW) and the New Zealand mid-upper gunner, F/S McGee (evaded) survived.[57]

75 Squadron's casualties accounted for 32% of the total losses on the Homberg raid. Forty-nine aircrew were lost, including forty-one killed. Some of those men had notched up an enviable number of ops. Henry Burtt had flown 26 trips. Howell had been on his eighteenth operation and his wireless operator, F/S Gerard Redwood, his twentieth.

Dying rarely got a mention. Familiar faces that were no longer around had simply gone for a 'Burton', 'got the chop' or 'bought it'. At first, Jim deemed the aloofness and arrogance of the more experienced crews unnecessary and it rankled him, but he later learned that when it was one of your friends who didn't come back, you really felt it. Most of the young airmen found it easier not to get too close to anyone and for that reason most crews remained quite insular.

Throughout July the crews were kept in a state of perpetual limbo thanks to continuous cold fronts sweeping across the UK. A raid detailed against Varies for 16 July only got as far as air testing the Lancs before bad weather postponed it. The crews were then kept on edge for 24 hours, stretching their patience to breaking point, before some bright spark with scrambled egg on his hat decided to scrub the operation completely.

Inclement weather didn't always get a raid cancelled. While it might be teeming down in Cambridgeshire, with the entire county boxed in by 10/10 cloud, it could be clear as a bell over Europe. 75 squadron's press-on attitude, and the desire to fly while the sparrows walked, resulted in a number of bad weather takeoffs, and with them the increased risk of collisions. Jim never saw a collision, but he'd heard enough gruesome stories about them to put the wind up him when taking off in the rain.

While a scrubbed operation might have encouraged disgruntled comments about the top brass, the crews were always thankful for the opportunity to go to the pub instead of the Ruhr Valley or some other heavily defended place in Germany.

Jim and his crew frequented the local pubs in Mepal and Sutton. London and Cambridge were out of reach without a 48-hour pass and they needed to

---

[55] Lancaster ND752 possible claim by Lt Josef Forster, 8. /NJG2, Tilburg - Hertogenbosch at approx 10,500 ft. 01.45 hrs. Possibly Forster's third Nachtjagd claim.

[56] Lancaster ND915 claimed by Hptm. Hermann Greiner, 11. /NJG1, S Hertogenbosch - Tilburg at approx 17,000 ft. 01.37 hrs. Greiner's thirty-sixth Nachtjagd claim.

[57] Lancaster ME752 claimed by Uffz. Bruno Rupp, 4. /NJG3, W. Monchengladbach at approx 17,000 ft. 01.14 hrs. Rupp's ninth Nachtjagd claim.

have completed five or six ops to earn one of those. On one occasion the Blance crew did manage to get to Ely after Frank commandeered a truck.

'We were joined by another crew', Jim recalled. 'You wouldn't credit it, but Frank turned out to be the only one with a driver's licence. We had twenty and twenty-one-year-old chaps crewing four engine bombers over Europe who didn't know how to drive a car.'

On the night of 22/23 July, six aircraft successfully laid mines in the Kattegat area and returned safely. Twelve other aircraft were detailed to attack a bombing target but the op ended up being scrubbed.

The night of 23/24 July saw twenty aircraft attack Kiel, all successfully bombing the target. It was a concentrated raid with reports stating that the glow of the fires could be seen from the Danish west coast on return.

Squadron records show that on the night of 24/25 July twenty-one aircraft took off as detailed to attack Stuttgart. Eighteen aircraft bombed the target with the aid of markers but the results appeared to be scattered due to intense A.A. fire concentrated over the target and fighters being fairly active. Two aircraft engaged in combats. One aircraft returned early with engine trouble and two aircraft, those captained by P/O J. McRae[58] & P/O K. Whitehouse,[59] failed to return.

Tragically, nobody from the McRae or Whitehouse crews survived.

Since the beginning of July 1944, 75 squadron had lost half its strength. Of seventy missing aircrew, fifty-six had been killed, and ten incarcerated in POW camps. Only four men had managed to evade capture. Despite the grim reading there would be no letting up and fourteen crews were briefed for a return to Stuttgart on the night 25/26 July.

The Blance crew weren't on the battle order for the op but it may well have been the trip Jim flew as a spare bod with another crew. All crews returned safely although only ten reached the target and dropped their bombs.

Squadron Operations Records detailed '...many fires and explosions. Heavy A.A. fire. F/S Smith claimed fighter (FW190) destroyed. Two a/c[60] landed at Ford. One with engine trouble, one with damage to petrol tank and rear turret. 4 aborts. 1 - Jettisoned after starboard engine caught fire. 1 - failed to see markers. 2 - had severe icing.' The succinct, impersonal remarks by the

---

[58] Lancaster HK575. Three possible Nachtjagd claims may account for the loss of this aircraft. (1) Hptm. Paul Zorner, Stab III. /NJG5, 50 km SE Kuli (Neunkirchen area) at approx 10,500 ft. 02.33 hrs. This would have been Zorner's fifty-seventh Nachtjagd claim. (2) Fw. Heinz Misch, 9. /NJG2, NE Metz/100-200 km NW Stuttgart at approx 12,500 ft. 02.24 hrs. It would have been Misch's seventh Nachtjagd claim. (3) Uff. Heinrich Buhlmann 11. /NJG5, 80 km WNW Stuttgart at approx 13,000 ft. 02.25 hrs. This would have been Buhlmann's first Nachtjagd claim.

[59] Lancaster HK568 claimed by Ofw. Gunter Scheidel, 3. /NJG7, Strasbourg at approx 12,500 ft. 02.11 hrs. Scheidel's first Nachtjagd claim.

[60] Aircraft.

squadron adjutant were very matter of fact and gave no real indication of what the crews had experienced.

On 27 July, twenty-one aircraft were detailed for a daylight raid on construction works at Coquereaux, but miserable weather postponed the op until the night of 27/28 July. In the end they scrubbed it entirely.

Chapter 14: The Fires of Hell

On the night of 28/29 July the Blance crew were back on the battle order. The erks[61] knew the young airmen faced a deep penetration raid, a little secret they were all too willing to share after being given orders to fully fuel the Lancasters.

The squadron was returning to Stuttgart for a third successive strike. Reconnaissance photos from the previous raids showed a number of the important factories turning out gyros and engines for V1 rockets had been left virtually intact. Daimler Benz and Bosch Electrical also had factories in Stuttgart manufacturing engines for everything from U-boats to aircraft. 461 Lancasters and 153 Halifax bombers were scheduled to hit the city.

75 squadron's fire and brimstone C.O. Jack Leslie had been far from impressed with the previous results and started the main briefing by castigating the squadron on their previous efforts. Bad weather, he said, should be no excuse for not reaching the target, implying that the crews hadn't tried hard enough, which caused some resentment.

For the third raid they would have to contend with rain and thunder clouds en route but designated flying altitudes would allow them to sneak beneath a heavy cloud base, thereby avoiding the bright moonlight. The Met boys assured them it would be clear over the target.

The crews were exasperated to be told they would be flying the exact same route as for the first two raids. Groans and incredulous cries of despair arose from those who'd been on the previous ops. So much disquiet arose that the C.O. had to bring the room to order.

Later, everyone emptied their pockets and deposited their letters and wills. They collected their escape boxes and flying rations, changed into layers of kapok and fleece, signed for their parachutes and boarded the transport to take them out to dispersal. The Waaf driving them out brought the truck to a lurching stop, throwing her charges around unnecessarily. 'Anyone for M-Mike?' she cried.

Jim jumped down from the truck and followed his mates to their charge for the night, which on this occasion was AA-M (ND756) whose regular crew[62] were on leave.

One of 600 Mark III Lancasters ordered from A.V. Roe (Chatterton), ND756 had been one of the first Lancasters delivered to 75 Squadron on 13 March 1944 when the squadron had converted from Stirlings. In fact, ND756 had

---

[61] Ground crews.

[62] F/O Ralph Brumwell, F/S Charles Busfield, F/S Max Ruane, W/O Ernest Armitage, Sgt. J. Nelson, Sgt. Arthur Limage, F/S Clayton Arthur.

notched up 229 hours and 45 operational sorties. She had flown on the raids to Homberg on 19 July, Kiel on 23 July and on both previous Stuttgart raids on 24 and 26 July.

Jim climbed aboard first and turned left toward his lonely station in rear turret while everyone else turned right and headed for the front of the aircraft. He settled himself in and went through his pre-flight checks.

A flare shot up from the tower giving the go-ahead to start engines. Once they were running, Ian's voice crackled over the intercom.

'Pilot to rear gunner, test your intercom.'

Jim flicked the intercom switch on the control column. 'Testing, one, two, three.'

John Swale, a rear gunner with 75 Squadron argued that RAF rear gunners should have been given the same type of throat mics the American crews used because the intercom switch on the Frazer-Nash control column often froze.

'You OK back there, Winkie?'

Jim traversed the turret and elevated and depressed the guns. 'All good, Skipper.'

He would much rather have been at the pub.'

Ian repeated the intercom drill with the others.

Take off was at 2200 hrs.

With the aircraft shaking under the tremendous power of its four Merlin engines, Jim sat in his lonely capsule watching the following Lancasters and listened to Ian and Bill go through their takeoff procedures.

'Brakes off,' Ian said. 'Taxiing out now. We're one of the last tonight, chaps. Keep a look out back there, Winkie.'

Stirring like a primordial beast the Lancaster crept out of its lair and onto the perimeter track. With most of the squadron taking off before them it took some time before Ian had the Lancaster lined up at the top of the runway.

'Pilot to crew, ready for take-off. Open throttle, Bill.'

The green light from the aldis lamp flashed from the caravan beside the runway.

'Full power, Bill.'

The engines erupted to maximum power and the bone-shaking monster lurched forward. Ian and Bill held the throttles wide open and Bill called out the ground speed as the Lancaster, loaded with bombs and incendiaries, thundered down the runway.

The usual small crowd of spectators and well-wishers flashed passed with a wave goodbye. The tail rose and then a moment later the undercarriage lifted and the heavily laden Lancaster hauled itself into the air. It cleared the boundary fence and climbed into the night. The undercarriage came up and once again Jim and his mates were heading into the unknown.

They encountered tracer as soon as they crossed the French coast, and from distant towns Jim saw sinister finger-like searchlights sweeping the clouds. He saw an aircraft caught in a beam, twisting and diving in an effort to escape the inevitable flak and night fighters. Occasionally a stream of brightly coloured tracer would whiz out of the dark from nowhere. He saw an aircraft blazing out of control in the distance. Bombers or night fighter? He hoped the latter.

The route had them climbing through heavy cloud to their bombing altitude of 20,000 - 21,000 feet. As they closed in on the target the intensity of the flak increased, the worst Jim had encountered. The concussion of exploding shells knocked the aircraft around and shrapnel rattled against the fuselage and tail. 'Heavens,' he admitted. 'I'd be lying if I said I wasn't scared.' There were no reports of damage.

Night fighters often penetrated the bomber streams during the inbound flights, but if the intelligence chaps were to be believed they wouldn't tangle with the bombers over the target for fear of getting clobbered by their own flak. Another great fallacy.

'Night fighters regularly dropped flares from above and in front of us to make it easier for the searchlights to pick us out,' Jim said. 'Then they attacked us over the target.' In some cases, the flak stopped to let the fighters finish off their trapped prey but more often than not the guns continued pounding and the fighters had to plough through a blizzard of flak just like the bombers. 'There must have been an acute rivalry between the flak batteries and the fighter pilots to see who could claim the most bombers', Jim said. 'Heaven only knows how many night fighters fell victim to their own anti-aircraft defenses. Those German pilots had guts.'

The bomb run; the part of the op every crew hated most. Committed to straight and level flight the bombers were vulnerable to night fighters, searchlights and flak. In the rear turret, Jim breathed heavily, gimlet eyes searching the sky.

The Met boys were bang-on about the cloud clearing over the target to give the bomb aimers an unobscured view. The Pathfinder flares drifted onto the aiming point like a cascading Christmas tree, and colourful tracer arced up from the ground and flak exploded all around the aircraft, Oscar gave his usual patter.

'Right …right …steady …left, left …steady …' After an age, he called, 'Bombs gone.'

The engines changed to a higher pitch as the Lancaster lifted in response to the release of the enormous weight and they continued over the target for a few more seconds to take their aiming point photo.

Jim found it difficult not to be distracted by the Pathfinders coloured T.I.s falling from the sky to meld with the hundreds of raging fires as brief, intense bursts of high explosive detonated across the target before evaporating to leave clouds of acrid smoke in their wake.

Jim spared a thought for the civilians caught in the carnage below.

'It must have been terrible. The sound of hundreds of Merlins overhead would have been bad enough, let alone the whistling of high explosive bombs and incendiaries.'

Those sheltering in cellars during a Bomber Command raid felt the mighty thud and tremor of high explosives falling about them, and the accompanying alternation of the suction-pressure they caused.[63] People cowering in the shelters learned to distinguish the sounds of the different kinds of incendiaries and bombs. A rustle like a flock of birds taking off represented a stick of incendiaries breaking apart as it neared the ground, sending individual incendiaries in all directions. An explosion like a sudden crack was a 12-kilogram fire bomb shooting out flames to a distance of eighty meters. A big splash was a 14-kilogram bomb, which spread liquid rubber and benzene over a radius of fifty meters. The sound of a wet sack flopping heavily down was a canister containing twenty litres of benzol. A sharp explosion heralded a 106-kilogram bomb that hurled out rags soaked in benzene or heavy oil. A 112-kilogram bomb ejected a thousand patties of benzol and rubber over the surrounding area.[64]

Ian banked the Lancaster away from the carnage below and Colin gave him a course for home. As the crew didn't talk unnecessarily, with no wisecracking or frivolous use of the intercom, Jim heard nothing for some time.

Ian dropped M-Mike down to the return flight altitude of 14,000 feet which took them into a 10/10ths cloud layer. While it hid them from the bright moonlight above it made spotting night fighters almost impossible. Thirty minutes into the return flight Colin's voice crackled over the intercom.

'Navigator to pilot, passing Strasbourg in twenty minutes.'

'Pilot to navigator, OK. Thanks Colin.'

Jim heard nothing more until sometime later a crashing roll of thunder almost drowned out the roaring drone of the Lancaster's engines and, at the same time, M-Mike shook violently. The surrounding cloud exploded in an orange glow so intense Jim could read the fuses above his head and he suddenly realized it hadn't been the sound of thunder at all. They were under attack. As the nose dipped and long ribbons of orange and yellow flames streaked passed his turret. Jim tried the intercom. 'Rear gunner to pilot, rear gunner to pilot.' He met foreboding silence, the intercom u/s[65].

He attempted to manoeuvre his turret and guns, but to no avail. That meant the fire had either severed the hydraulic lines to the port outer engine or the engine had quit.

---

[63] Beck, *Under the Bombs,* page 60.

[64] Ibid, Page 62. Beck is describing the experiences by Josef Fischer, a citizen of Cologne who made a record of his experience under bombing.

[65] Unserviceable

He frantically tried the intercom again only to be met with further silence. He had no idea what was happening at the front of the aircraft but when the nose came up and then dipped again sharply, he knew it wasn't good. As smoke started to seep into his turret all his bravado about never jumping went out the door.

He disconnected his suit from the electrical socket, ripped off his thick gauntlets, oxygen mask and helmet, and released his safety strap. With the turret already facing dead astern, he slid open the doors and reached back for his parachute. Beyond the anti-draught doors an appalling, impenetrable wall of fire engulfed the aircraft and the ammunition in the storage tanks mid fuselage, plus the ammo in the long ducting that supplied his turret, had started to ignite.

'My God! he thought. Hopefully Frank had already bailed out. But he didn't have time to dwell on the matter as he reached back into the fuselage to retrieve his parachute. With no chance of escape from the main door, exiting directly from his turret became his only option.

As he fought to attach his parachute, the mortally wounded Lancaster suddenly lurched forward and pitched down through the cloud. As it tore through the base of the cloud and into clear air, Jim saw the frightening sight of JU88 night fighter breaking out of the cloud behind them.

'I could see the pilot's face as plain as day,' he recalled. 'It may have been the blighter that had shot us up but thinking about it later, I didn't think so. I don't believe he would have had time to break off from his first attack and get around behind us again so quickly.'[66]

With no time to consider the irrevocable peril he might be putting himself in, he dumped his parachute and turned to face the danger. It defies belief that with his aircraft plunging in flames his thoughts were focused solely on dealing with the night fighter. Averting from any notion of heroics, he said, 'I just didn't fancy jumping in case the blighter started shooting.'

He released his guns from their hydraulic mechanism, knowing he might have sufficient fluid left in the severed hose to get the servo feed pulling the ammunition through the guns for an initial burst. After that, they would remain firing as long as he held the triggers down.

Already facing dead astern, he quickly raised the guns manually, took a quick sighting and jammed down on the triggers. The four Brownings were impressively devastating at close range. They sent a long burst of tracer and armour-piercing bullets smashing into the JU88's port engine which instantly exploded in flames.

In all likelihood the German pilot had been chasing the crippled Lancaster down to confirm the kill only to be met by a burst of machine gun fire for his

---

[66] See Author's notes, Chapter 14 – Into the Fires of Hell.

trouble. The fighter peeled away in a dive with flames cascading from its wrecked engine.

Jim was always amused by the account of the episode as written in the Official History of New Zealander's with the R.A.F. That version recounts how '...closing in for a second attack, the fighter met determined fire from the Lancaster's rear guns and down it went.'[67] Determined?' Jim laughed. 'More like just plain scared.'

With the JU88 dealt with, he faced the unenviable task of escaping the burning Lancaster, which had fallen into a steep dive with the smoke getting thicker and the heat from the flames beginning to penetrate his suit. With perspiration running down his face, and struggling to breathe, he reached back for his parachute, thankful the flames hadn't breached the anti-draught doors.

Struggling against the mounting G-forces provoked by M-Mike's dive, he desperately groped to hook on his parachute. One of the D-rings clicked into place on the harness clip without difficulty, but the other refused no matter how hard he tried. Then he remembered the old axiom, 'more haste, less speed'.

He forced himself to relax for a second, just to breathe, and then tried again. This time the D-ring snapped firmly into place. That proved to be the easy part. Now he had to get out.

Without electrical power, he had to traverse the turret manually using the rotation gear situated above the hydraulic motor on his right-hand side. It seemed to take forever to get it round to port, by which time M-Mike was plunging wildly.

Abandoning the aircraft wasn't as easy as he'd been led to believe during training when it had simply been a matter of, 'Oh, just pop your turret around and fall out backwards.' They had forgotten to mention that he, like many other airmen, would have to fight for his life against a ferocious slipstream and damning G-forces.

Clawing at whatever he could get a hold of, he squeezed his head and shoulders out of the turret. Flames and smoke streaked past and a raw wind bruised his face as the G-force, like an invisible iron hand, pinned him hard against the side of the turret.

Writhing and squirming, he struggled back inside for another attempt. In all likelihood, his last. Flames and pungent smoke had already burst through the floor of the turret.

Battling the howling slipstream, he fought to get out again, this time latching onto a small radar antenna on the fuselage above his turret and lifting his feet up onto the seat.

---

[67] Thompson, Official History of New Zealand In the Second World War. New Zealanders With the Royal Air Force, Volume II, Pg. 410.

'Thank goodness for being so short,' he reflected. 'Any taller and I wouldn't have been able to get up on the seat.'

With a gale of flames pouring from the aircraft and a deafening, bitter wind pounding in his ears, he heaved on the antenna and pushed against the seat with every excruciating ounce of strength he had left. Then suddenly he lurched clear of the flaming death trap and somersaulted through the air, free of the ravaging slipstream and unshackled from certain death. Remarkably, he didn't have the sensation of falling. If anything, it felt like an invisible hand had grabbed him, determined to drag him upward. Per ardua ad astra[68] indeed. He reached for the ripcord and to his horror discovered it wasn't there!

---

[68] Motto of the Royal Air Force and other Commonwealth air forces, meaning 'Through adversity to the stars', or 'Through struggle to the stars.'

Chapter 15: Into the Silk

In later years, Jim read plenty of stories about aircrew who described in great detail the sickening realization that they were standing upon the threshold of death.

'But the trouble with that sort of stuff,' he said, 'is that it's written in the wonderful world of hindsight. In reality you don't have time to get philosophical. At least I didn't.'

In fact, Jim hadn't had time to consider what had gone wrong before he heard a wild flapping like an explosion of geese taking to the air above his head. An instant later he heard what sounded like a whip cracking and without warning a powerful bone-shaking jerk ripped him abruptly upwards through the air, cutting his parachute harness into his groin. Then everything went calm and he found himself under a huge white canopy with the ripcord handle clutched in his left hand.

Being right handed, he had stowed his chute so the ripcord handle would be on the right-hand side when he picked it up. However, when he'd dropped it in his haste to tackle the night fighter it had fallen the wrong way and he simply hadn't noticed he'd put it on with the handle to the left. He always believed his guardian angel must have pulled it.

Despite his long-held fears, his canopy had deployed perfectly. But the reprieve of seeing it in full bloom became quickly overshadowed by concern for his crew as their blazing Lancaster hurtled to earth. He watched it until it fell from sight.[69] He prayed everyone had escaped, but in his heart, he knew that was almost impossible.

Adrift in an empty black sky, the visual absence of terrain and horizon left him devoid of any sensation of descent and it felt like he might float off into the darkness to wherever the winds took him. Fretting that he might not be heavy enough for the parachute do its job properly he wrenched down on the cords to let some air out of the canopy. This should have accelerated his descent but he didn't feel any appreciable increase of velocity until without any warning he became embroiled in a crashing blizzard of snapping branches and boughs as he plunged through a tree at high speed and came to an abrupt, excruciating halt, his parachute snagged.

He swung in his harness and regained his breath, barely able to see his hand in front of his face let alone the ground below. With no idea how high up he was dangling it would have been foolhardy to release himself from his harness, but hanging in a tree until morning didn't have much appeal either. He'd heard tales about aircrew being caught up trees. Some were left where they were

---

[69] See Author's notes, Chapter 15 – Into the Silk.

found while others had been used for target practice. He had no idea if the stories were true and he had no intention of finding out. But how to get down? If he could find a branch to sit on, he could at least assess his situation in a measure of comfort.

He began to swing to and fro, groping blindly in the dark. A chorus of cracking branches erupted above his head and his parachute shredded and dropped him a few feet. Broken limbs clattered past his head. Fearing a plummet to earth, he arrested his movement and hung motionless for a couple of minutes. He strained his eyes for the merest hint of what lay below but he couldn't distinguish a single feature.

Satisfied his parachute would hold, he began to swing again. More branches snapped and his parachute tore some more, dropping him a few more feet. Not knowing how much longer his parachute would hold, or how high he hung, he decided to chance one more attempt. This time, as he began to swing, his feet unexpectantly scraped the earth. He hadn't been more than six feet above the ground. With a sense of relief, he gave one good tug on the parachute cords and finally had his feet firmly planted on the ground.

A normal parachute landing, they said, equated to jumping off a 10-12 ft. high wall, so on reflection the tree had done him a favour. Perhaps it had saved him from a twisted ankle, or worse. He'd been lucky. He'd landed in one piece and avoided injury. Many unfortunate airmen also lost their boots when bailing out. They'd been torn off in the slipstream of their doomed aircraft or when their parachutes jerked open, but he'd not only managed to keep his boots, but also the knife he'd strapped to his right leg.

He released himself from the heavy canvas harness and dragged his parachute out of the tree. Escape and evasion lectures had stressed that if he was to stand any chance of avoiding capture, the first 48 hours were crucial. But sitting in a lecture room, perhaps a little sleepy in the afternoon sun, turned out to be a far cry from the reality of the situation in which he now found himself.

He stood breathing hard. He was a little shaken from his ordeal but quickly regained his composure. With no means of burying his parachute, he decided to cover it with the leaves he could feel underfoot. When he started to clear them, he found their undersides glowed with phosphorus fungi so bright he could clearly read the time - 1.40 am. A pile of glowing leaves was hardly ideal for camouflaging his parachute, and as he doubted the Germans would be searching before daylight, he decided to wait until morning when he could get a better gauge of his surroundings and do a decent job of hiding his gear. Besides, he risked serious injury attempting to walk out of the woods in pitch blackness. He groped around in the dark and sat down against a tree, thankful for his multiple layers of clothes, and settled in for the night.

Remnants of AA-M (Mike) scattered on a hillside near Millery, N.W. France. Lebel Collection

Gerard Lebel's mother (left) and her cousin collected donations for flowers. Lebel Collection

People from the village of Millery carry the bodies of the deceased crew members Ian Blance (RNZAF), Fred Climo (RNZAF), Frank Jenkins (RNZAF) and Ronald (Oscar) Spencer (RAF) to Millery Communal Cemetery. Lebel Collection

113

Funeral cortege, 1944. Lebel Collection

Funeral cortege making its way to Millery Communal Cemetery. More than 1,500 people attended the funeral for the four deceased airmen. Lebel Collection

Flowers and wreaths for the fallen airmen. Millery Communal Cemetery. Lebel Collection

Crosses and wreaths at Millery Communal Cemetery, 1944. Lebel Collection

Chapter 16: Evasion

Jim slept fitfully. He would drift off only to wake again with his escape playing on his mind. Back at Mepal, the skipper's name would have FTR chalked up beside it. Eventually it would be wiped off. Just another casualty of war. His mother would receive a telegram from the Minister of Defence and a letter from the Air Ministry sympathizing with her over the loss of her son, but neither would be able to shed any light on his fate. Later, she would receive an empathetic letter from Wing Commander Leslie containing standard condolences but again, no clue as to what had become of him. [70]

Eventually he succumbed to overwhelming fatigue, and the next time he woke he found himself in a heavy forest with sunshine filtering through tall trees glistening with Christmas tinsel. What the heck?

He sat up, heavy-eyed and bemused, and it took him a moment to realize the trees were in fact festooned with window. He'd never given any thought to where the aluminium strips might end up after being shoved down the flare chute.

A faint metallic clanging somewhere in the distance brought him to his feet. Noise suggested the presence of people, and that could pose a problem. Allowing for the short time it had taken him to plunge through the tree after bailing out, the wreckage of his Lancaster couldn't be far away. The Germans might already be on the scene. When they discovered the rear turret empty and his parachute missing, they'd be on the hunt.

He quickly stripped off his layers of flying gear and, in an effort to appear less conspicuous, rubbed his Persil-white jersey in the dirt before pulling it back on over his battledress blouse. Then he dirtied his trousers and tugged them down over his thick woollen socks and boots. If spotted, he would hopefully pass for a mucky farmer, at least at a distance.

Unable to bury his gear, he had no choice but to hide everything beneath piles of leaves and rotting logs. [71] While not the most ideal solution it at least reduced the risk of it being discovered. Landing in a forest had its advantages.

He examined his escape supplies. The Pandora Box contained a rock-hard concentrated fruit bar, chewing gum and liver tablets, enough food to keep him going for a couple of days. It also included a rubber bag with a drawstring for collecting water. Directions would not be an issue. The Pandora Box also contained a compass and he had two others concealed on his uniform, one hidden in a tunic button and the other secreted in his collar stud. Complementing his compasses, he carried a detailed silk map. He also had

---

[70] See Author's notes, Chapter 16 – Evasion. Note 1.

[71] See Author's notes, Chapter 16 – Evasion. Note 2.

Dutch, Belgium and French currency, but that would only come in handy if he could find help. He took one last look around to make sure he had hidden his gear adequately then struck out in a southerly direction with Spain or Switzerland a distant goal.

An eerie, fragile silence pervaded the forest, punctuated only by the sound of his boots scraping up the dry leaves underfoot or the flurry of a bird exploding from a tree which ratcheted up his heartbeat. An hour later he stumbled across what appeared to be a long-forgotten path. He followed it at length before stumbling across a clue as to his whereabouts. It was a crumpled, soiled letter written in French, which suggested he had landed in France, although he couldn't be exactly sure where. He remembered Colin telling Ian just before they were attacked that they would soon be passing over Strasbourg, so he may have landed somewhere in the Alsace-Lorraine region.

Finding help in France would be infinitely easier than Germany, but the Alsace-Lorraine region posed its own unique problem in that it shared a border with Germany. In fact, Alsace-Lorraine had once been considered an ideal independent buffer state between France and Germany. As a result, many Alsatians sympathized with the Germans, while others sided with the French. It would be incredibly difficult knowing who to trust.[72]

The letter gave Jim a vague idea as to his location, but as he couldn't read French, he found it of no other use - at least not at the time - so he discarded it. Not long afterwards the path terminated at a T with the intersecting path running east to west. Pausing to decide which way to go, he suddenly heard voices carrying through the trees. He ducked off the path and threw himself down amid some long grass behind a decaying log.

He watched two men walk past. Their accents sounded French, but he nonetheless remained motionless. He waited five minutes for them to get well clear then scooted off in the opposite direction. It had just gone 9 a.m. on Sunday. By mid-morning his hunger had mounted and his feet were aching. He slipped off the path and sat down on a log among the trees. Suede, fleece lined boots were fine at 20,000 feet, but they weren't much chop for hiking. A pair of the escape boots with their cut away uppers seemed pretty inviting right about then.[73]

He soothed his bare feet in the grass and attacked the concentrated fruit bar from the Pandora Box. It had been baked as hard as concrete, no doubt to prevent scoffing because it was supposed to last 48 hours. But that didn't account for a desperate man with a knife. He cut it in half, saving one half and carving the other into bite size pieces which he polished off in one sitting.

---

[72] In 1871 Germany regained a part of Lorraine (Bezirk Lothringen/Department de la Lorraine, corresponding to the modern department of Moselle). The department formed part of the new imperial German State of Alsace-Lorraine, which gave rise to a revanchist movement to recover it in France.

[73] See Author's notes, Chapter 16 – Evasion. Note 3.

After a suitable rest, he continued his trek. Later in the morning he emerged from the forest to be confronted with an expanse of paddocks. He pulled out the silk map and a compass, but except for a few houses in the distance there were no obvious landmarks from which to get a fix. It didn't help that he'd never been a great map reader. He didn't fancy the prospect of crossing open country in daylight, but with the protection of the forest behind him he didn't have much choice.

He walked for much of the day, scooting over paddocks and risking the odd trek on the open road while dodging any signs of habitation. Using the roads presented a greater danger of being spotted but it meant he could move faster and put more mileage behind him.

Around mid-afternoon he found himself crossing a paddock shadowed by some inquisitive cows. On the far side of the paddock he came to a wide dirt road with yet another paddock beyond it and then more forest. The deserted road ran for a reasonable distance in both directions and swept into a blind bend off to his left. He had not got more than halfway across the road when a platoon of German soldiers came around the bend at a brisk march.

Jim froze, afraid that any hasty movement would raise the alarm. Then he slowly moved back to the verge of the road where he picked up a stick as casually as his racing heart would allow. He walked back into the paddock toward the milling cows with a theatrical display of herding them back the way they'd come. By the time the platoon reached the point in the road where he'd been standing moments earlier, he had the cows back on the far side of the paddock.

As his heart thumped in his chest, he flashed the platoon a cherry wave with his stick. 'The officer in charge, who marched to one side of the platoon, waved back and barked an order at his men who responded by breaking into song,' he recalled. 'Further down the road, the officer rapped out another command and the singing abruptly stopped.'

Jim couldn't help thinking, with some amusement, whether the Germans would have remained in such high spirits had they realised they'd just marched straight past an evader. As soon as they were out of sight he scurried back to the road and scooted across. He hurried over the next paddock and into the sanctuary of the trees, promising himself that future cross-paddock ventures could wait until dark.

By evening he had devoured the last of the fruit bar. He would look for more food later but right now he needed water. He hadn't had a drink since Mepal. A creek; a stream; a puddle; anything would do. He went on the hunt until nightfall before he abandoned the search, determined to resume it again with some urgency at first light.

He emerged from the trees again and slept that night in a haystack, which didn't turn out to be anywhere near as romantic or as fun as they made out in the movies. The air hung heavy with musty humidity and the hay scratched and prickled him. Then it rained and ear wigs dropped out of the hay into his face. He attempted to collect some rainwater in his cupped hands but only managed enough to moisten his lips. He found relief when morning arrived and he could get cracking.

He thought that after the rain he wouldn't have any problem finding something to drink, but he had to wait until mid-day before he came across a shallow puddle swimming with bugs. He threw some water purifying tablets into the dirty water and without bothering about the ten minutes the instructions suggested he wait before drinking, he fell flat on his stomach and slurped up the filthy water, bugs and all.

His luck improved a couple of hours later when he found a large concrete tank buried in the ground at the edge of a wood. It had a heavy steel padlocked lid, but he found a gap big enough to push through a large stone about the size of a tennis ball. Cheered to hear the echo of a hollow splash, he took the rubber bag from his escape box, tied the fishing line to it, and fed it through the gap. He waited a few minutes after the string went limp then pulled the bag up to find it tantalizingly wet but empty. What a twit, he thought, it's just floated.

Learning from his failure, he weighted the bag with a few stones and tried again. This time he felt the string pull taut. After a minute he hauled up a bag heavy with water. He lost half of it pulling it out between the lid and the rim but there remained plenty for a decent drink.

He prudently dropped a purifying tablet into the bag and this time gave it five minutes before drinking. After the muddy cocktail he'd happily slurped down a couple of hours earlier, this tasted pure and sweet. With his thirst quenched, he refilled the bag and set off with the sun digging its claws into his back like a scared tomcat.

He found being on the run in occupied territory, where capture or something worse could happen at any moment, a far cry from the exercise he and his crew had played back home. Nothing worse than being apprehended by an overly enthusiastic police bobby ever happened on an exercise. Even then you might get a cup of tea out of it.

He found the real thing mentally and physically exhausting. He perspired heavily in the summer heat, but dared not remove his jersey. He couldn't carry his battle dress blouse in case someone saw it. Nor could he dump it because he needed it for the chilly nights. His feet ached, but he walked until dusk when he found a place beneath a stone wall to curl up for the night.

Nights on the continent could be frigid and he kept waking up stiff and cold. He thought about his flying suits hidden back in the forest. One of them would have been handy but it would have been impractical carrying it all day. With a clear moonlit night, he took the opportunity to get warm by putting some miles behind him.

He used the roads sparingly and avoided any signs of habitation. Come morning, his hunger returned with a vengeance and he regretted having eaten the entire fruit bar. Just after dawn he found a potato paddock. Unfortunately, the potatoes were green and tasted foul, and he had to use his remaining water to flush the starchy taste from his mouth.

He tramped all morning until just before noon when he found a river, most likely a tributary of the Moselle. After a good drink, he refilled his water bag, threw in the last of the purifying tablets and struck out into a forest, heading south with the Spanish border a vague goal.

By mid-afternoon, thoughts of getting home were playing second fiddle to a tormenting hunger and overwhelming tiredness. No wonder so many men who were shot down never made it home. He emerged from the woods near a small orchard overlooking a village. Fat green apples hung from the trees. They weren't ripe but they were a great improvement on the potatoes. A stone wall separated the orchard from a cemetery. With nobody about, and with a distinct lack of activity in the village, he climbed over the cemetery wall and concealed himself behind a large headstone. He hadn't had a decent sleep since being in his bed back at Mepal three nights earlier. Now he allowed himself to lay down and fall asleep with the sun on his face.

Chapter 17: Roll of The Dice

Later, Jim woke to the sound of children's voices. They were the first voices he'd heard since the singing Germans. He listened, expecting to hear adults at any moment, but when none eventuated, he chanced a peek over the cemetery wall.[74]

He saw three young boys scampering around the orchard throwing apples at each other. They were wearing ribbons of red, white and blue on their sleeves. Jim thought it odd they should be flaunting British colours, until it dawned on him, they were French tri-colours. That was promising. Surely, they wouldn't be wearing them if the Germans were in the immediate vicinity. Still, he couldn't be sure. The boys might be able to help, but on the other hand they might get him a quick introduction to the local German commander. He sat down to weigh his options, well aware that if he wanted to avoid a prison camp, he would have to roll the dice sooner or later.

'Well,' he thought. 'If there's any trouble, I shouldn't have too much difficulty getting away from three young lads.'

His escape kit included a card containing a list of English phrases with translations in Dutch, German, Spanish and French. It carried the warning, *'Not to be Produced in Public'* but as he didn't consider three lads in shorts 'the public', he climbed over the wall into the orchard.

'Hey there,' he called.

Goodness knows what the boys thought when they saw the dishevelled wreck scrambling over the wall. Perhaps they thought he owned the orchard because they drop their apples and bolted.

He waved the card. 'Parlez-vous Anglais?'.

The eldest looking boy, who Jim considered to be ten or eleven years old, stopped in his tracks and turned around. His face fluctuated between airs of suspicion and curiosity. Jim beckoned him closer and pointed at the card. 'Parlous vous Anglais?'

The boy made a few tentative steps toward him, and at the same time encouraged his younger, less ambitious friends to back him up. When they were close enough to read the card, Jim pointed out the English phrase, *Where am I?*

The eldest boy pointed to the tri-colour on his sleeve. Then he took the card. After a brief study he picked out the phrase, *Can you hide me?* And pointed at Jim.

Jim lifted his jersey to show them his air gunner's brevet and the boy's initial suspicion evaporated as excitement lit up his face. He beckoned his friends closer and they crowded around staring at Jim, and examining the card.

---

[74] See Author's notes, Chapter 17 – Roll of the Dice. Note 1.

One of the younger boys ran his finger down the list of phrases and stopped on *I am hungry; thirsty.*

Jim nodded and rubbed his stomach.

The eldest boy took charge and motioned everyone to sit down. When they were settled, he indicated skyward, then fluttered his hand to the ground and pointed inquiringly at Jim.

'Oui,' Jim nodded.

The three boys chattered among themselves before the eldest leapt to his feet and pumped Jim's hand.

'Bon comrade, bon comrade,' he cried.

Then he brushed off his shorts and pointed toward the village. Without another word he vaulted the wall and raced down through the cemetery, leaving the two younger lads to keep Jim company.

They sat under the trees exchanging phrases and trying as best they could to communicate for the best part of an hour before the older boy returned in the company of two men. Jim jumped to his feet to greet them. The men didn't speak English and tried to connect through the use of crude sign language. Apart from making it understood that he'd abandoned his aircraft, Jim might as well have been communicating with Martians.

Word of his arrival must have spread quickly because a short time later another group of men turned up. One of them had a French/English dictionary and pencil and paper. However, using a dictionary to translate proved just as tedious and frustrating as sign language. A few words strung together, which made perfect sense in English, didn't necessarily translate well into French.

It didn't help being constantly interrupted by a steady procession of villagers turning up, with everyone wanting to shake his hand and give him food and wine. Having survived three days on meagre escape rations, he now faced a banquet of black bread, beef, biscuits, cubes of sugar (which he later found out were a luxury in occupied France) cheese and bottles of wine.

For the moment, the only people to turn up were from the village, but Jim had to wonder how long it would be before the inevitable arrival of the Germans. He didn't fancy spending the rest of the war in a prison camp. He began formulating an escape plan which hadn't got beyond making a mad dash for the woods, when a man's voice said, 'Who are you?'

They were the first English words Jim had heard since Colin had told Ian they'd soon be passing Strasbourg.

A man of about fifty, dressed in a suit and tie, stepped out of the crowd. At six feet tall and well-built, he had a very strong, no-nonsense face. Jim noticed missing fingers on his left hand. He later learnt the man managed an iron mine, and the faint metallic clanging he'd had heard on that first morning had come from the mine.[75]

---

[75] Maurice Schwartz managed the iron mine at Saizerais.

The man introduced himself as Maurice. No surname.

'What is your name?' he asked Jim.

Jim replied with his name, rank and serial number.

'Where were you shot down?' Maurice asked.

'I don't know.'

'Where is your parachute?'

'I hid it.'

'And your flying suit?'

'I hid that, too.'

'How long have you been walking?'

'Three days.'

'When were you shot down? What time?'

Jim shrugged.

'How many of your crew escaped?'

'I can't tell you,' Jim said. 'We were on fire and out of control when I bailed out.'

'You were the rear gunner?'

The question surprised Jim, but he remained composed. 'I can't say.'

'I appreciate that,' Maurice said. 'But you must understand, we need to be very careful who we help. For all we know, you could be a German posing as a British airman.'

'I'm sorry, but I can't tell you anything about my crew.'

'Well, then,' Maurice replied. 'I'll tell you.'

To Jim's astonishment, Maurice rattled off the serial number and code letters of his Lancaster.

'I am sorry to tell you that four of your comrades died,' he said. 'Your pilot, wireless operator, bombardier and gunner.'

Ian, Oscar, Freddie and Frank all killed? Jim felt sick.

'I cannot tell you if they were killed during the fighter attack or when the aircraft crashed,' Maurice said. 'We had a big funeral for them. Normally, the Germans forbid such gatherings. They fear they may encourage unrest. But on this occasion, they did not intervene. Many people came and there were many flowers. Your friends are part of our community now. We will look after them. They are buried not far away in a small cemetery.[76] Hopefully, one day you will be able to visit.'[77]

'And the rest of my crew?' Jim pressed.

'Your flight engineer is in safe hands. Unfortunately, there has been no word concerning your navigator. Perhaps he is still at large. But now, we must do something about your situation.

---

[76] See Author's notes, Chapter 17 – Roll of the Dice. Note 2.

[77] See Author's notes, Chapter 17 – Roll of the Dice. Note 3.

Chapter 18: In Safe Hands

Jim absorbed the news about his crew with a hollow sense of disbelief. But he didn't get time to dwell on the matter as people continued to turn up at the orchard 'like they were on a Sunday picnic.' They all wanted to shake his hand and thank him as if he guaranteed their inevitable liberation.

It took a couple of hours before the congregation began to disperse. As it did, Maurice started making arrangements to hide Jim - arrangements that changed a number of times as the crowd dwindled, until in the end nobody knew for sure who would be hiding him.

At this time, Maurice also asked Jim to change into civilian clothing. From a practical point of view, wearing civvies provided the only means of being able to move around without arousing suspicion. However, if he was captured out of uniform the Germans might be tempted to shoot him as a spy. It had happened to unfortunate evaders in the past. After balancing the risk of getting caught out of uniform against the dire consequences faced by the people who were risking their lives for him, Jim agreed to change. After all, he still had his dog tags.

A selection of clothes miraculously appeared from out of the crowd and the fun began. As Maurice helped him select a suitable attire, the callow Kiwi began by removing his grubby white jersey. Someone snatched it up the moment he put it on the ground.

He then removed his battle dress blouse, and had no sooner pulled a wad of foreign currency from the breast pocket before the blouse vanished. As he handed the money to Maurice, he was amused to see someone produce a pair of scissors and start removing the insignia from his blouse.

Maurice tucked the money inside his jacket. 'Merci, bon comrade.'

At that moment, Jim remembered the escape photos he'd sewn into the waistband of his blouse. As soon as he mentioned this to Maurice, the Frenchman ordered the immediate return of the blouse. It had only been in the crowd for thirty seconds, but when it reappeared it had been stripped of all its insignia and buttons, including the button that contained the compass.

Jim had never used the station tailor. He had meticulously sewn on his own insignia, including his stylish New Zealand air gunner wing.

'All my handiwork had been undone in a matter of seconds' he bemoaned. He wondered if anyone ever discovered the compass in the button.

He sliced open the blouse with his knife and found the photos in perfect condition. He gave them to Maurice who examined them briefly. 'Good,' he said, and handed them back. 'Don't lose them, we'll be able to use them soon.'

Next, Jim kicked off his boots, removed his socks, and stripped off his shirt. There he stood, all five feet three, barefoot and stripped to the waist, save for his long johns.

'You will have to change your trousers,' Maurice said.

There were still a number of young women present whose incessant giggling Jim had already found embarrassing, so he was loathed to strip down to nothing but his unflattering long johns in front of them.

'Ah,' acknowledged Maurice. He addressed the women sternly, the hilarity ended abruptly, and a shirt flew out of the crowd at Jim. It hung to his knees, but with his modesty now adequately covered, he slipped out of his air force trousers and into a civvy pair. They were far too long and had to be turned up several times at the cuffs but they were a great deal more comfortable than standing around in shirt tails. A pair of oversized shoes and a woolen jacket completed the makeover and all the young women gave him a rousing cheer.

Jim tucked his knife into the small of his back. Maurice said, 'Keep it well hidden, my friend.'

When most of the crowd had departed, Maurice introduced Jim to a man named Ugo. History often vilifies the French, but the people Jim knew were the bravest and most loyal he'd ever met. Of all those dauntless characters, Ugo topped the list.

'He was a little taller than me and slightly built,' Jim remembered. 'I guessed him to be in his late twenties. From what I later learnt about him, I would say his exploits were enough to fill a dozen books.'

Over the next half an hour the crowd drizzled away until only Maurice, Ugo and Jim remained in the orchard. Even the three boys had disappeared. Jim never knew their names, never had a chance to thank them, and never saw them again. Maurice told him, 'You will stay with me and my wife for a day or two while we make further plans. Ugo will be your guide. You must follow his directions without question.'

Escape and evasion lectures had stressed the imperativeness of that. The evader who questioned a decision, or thought they knew better, inevitably met with disaster.

Ugo, who didn't speak English, spoke directly to Jim in French while Maurice translated.

'I need to know where you hid your parachute,' Ugo said.

Not only would the parachute confirm Jim's story, but silk had become a rare and valuable commodity.

'I'm not exactly sure where it is,' Jim said.

'Anything you can remember will be of great help.'

'I buried it with my flying suits under piles of leaves at the bottom of a tree. I put logs over them.'

Jim then retraced his movements through the potato field, over the cow paddock where he'd come across the Germans, and along the path through the forest where he'd encountered the two labourers.

After a brief conversation with Maurice, Ugo turned to Jim. 'How far did you walk on the path?'

'About two or three hours,' Jim said. 'I found a letter written in French. I couldn't read it so I threw it away.'

'On the path?'

'Yes.'

The discarded letter pleased Ugo. If he found it, he could be assured of literally being on the right track. 'Anything else?'

'I found a water tank with a steel lid.'

Maurice and Ugo had another short exchange.

'Ugo knows of two or three such tanks in the area,' Maurice said. 'He will go and look tomorrow. If anyone can find it, he can. Now my friend, we must get you away from here.'

As they were leaving the orchard, they were joined by a fourth man. Jim wasn't given his name. He chatted briefly with Maurice and Ugo before shaking Jim's hand. 'Bon comrade,' he grinned. 'Bon comrade.'

Leaving the orchard, the four men were approached by an attractive, dark haired woman who greeted Maurice warmly and acknowledged Ugo and the other man in a manner that suggested they were well acquainted.

'This is my woman,' said Maurice. By which Jim supposed he meant his wife. She looked askance at Jim as Maurice spoke to her. Jim had no idea what he said, but it must have been reassuring because his wife extended him a demure hand. 'Bonjour,' she said.

Without another word, she accompanied them down the hill, content to let them talk while she walked ahead scanning the ground. Every so often she stopped to pick large orange slugs or some other variety of invertebrates from the dirt.

'What's she doing?' Jim asked.

'We salt them in barrels, like we do the snails,' Maurice said. 'For eating. Do you like snails?'

'I've never tried them.'

Maurice looked at him, shocked. 'Never? Well, let me tell you, they are very good. I'm sure you'll agree once you've tried them.'

Suddenly raw potatoes and unripe apples sounded tremendously appealing to Jim.

As they neared the village, Ugo gave Jim a hearty handshake and took his leave.

'He will join us again soon at my house,' Maurice said. 'It isn't wise for all of us to be seen together.' He cast an eye on Jim. 'You may look like a little Frenchman, but you don't sound like one, so it is very important that you do not say anything more until we reach my house. Just walk along and pretend you are listening to our conversation,' he said, indicating toward his nameless friend. 'Nod or shake your head if you please. But do not say anything.'

Jim nodded.

'Very good,' Maurice said. 'Now we had best move along.'

Chapter 19: The House of Maurice

Maurice and his wife France (pronounce Frounce) lived in Custines, a small town on the Moselle. Their modest two-storey house had a kitchen, a dining room and a lounge downstairs, and bedrooms and a bathroom upstairs.

'Come down to the basement,' Maurice told Jim.

Jim followed him through a door off the passageway and Maurice snapped on a light and led him down some concrete steps. The dimly lit basement contained an assortment of discarded household paraphernalia as well as three enormous wine barrels, but nothing to suggest it would be a comfortable stay. No bed. Not so much as a mattress.

Maurice read Jim's obvious consternation. 'Oh no,' he said. 'This is not where you are staying. I wanted to show you these.'

He stopped beside the barrels and lifted the lids. Two of them were crammed with layers of snails and slugs while the third was a quarter full.

'You were interested in what my woman does with the slugs she collected,' Maurice said. 'She is upstairs washing them as we speak. When she is done, she will bring them down here. Look.'

He demonstrated how each layer of snails and slugs had been covered in salt to suffocate them. 'The best way to kill them,' he explained. He plucked out a snail, blew away the salt, and pushed it under Jim's nose.

After green potatoes and unripe apples, Jim didn't think his palate could tolerate much more French cuisine, and he politely declined.

'Very wise,' laughed Maurice. 'They're much better with frog's legs.' He replaced the lids and ushered Jim back up the steps. Ugo had returned and was waiting for them in the lounge. Maurice poured them all wine and they sat down to discuss Jim's adventures and the state of the war. Maurice and Ugo were delighted with the Allied advance and Ugo remarked how wonderful it would be to see Paris liberated.

'The Germans are withdrawing toward the Rhine but there is still much fighting to be done before Paris can be liberated,' Maurice cautioned.

'Won't the German retreat make it dangerous for you?' Jim asked.

'We are ready,' Ugo declared.

While they were discussing Allied strategy and what a German defeat would mean for the world, delicious aromas drifted from the kitchen. Jim had visions of frog's legs and slugs sizzling in butter but when it came time to eat, France presented him with omelettes and bread.

With eggs being scarce, France had used one egg to one-part egg powder, but even so, Jim, whose last hot meal had been bacon and eggs back at Mepal, thought they were the most delicious omelettes he'd ever had. When they'd finished eating, and had polished off a bottle of wine, Maurice said, 'You most likely want to sleep.'

'Yes, if you don't mind,' Jim said. 'It's been a while since I managed a good kip.'

'And a bath?'

After three days on the run Jim guessed he didn't smell the freshest. Maurice led him upstairs to the bathroom where France ran him a hot bath, another luxury in occupied France.

He washed away three days of grime and tension, after which France showed him to a bedroom where an enormous bed occupied the middle of the room. A pair of pyjamas had been laid out for him. After three days in his uniform, the pyjamas provided a light and refreshing caress against his tired body, and with the bed feeling like a cloud of feathers he slipped between the sheets and fell asleep within seconds.

After what seemed like a few minutes he felt a sharp tapping on his chest and woke with a start to find an old white-bearded man hovering over him with a stethoscope. It took him a moment to get his bearings. When he did, his initial thoughts were of betrayal.

He sat upright, afraid and confused at the chilling thought of capture. Who was it? Gestapo? Police? He thought it bizarre they'd send someone so elderly to arrest him.

'You've been asleep for two days,' Maurice said reassuringly. 'We were worried when we couldn't wake you, so we fetched the doctor.'

Two days? It had seemed like two minutes.

Jim watched the old doctor remove the stethoscope from around his neck and tuck it in a little brown leather bag, all the while speaking to Maurice and France at the foot of the bed. It hadn't taken the him long to conclude that exhaustion had put Jim to sleep and now, satisfied his patient wouldn't die, he closed his little brown bag, gave orders for Jim to rest some more, and departed.

Jim went straight back to sleep.[78]

He woke up a few hours later in the early evening feeling invigorated and refreshed. But, getting out of bed, he found all his clothes missing. He had just started to contemplate spending the rest of the war stuck in a room with nothing to wear but a pair of oversized pyjamas when there was a candid knock at the door and France came in with his clothes all washed and ironed. She lay them on the bed for him and illustrated with sign language that after dressing he should come down for dinner.

When Jim entered the living room downstairs, he found Maurice and France entertaining half a dozen people.

'You have woken in time for dinner,' Maurice said. 'We have guests. My very close friends. They have been looking forward to meeting you.'

---

[78] See Author's notes, Chapter 19 – The House of Maurice.

Maurice obviously trusted these people beyond measure, because the repercussions they faced if they were caught with an evader in their midst were dire. Maurice introduced Jim to everyone in turn. Never that great at remembering names, Jim promptly forgot them all. He didn't consider it a problem as he suspected they had all furnished him with aliases. But he didn't forget the name of Marie, whom Maurice took particular pleasure in introducing to him. All the other guests were middle-aged, but Marie, a striking, raven-haired creature with exquisite dark eyes and a quiet demeanor, was about Jim's age. He certainly had no complaints about being seated next to her at dinner.

The meal France produced made a mockery of the wartime rationing. Not that Jim had much time to indulge. His hosts and their friends bombarded him with a continuous barrage of questions, wanting to know about his family, his upbringing, New Zealand, and how much longer before the war would be over. With his French being limited to a couple of phrases, it fell to Maurice to translate everything.

Marie was sitting close to Jim, obviously enjoying his company, when Jim noticed her wearing an engagement ring. A smile lit her face when he touched her arm to get her attention, but it died when he tapped her ring and indicated inquiringly around the table, as if to say, 'Who?' All the men looked far too old for her. She slipped her hand over his and shook her head, then turned and spoke to Maurice. When she had finished, Maurice nodded.

'Marie wishes me to explain that she is engaged to a boy from her village. But she has not seen or heard from him since he was sent to a labour camp in Germany.'

Jim looked at Marie. 'I am sorry. I hope you will be together again very soon.'

Maurice passed on his sympathies and Marie gave Jim's hand an appreciative squeeze and then held it for a long time. At the end of the night, all the guests, except Marie, bid Jim and their hosts goodnight and departed.

'Won't Marie miss the curfew?' Jim asked.

'It is all right,' Maurice said. 'She will be staying here tonight.'

Jim didn't think much of it, assuming Marie must be a good friend of the family. Despite two days sleep, he felt himself start to fade rapidly. He said goodnight to Maurice and France, kissed Marie goodnight on the cheek, and retired upstairs. No sooner had he entered his room when Marie appeared in the doorway. She stood there for a quiet moment then moved into the room and closed the door softly behind her. She came to Jim without a word, took him by the hand and led him to the bed. With the sort of bewildering alarm appropriate for a naive twenty-one-year old, he suddenly appreciated the real intent of the evening.

Marie drew close to him with a vulnerable, sad, almost resigned silence. He sensed an urge to take her in his arms and hold her but his inexperience saw him offer her no more than a bashful kiss on the cheek and a coy, 'Goodnight.'

Marie gave him a bemused smile. She pointed at herself, then at Jim and the bed. Not wishing to further betray his naivety, he pressed his hands together against his cheek, indicating he wanted to go to sleep. Again, Marie indicated that she would join him.

Not only did Jim's innocence restrain him, but so did the thought of Marie's fiancée. A lot of blokes wouldn't have given tuppence about him, but he did. Or at least that's what he told himself. Perhaps if he'd been more adept in such matters, he might have chosen a different path.

He lifted Marie's hand, tapped her engagement ring and shook his head. Her face brightened, like a weight had been lifted from her shoulders, and she threw her arms around my him. 'Merci. Merci.'

Jim pondered that night many times over the years. He speculated on what might have been, and often wondered if Marie had ever been reunited with her fiancée.

The next morning Maurice asked him if he had enjoyed the evening. Did he and Marie appreciate each other's company?

'Marie's lovely,' Jim said.

'Good, good. We thought she would please you.'

Jim smiled. Perhaps one day Maurice would find out what never happened.

Over the next couple of days, Jim kept mainly to his room. On the second day France turned up with a measuring tape and fitted him with one of Maurice's suits which she altered into something fashionable and elegant. When she had finished, Jim looked smart enough to be going to the office. Not that he could leave the house.

When Maurice returned from work on the second evening, he asked Jim for his escape photos.

'We will put them to good use.'

Jim assumed that meant false papers, but he knew better than to ask.

'You will need a new name,' Maurice said. 'Aubrey is not suitable for a Frenchman. Do you have a second name?'

'Charles.'

'That is better, and it will be easy for you to remember. You will be Charles Leroy.'

In fact, Jim had rarely, if ever, been known as Charles. Growing up he had been known as Jimmy or Little Jimmy Boy. Latterly everyone had called him Winkie.

'You will be an agricultural worker. A farm worker as you might say,' Maurice said 'That will explain why you are not in a prison camp, or a labour camp. Also, you will be a deaf mute. That way you will be excused for not understanding if anything is ever asked of you. You will not have to answer any awkward questions. Your date of birth will not change.'

After dinner Maurice made another announcement, 'We're moving you to another safe house tonight. It isn't a good idea to stay in one place too long. My wife has made you up a parcel of clothes. I have a new pair of shoes for you. Try them on.'

The shoes were a couple of sizes too big, but nothing three pairs of socks couldn't fix. They were certainly more comfortable than flying boots.

Shortly after, Ugo arrived to escort Jim to the next safe house. He looked particularly pleased with himself as they greeted each other with smiles and a handshake.

'Ugo followed your directions and found your parachute and flying suits,' Maurice said. 'He also found the letter you threw away.'

Amazing, Jim thought, as France presented him with a handkerchief and scarf she had made from his parachute.[79]

'Keep them hidden,' Maurice told him. 'Silk is a valuable commodity and there is only one place it could come from' He also reminded Jim, 'Remember, never question anything Ugo tells you. And never speak in public.'

In Lorraine there were many people who supported the Vichy government, while others pinned their colours to the Gaullists. A wrong word at the wrong time could be catastrophic.

Jim regarded Maurice and France as friends. Without their help he'd still be wandering the countryside, tired and hungry. They laughed when he told them he'd been heading for Spain. Marie arrived to say goodbye. Jim, who hadn't seen her since the morning after 'that night', gave her a kiss and a huge hug.

'Au revoir, Marie.'

Ugo waited eagerly at the front door. With a curfew in place from 10 pm until 6 am, he wanted to crack along. With a melancholy heart, Jim left the house. Despite his best intention to return, he never saw Maurice, France or Marie again.

---

[79] The rest of the parachute was cut up and used to make a First Communion dress which was worn by several young girls in the village in the years after the war.

Chapter 20: Burying the Old Life

Two hours before curfew, Ugo and Jim left Custines and hastened on foot toward the village of Frouard. Ugo had purposely left their departure until late in the evening when there would be fewer people on the streets. They passed through the small town of Pompey and crossed a wide bridge over the Moselle into the Frouard[80] where, a little over an hour after leaving Custines, they reached a small boot repair shop.

A 'closed' sign hung in the door, but it opened without delay as though the middle-aged man who answered Ugo's knock and ushered them inside with a furtive glance up and down the street, had been waiting at the door for them. He introduced his wife without giving her name and she quickly disappeared. Jim didn't need to know their names and it made things safer for everyone if he didn't.

The couple didn't speak English and were far more reserved and circumspect than Maurice and France. Using simple sign language, Ugo conveyed to Jim that he'd be back in two days.

After Ugo left, the man led Jim upstairs to a small, spartan room with bare floorboards, a threadbare mat, one small window, comforts and just enough space for a bed and dresser. There were some basic and a small alcove hidden behind a curtain where Jim could hang his clothes. An enamel basin and jug sat on the dresser.

The window had storm shutters and two sets of curtains, a heavy set that were only drawn at night so as not to arouse suspicion by having them closed during the day, and a flimsy lace set to be kept closed at all times.

The man patted Jim on the shoulder and made it clear what he expected of him by putting a finger to his lips. Next, he pointed at Jim's feet and shook his head.

'I sat down on the bed and removed my new shoes,' Jim recalled. 'Then the man closed the curtains, and made it quite clear I was to keep well clear of the window.'

The man's wife came into the room carrying a plate with bread, a small piece of cheese and a cup of black coffee. Jim had never cared much for coffee but he would soon learn to tolerate it. The woman placed the meagre meal on the dresser and retreated to her husband's side. Satisfied the house rules had been made clear, they left Jim alone in what would be his home until his false papers and permits could be organized.

He stayed in the room for two days. The couple were busy in the shop most of the time and only came to see him with food or when changing his washing

---

[80] See Author's notes, Chapter 20 – Burying the Old Life. Note 1.

water. There were no creature comforts and the fear of being caught hung over him like a black cloud.

He kept clear of the window, except for one occasion when the arduous lack of any engaging distractions tempted him to take a peek at the street below. He pressed his face to the wall and spied through a crack between the curtain and window frame. The sight of a company of German soldiers passing in the narrow street below rapidly curbed his inquisitiveness, and he rebuked himself for taking such a risk.

Disquietingly, most of the customers coming into the shop were German soldiers needing their boots repaired. There were many times when he heard the shop door open and German voices drifted up the stairs. He would sit motionless and apprehensive on the edge of the bed, entertaining dark thoughts of what would happen if the Germans decided to do a random search for illegal wireless sets or firearms, as they were known to do. His existence came as close as he could imagine to living on a knife edge.

His continued freedom, and the lives of the couple hiding him, depended on him making the right decision on every occasion. Even mundane tasks, to which he wouldn't normally have given a second thought, were tackled with meticulous care. Washing meant picking up and placing the water jug with caution. He walked about only when absolutely necessary, and when he did so it was with precise, light steps in stocking feet. If he needed to use the toilet - the sort of detail often omitted from evasion stories – he had use of a small bathroom next to the bedroom. However, it required either the man or his wife to be upstairs when he was using it as it would have aroused suspicion if they were both in the shop when the old plumbing started rattling with sound of running water. To avoid making any needless noise, he spent most of his time laying on the bed staring at the ceiling.

Ugo returned two days later and flashed Jim a satisfied smile as he pulled out an envelope containing a French identity card displaying one of Jim's escape photos, a travel permit, a certificate exempting Jim from forced labour, and the remaining unused escape photos. He had Jim sign the identity card in an easy to remember style and supply a couple of fingerprints. When Ugo had finished with him, Jim folded the envelope around the unused escape photos and tucked them in his shoe. He might need them later.

Ugo didn't stay long. After he left, Jim sat down on the bed and studied the identity card. It described him as Charles Leroy, a deaf-mute agricultural worker. He had gone from being a Christchurch apprentice butcher to a French farm labourer. He doubted the forgery would cheat a vigilant identity check, but something had to be better than nothing.

Ugo returned later that day, bringing him a change of clothes more in keeping with his new identity. He also brought news that another safe house had been organized for him.

'It seemed a shame to discard my suit after the trouble Maurice's wife had gone to fitting it for me, but I don't suppose there were too many farm labourers waltzing around in such well-tailored attire,' Jim reflected.

Ugo then beckoned Jim to surrender his watch, wrist chain and dog tags. 'My watch, and my wrist chain with its inscription and greenstone, were understandable,' Jim said. 'But my dog tags were a different matter. Without them I couldn't prove I was a genuine evader. I wouldn't have been the first evader to be tortured and executed on suspicion of being a spy or saboteur.'

Despite his disquiet, he knew there were people who had risked their lives for him: Maurice and his wife; Ugo; all the people he'd met at dinner; the owners of the boot shop; the three boys in the orchard; Marie. The Germans could have rounded them all up and shipped them off to concentration camps or simply shot them out of hand. With that thought, he surrendered everything.

Ugo put the items in a small tin, and Jim followed him out to the back garden where he watched his old life get buried unceremoniously among the flowers.[81]

With his past hidden, Jim said goodbye to the brave couple who had hidden him for two days. While he greatly appreciated the enormous risk they had taken, he had never felt comfortable living above the shop and he felt greatly relieved to be leaving.

What some of the French people endured in their efforts to help men like himself never failed to amaze Jim. There were those who openly aided and abetted the occupiers, but others only feigned collaboration in order to disguise the dangerous work they undertook in aiding escaping POWs and evaders.

It remains a tragedy and a great miscarriage of justice that some of the people who had risked their lives helping downed airmen, were killed or otherwise punished by vengeful communities who were unaware of their activities. Some of the lucky ones still had evaders in hiding when liberation came.

---

[81] See Author's notes, Chapter 20 - Burying the Old Life. Note 2.

Chapter 21: Up Close with The Enemy

Not long after leaving the boot shop, Ugo and Jim were approached by a man dressed in a dark jacket and trousers, and sporting a black beret. He crossed from the opposite side of the street, fell into step beside them, and began chatting to Jim like they were old friends.

'I'd picked up a few simple French words and could string together one or two phrases, but I had no idea what this bloke was on about,' Jim said.

Ugo interrupted Black Beret who, suddenly realizing Jim didn't speak French, shook his hand apologetically. Thereafter, he simply made the pretense of involving Jim in the conversation, and Jim responded with his pretentious act of interest.

Coming to a small café, Jim wondered if he had reached his next safe house. A little bell jingled above the door as Ugo pushed it open, and Jim followed him and Black Beret inside.

On the left, a counter ran the length of the room, while on the right there were alcoves with tables and chairs. Either there had been a power outage, or the owner had gone for some sort of rustic ambience, because the lights were off. There were half a dozen unlit candles placed along the counter and one on each alcove table. There were no other customers in the place.

A middle-aged man appeared from a backroom and slipped behind the counter to serve them. Ugo didn't speak to him except to order coffees. Hardly what Jim had expected if they were going to hide him there. Ugo then selected the trio an alcove table obscured in shadow where he and Black Beret chatted while Jim sat silently on the sidelines feigning interest.

The proprietor brought over their coffees and lit the candle on their table. He had just slipped back behind the counter when the front door opened to the jingle of the bell. Jim peered over the rim of his cup, flabbergasted to see two SS officers walk in. In their immaculate, menacing uniforms, they oozed coercion and intimidation, and Jim's heartrate ratcheted up three or four notches. Ugo and his mate offered the SS men no more than a cursory glance.

One of the officers carried a leather satchel which he placed on the counter. Then, like a scene from a movie, both officers removed their hats, dropped their gloves into them and positioned them delicately upside down on the counter.

The officer with the satchel pulled out some documents and spread them on the counter while the second one spoke to the proprietor who had started making them coffees without being asked. He paused as the officer spoke to him, looked around speculatively, and then pointed toward the three men at the table. Jim felt his heart ready to explode out of his chest. What had given him away? It could have been the simplest of mistakes. For example, during his escape and evasion lectures he'd heard about an evader who had slipped up by pouring milk into his cup before the coffee, the opposite of how continentals do it. But Jim had been very careful to copy Ugo in such matters.

He didn't think he could muffle the sound of his pounding heart as the SS officer swung on his heel and strode deliberately over to the table and slapped him on the shoulder. It sent a cold shiver down his back and the hairs on the back of his neck prickled. He had an urge him to bolt for the door, but the way Ugo and Black Beret continued to gossip like two old women in the Marigold Tearooms, and their complete disinterest in the Germans, curbed his overzealous desire to run.

When the German squeezed his shoulder, Jim felt his heart plummet to his stomach. Fortunately, he had his back to the German because he was sure his expression would have betrayed him. He wanted to hear the officer say something comfortingly cliché like, 'For you, my friend, the war is over.'

But he didn't. Instead, with his hand firmly on Jim's shoulder, the officer said something in French. Unable to reply, Jim glanced at Ugo for a cue. Ugo looked up at the German and nodded. The SS man then reached across the table and picked up the candle. He patted Jim's shoulder and took the candle back to the counter where his friend waited with the documents. They stood reading by candle light and drinking their coffees while Ugo and his mate continued their conversation as if nothing out of the ordinary had happened. Jim may not have been in the dire danger he'd imagined but under the table his hands trembled like tambourines. He didn't dare try drinking his coffee. He later discovered Ugo spoke German and knew the SS only wanted the candle after the proprietor had told them he had no matches to light them one.

When the Germans had concluded their business, the same man returned the candle and patted Jim on the shoulder again with a polite, 'Merci, monsieur.' To which Jim, acting the deaf mute, did nothing. The Germans then finished their coffees and left. Not, Jim prayed, for reinforcements.

The SS men hadn't long departed when a little Frenchman entered the café. He came straight to the booth and slid in next to Ugo. The three Frenchmen spoke briefly in low, conspirator-like tones and then the new man reached over and shook Jim's hand.

Without any formal introduction, they all got up and left the café which, contrary to Jim's vivid imagination, hadn't been surrounded by Germans. They hustled down the street to an old car parked at the curb. With his heart rate returning to somewhere near normal, Jim crammed himself into the back seat with Black Beret. Ugo climbed into the front passenger seat and the little Frenchman drove them away.

Shortly after leaving town, Ugo directed the little Frenchman to pull over at the verge of the road and had everyone get out. Now what? Ugo then lifted up the back seat to reveal a cache of rifles and handguns.

'This was mind boggling,' Jim recalled. 'We could have been stopped at any time.'

Ugo issued everyone with a rifle and also stuffed a small Belgium-made automatic pistol into Jim's hand. Jim made sure the pistol was loaded, double checked the safety catch, and slipped it into his jacket pocket, praying he wouldn't have to use it.

He had never shot at anyone before, at least not anyone he could see. In the air things were different. It had been impersonal. He had been shooting at another aircraft, one machine against another. He had never considered the human element. He didn't think Ugo would hesitate to use his weapon, and if some of the stories he'd heard about him were true he'd most likely do so with a great deal of alacrity.

The men climbed back in the car, stowed the rifles out of sight, and carried on 'armed to the teeth' as Jim described it.

Not too much later, the very situation Jim had been dreading presented itself when, rounding a bend in the road, they found themselves coming up rapidly behind a platoon of German soldiers. Expecting the driver to slow down, Jim nervously felt for the pistol in his pocket. It would be more effective in the confined space of the back seat if they were seriously challenged. But instead of reducing speed, the driver accelerated, coming up behind the platoon with a long blast on the horn.

The consequences of being stopped petrified Jim, but then he suddenly found it the funniest thing to see the Germans hurriedly move aside to let the speeding car pass unhindered.

They travelled onto the town of Pont-a-Mousson where they alighted from the car. The little Frenchman stayed with the car while Ugo and Black Beret led Jim down a narrow street and stopped outside a three storey L-shaped building standing behind a high rendered wall. An ornate arched entrance with a heavy wrought iron gate guarded the property.

The house belonged to Charles Francois, a short, stocky solicitor with swept back black hair and an erudite, no-nonsense countenance. He lived with his wife and young daughter and Jim became their guest for two days. He never knew that Francois held the rank of Colonel-in-Chief of the Resistance for the Pont-a-Mousson sector.[82]

---

[82] See Author's notes, Chapter 21 – Up Close with the Enemy.

Chapter 22: Bill's Story

After spending two days under the roof of a Resistance leader, Jim travelled forty kilometers south to his next safe house in the town of Toul where Ugo introduced him to veterinary surgeon named Grigoire (Jim knew him as Maurice)[83] who lived with his wife and 3-year old daughter in a sprawling house.

Ugo left immediately after the introductions and Grigorie led Jim to the living room. As he opened the door, he said, 'There are two other people also staying with us who you need to meet.'

Jim followed him into the living room and someone called, 'Winkie!'

Jim couldn't subdue his surprise when Bill Hyde stood up from a chair.

'Bill!'

They embraced heartily. In his shock and delight at finding his friend alive, Jim had overlooked the other man in the living room and Gregorie had to interrupt him and Bill to introduced Emile Dubois, an immaculately groomed, aristocratic-looking individual who reached out and shook Jim's hand.

'Captain Chester Williams,' he said. 'British army. Emile is the name the Frenchies have given me.'

'Flight Sergeant Jim Kirk, Royal New Zealand Air Force,' Jim said. 'Otherwise known as Charles Leroy.'

Williams told Jim about his escape from a POW camp in Poland after being captured while serving with the tank corps in North Africa. Jim discovered Emile spoke fluent French and was free to come and go from the house as he pleased.

'Come,' Grigorie said. 'I will show you upstairs to your room, Charles Leroy. You will share it with your friend.

He paused halfway up the stairs to show Jim a secret cupboard hidden behind one of the wall panels.

'If there is any trouble, you and your friend must get in here. Do not ask questions. No hesitation, ok?'

Jim had no worries that Captain Williams had the ability to pass himself off as French and would not need to share the cupboard. Which was just as well, because it hardly seemed barely big enough to accommodate one man let alone three.

Jim moved into a small room with Bill at the top of the stairs, while Captain Williams had his own room down the passage. They all shared one small bathroom. When Bill and Jim were alone, they recounted their adventures.

---

[83] Most of the men introduced to Jim used the alias Maurice. That way he couldn't reveal any real names under interrogation. The only man whose real name was Maurice was Maurice Schwartz.

'Well, old mate,' Jim said, after telling Bill his story, 'what the heck happened to you?'

'I was checking the engine gauges and temperatures when all of sudden we were on fire,' Bill said. 'I turned to Ian to see if there was anything I could do to help, but the intercom was u/s. He shouted that the controls had gone and I needed to get out. I put my parachute on and tried handing him his but he waved me off. 'Get out!' he hollered.

'I scrambled down into the nose and released the escape hatch cover but when I tried to throw it out it went at an angle and got stuck. It wouldn't budge. I was trying to free it when Oscar arrived and we tackled it together. It still wouldn't shift. I stood up and began kicking and stomping it. The next thing everything went black. When I regained consciousness, I was floating down in my parachute. I'm not sure what happened. I think the hatch cover must have come free, and when it fell, I went with it. I must have hit my head on the way out because I had a large bump on my forehead. I don't remember pulling the ripcord. The next thing, I saw the ground rushing up. I hit with a thud. I'd landed in a paddock.[84] I released my parachute and I was busy gathering it up when I found myself surrounded by some men who pitched in to help. I had no idea where they had come from, especially at that time of night. I was taken to a farmhouse and given food and clothes before being transferred to another house a few days later.'[85]

Bill's escape from the blazing Lancaster is one of the many miraculous tales of survival that litter the annuls of aerial warfare. In a letter he wrote to Ian's mother, Ivy Blance, and according to his escape report filed with MI9 upon his return to England, some of the details differ from what Jim remembered Bill telling him. In both the report and the letter, Bill stated that he hid in a ditch for two days before finding help from local farmers who put him in contact with the Resistance. But whether he hid in a ditch or was picked up straight away has no bearing on the rest of his story. He found refuge with M. Hardy, a local farmer, and his two sons. After contacting the Resistance, M. Hardy had his sons disguise Bill as an onion seller and escort him to a safe house. One of M. Hardy's sons recalled, 'We had the Englishman walk a few yards in front of us, while we followed with a revolver in case it was a Bosch trick. In this manner, we passed through the village of Bellville and down the road to Millery.'

From Millery, Bill and a local member of the Resistance kayaked fifteen kilometers down the Moselle River to Pont-a-Mousson where they came ashore at the Nautical Club. As they clambered ashore, they were approached by a German soldier who slung his rifle over his shoulder and offered to help stow their kayak in the boat shed!

---

[84] . Many years later Bill told his then son-in-law John Thorpe that he had no recollection of pulling his ripcord and woke up in a field clutching his bible.

[85] See Author's notes, Chapter 22 – Bill's Story.

Chapter 23: A Shot in the Dark

Jim, Bill and Captain Williams stayed at Gregorie's house in Toul for nearly a week. During that time, Captain Williams (Emile) struck Jim as a rather haughty individual, rather confident in his own abilities and somewhat aloof. He didn't let Bill or Jim forget his rank, reminding them that as NCOs they were under his command.

'He seemed to think he had some sort of clout over us,' Jim remarked. 'The fact that he came and went as he pleased only added to his air of arrogance.'

For the first few days a cordial relationship existed between the three men, but that came to an abrupt end one morning when Jim went into the bathroom to find it looking like a pigsty. Normally Captain Williams used the bathroom first in the morning, followed by Bill and then Jim. But this particular morning Jim went in before Bill and found the basin full of dirty water with the captain's lather-clogged shaving brush and unrinsed razor sitting on the edge of the basin. He went straight to Williams's room and confronted the indolent captain.

'I don't have to clean it up,' retorted Williams. 'That's Bill's job. He's the sergeant. I'm the captain. I hold a King's commission which, I might remind you, puts you and Bill under my direct command.'

Jim saw red. 'Bill is not your batman, and neither am I,' he exploded. 'When we left our aircraft, we were on our own. Our only duty has only ever been to get back to England. You do realize that as an escaped prisoner of war, it's also your duty?'

At the time, Jim thought Williams could have arranged his way back to England without much difficulty, but he seemed quite content living with the French. In hindsight, he admitted that Williams may have been doing his duty in some other covert manner to which he wasn't privy, but at the time it never entered his mind.[86] He didn't recall exactly how the rest of their conversation went, but they were very cool toward each other afterwards.

Jim told Bill he should not be expected to clean up after Williams, but Bill played it down. 'It's a very English thing,' he said. 'Being a Kiwi, Winkie, you don't understand. It's just the way it is.'

'He certainly got that right,' Jim said.

Bill continued to pander to Captain Williams but Jim wouldn't do anything for him.

'Not that it mattered,' Jim said. 'Because Williams spent much of his time away from the house doing heaven knows what.'

Bill and Jim had the run of the house, with the exception of the front room which Gregorie used as a surgery. They quickly learnt to be very careful when speaking to each other because Gregorie's little girl had picked up a few

---

[86] See Author's notes, Chapter 23 – A Shot in the Dark

English words, her favourite being 'yes'. She started saying it regularly, much to her parent's horror. With most of Gregorie's clients being Germans bringing in their dogs, the consequences of the little girl being overheard repeating something in English did not bear thinking about. Bill and Jim decided it best if they only spoke to each other in their room, or with the little girl well out of earshot.

After three days, they began to feel somewhat relaxed. But if a sense of laissez-faire at keeping one step ahead of the Germans had set in, it got curtailed late one night when they were climbing the stairs to their room. A rifle shot rang out from the street below and a bullet smashed through a small window above their heads on the first-floor landing, showering them with glass. They bolted for the hidden cupboard and crammed themselves in.

A loud thumping at the front door reverberated through the house and a someone barked angrily in German.

Bill whispered, 'After all we've been through, only to be arrested in a cupboard.'

Jim would have laughed in less nerve-wracking circumstances. They heard Grigorie open the front door and someone spoke in heated German. After a minute the talking stopped and they heard the front door shut. They were in the cupboard for what seemed an age before Gregorie opened the door.

'It's all right. A German soldier saw a light shining through the window. That is how they warn you to keep the blackout curtain in place.'

The next day Captain Williams returned from one of his frequent excursions. 'We're moving,' he announced. 'The Germans are retreating from this area and they're breaking into a lot of houses ransacking for food. It's too dangerous for us to remain. We'll be joining one of the local maquis.'

Jim and Bill were well aware of the Underground, but had no knowledge of the maquis or how it operated. It sounded like a rather nefarious organization. In the eyes of the Germans, the maquis were troublesome groups of guerilla fighters that needed to be eradicated without mercy. Many of the groups had started life as links in extensive escape routes, helping downed airman return to Britain. The Resistance in the Pont-a-Mousson sector had operated as part of such an escape line. It had stretched all the way to the Pyrenees, but by 1944 it had, along with most other escape lines, been compromised by the German retreat. Even the secret airfields that had been used to smuggle evaders out of the country could no longer be maintained. Someone decided it would be safer for evaders to join a maquis, or hide out in the forests and wait for the advancing Americans. For example, in the Forest of Freteval, midway between the highway from Cloyes to Vendome, in the Department of Loir-et-Cher in central France, a secret camp had been set up for downed airmen.

It had been the brainchild of a Belgium baron, Jean De Blommaert. After the capitulation of his country, De Blommaert had joined the Resistance and had been an active organiser of the famous Comet Line. The Germans nicknamed him The Fox. In 1944, De Blommaert made his way to London, impressing MI9 with his idea of setting up a series of camps for evaders in maquis areas. From there they could be gradually processed into Brittany where they could be put on boats to Britain. With the invasion of Europe imminent, MI9 shelved the plan and told De Blommaert to hide the airmen and wait for liberation. It turned out to be one of the trickiest but most successful schemes of the war, with 150 men allied evaders and escaped prisoners of war sitting out the war in splendid isolation until they were liberated in August, 1944.

Gregorie and his wife laid on a fabulous farewell dinner for their guests, a posh affair where they not only had several crystal glasses for water and various wines, but also crystal cutlery the likes of which Jim had not seen before, nor seen since. Their glasses were never empty.

The next morning, Jim woke up with no memory of the last part of the evening. 'Well, we were drinking champagne,' Bill reminded him.

Later that afternoon Ugo arrived to take them to their next location.

They went by car through Toul to a warehouse where two large doors swung open. They drove in and the doors shut behind them. A high-sided truck with a canvas canopy waited for them. Ugo threw open the flap at the back of the truck to reveal nearly a dozen men sitting inside, all evaders or escaped prisoners who had arrived via an escape line. Ugo directed Jim, Bill and Captain Williams to climb aboard.

With the exception of Captain Williams, who looked like a dapper Frenchman, everyone on the truck looked like a farm labourer. Among the contingent were three Canadian escaped POWs, a 17-year-old Polish lad who spoke enough broken English to explain he had been living rough for some time after his family had been killed in Warsaw, and two American airmen who'd walked out of Germany after their B-17 had crash landed.

The Americans introduced themselves as Dan and Ben, both waist gunners on their aircraft. They had a similar story to Jim's, except they had been on the run much longer. Dan was a particularly 'tough looking nut' while Ben appeared more reserved. They struck up an immediate rapport with Jim and Bill and they were to become very close pals. They would share more adventures in a few short weeks than most friends would share in a lifetime.

The canvas flap on the back of the truck came down, the warehouse doors swung open, and the truck rolled out into the street, full of evaders and escapees.

Chapter 24: Dan and Ben's Escape

On 28th May, 1944 Daniel Dunbar and Benjamin Norris climbed aboard War Eagle, a B-17 operating with the 365th Squadron of the 305th Heavy Bomb Group out of Chalveston, England. They were embarking on their fifth mission as waist gunners under the command of 2nd Lt. Julius Herrick. Their target: the synthetic oil refinery at Ruhland south of Berlin.

War Eagle reached the target without incident, but during the return trip an engine cut out, most likely due to mechanical failure because according to an eyewitness, 1st Lt. Gerald V. Vega, a navigator on another 305BG aircraft, *'there was no flak or enemy aircraft in the vicinity...'*

Losing an engine so deep in enemy territory did not pose an insurmountable problem, but it did leave Herrick with the invidious task of nursing his aircraft home on three fans. It made for a long, dangerous haul with the aircraft not only steadily losing height and speed, but also losing the protection of the formation. However, according to 1st Lt. Vega, *War Eagle* wasn't left to straggle. *'When last observed, A/C 42-39878 was reported behind our formation, being escorted by friendly fighters back toward England.'*

With fighter protection, Herrick's crew stood a good chance of getting home, but unfortunately more engine trouble saw *War Eagle* lose further height. Herrick left the decision to bail out too late, leaving him and his co-pilot, 2nd Lt. Lloyd Saunders, no choice but to crash land their crippled aircraft. At 16.45 hrs they put *War Eagle* down in text book manner in a wheat field near a forest at Hentern north of Zerf, about 90 miles east of Trier. Remarkably, the only minor injury occurred when Daniel Dunbar suffered a sore back.

Keeping with standard procedure, the crew split up to give themselves a better chance of evasion. Waist gunners Dan and Ben paired up, as did Ball Turret gunner Orval Busby and Engineer Charles Gillespie, while Tail gunner John Napier went with Radio Operator William Schwartz. Herrick, Saunders, and the other two officers - navigator, 2nd Lt. Leon Lobdell, and bombardier, 2nd Lt. Herbert Borax - stayed behind to destroy everything of value. After an unsuccessful attempt to set War Eagle on fire they were captured with the aircraft intact.

Most of the enlisted men didn't stay at large very long. Busby and Schwartz were on the run for 24 hours before being caught near Zerf, while Napier and Gillespie remained at large for 48 hours, getting as far south as Merzig. It had been Gillespie's 28th mission, but his first with the Herrick crew after being drafted in for the regular top turret gunner Sgt. Tubbs who had been ill. Napier had replaced Sgt. Green as tail gunner for the same reason.

Tubbs and Napier had been called in at such short notice that neither Ben Norris nor Daniel Dunbar could remember their names when they later filled out I.S.9 reports. Many years after the war, Lloyd Saunders recalled being interrogated at the crash scene. His refusal to say anything about the missing members of the crew met with a rifle butt in the mouth and the loss of several teeth.

Daniel Dunbar and Ben Norris's escape reports filed after their return to England give a brief glimpse of their time on the run.

Dan: *A village and railroad stood between us and the first river we had to cross but we marched through boldly and got away with it. We crossed over the river by a bridge about 02.30 hrs. We drank from a trough in the village. We stole a boat to cross the second river, and we were lucky to do so. We crossed the border where there were no guards. Norris and I were nearly captured again at Thoinville, which had been bombed three days before we crashed. All this time we were travelling in flying suits, and it was weeks from the time we crashed until we reached France. Since there was a reward of 25,000 francs for anyone who would turn us in to the Jerries we took care to wait until it was dark and everyone was off the street before we asked for food. It was one month from the time of crashing until we got in the hands of the underground. I was issued with an aid box and used everything in it. My money from a brown purse was used in expenses.*[87]

BEN: *The food in the escape kits are very nourishing. I found the water bag and Benzedrine tablets useful, and also the compass and maps. We travelled in flying suits and wore GI shoes. We crossed the Siegfried Line just before we came to the Saar River, but it was just pill boxes and concrete block houses at that point and entirely deserted. We walked through a village and crossed the Saar River on the main highway bridge. The bridge was unguarded. There were several people in the streets of the village although it was midnight, but we were not recognised. All villages and towns are completely blacked out and even the farm houses. The people work from daylight to dark. We crossed the Maginot Line just before we came to the Moselle River. It too was deserted, but much more heavily fortified than the Siegfried. The big guns were all gone though. The Moselle Valley from Thoinville to Metz is quite an industrial area and people were on the streets all night but we weren't bothered. We stole a boat and crossed the Moselle River about halfway between Thoinville and Metz. Thoinville was pretty well bombed and filled with German soldiers. After we crossed the Moselle River, we headed due west and were in France the next morning. The section of the frontier where we crossed was not patrolled. The first village we came to was Avril... I carried a brown purse, the money from which I used for toilet articles, food, tobacco and drink. I had been briefed both in America and England and these lectures proved to be very useful.*[88]

---

[87] E&E Report No. I.S.9 (WEA)/6/460/1572
[88] E&E Report No. I.S.9 (WEA)/6/460/1573

The reports give a brief overview of Ben and Dan's evasion but a more comprehensive account is offered by Daniel Dunbar in his post war memoir.

As in Jim's case, Dan's recollections are at times contradictory to what he stated in his official Escape and Evasion report, but a more detailed and clearer picture emerges of what happened to the two men from the time they left their aircraft until when they arrived at the warehouse where Jim met them.

The two gunners had laid up in the woods until dark before heading away from the search area in a south-westerly direction. They kept off the roads and avoided the villages as much as possible. They encountered a couple of German civilians early on but managed to evade search parties and capture thanks largely to Dan's upbringing.

Danny Dunbar explained, 'Dad had Cherokee Indian blood and had been raised around some of his cousins who had taught him how to survive in the woods. At school they had nicknamed him Tarzan, and like his namesake he was well built and tough as nails.'

Ben and Dan marched by night, navigating by compass and the stars, and rested during the day, surviving on the contents of their escape kits and water collected from streams.

'We made the concentrated food in our escape kits last three days,' Ben Norris later stated. When their escape supplies were exhausted, they resorted to raiding gardens. Daniel Dunbar: 'We dug up seed potatoes which was all we had to eat from then on. Most of the potatoes were half rotten.' His son Danny recalled, 'Dad would not touch another potato for the rest of his life!'

When the weather turned bad, they hid in barns or ditches, using cut grass or hay to cover themselves. Like Jim, they discovered that nights on the continent in the middle of a blackout were very dark indeed. Walking along a road one night, Dan stumbled into Ben who had stopped suddenly in front of him, convinced he had heard something coming down the road. To their relief, it turned out to be a calf on the loose.

They inevitably faced an evader's biggest concern - finding help. A successful escape hinged on it. They considered crossing the Pyrennes into Spain, but decided they stood a better chance of finding help in occupied France, even though this posed the daunting prospect of passing through a number of large towns, negotiating the Siegfried and Maginot Lines, and crossing the Saar and Moselle Rivers.

They continued their trek west hoping to meet a Resistance organisation. Although food became scarce, they didn't have the same problem with water, as they came across many tributaries from the main rivers, in particular the Rhine. Dan's memoir tells how there were frogs and small fish in these little branches, but without the means of making a fire he saw no point in catching anything. The half breed Indian, as Dan described himself, said he could have started a fire without matches but it would have taken time to find the necessary material. They made their way to where the Rhine joined the Moselle. After a quick recce of the river bank they found a haystack that could accommodate them until nightfall when they could attempt a river crossing. The haystack happened to be home to a number of rats, making it a rather unpleasant few hours until they could get down to the river.

When night fell, Dan stripped off. Being a powerful swimmer, he swam across to reconnoiter the far bank. With it all clear he returned for Ben who couldn't swim. Having had no food for several days, Dan displayed incredible endurance to swim the river three times in one night. Safely on the other side, they held up in an old barn for the rest of the night and all the next day while their clothes dried.

One sunny afternoon during their third week on the run, they came across a priest in his village church.

'This priest, must have been in his mid to late sixties,' recalled Dan. 'He could speak broken English and invited us in for wine and bread. We stayed until daybreak when he gave us more bread to continue our journey.'

That took them to Thionville, a town still occupied by the Germans. Although neither Ben nor Dan elaborated on what happened, it appears, according to Ben Norris's escape report, they came close to capture. The most Daniel Dunbar offers in regards to Thionville is that they 'back-tracked out and around where the Germans had set up camp.'

Later, near the town of Metz, they came across some French labourers cutting up fallen trees. One of them spoke reasonable English and told them to wait a few minutes while he went for help. He returned with some people who brought food and drink and offered to put a roof over their heads.

Ben and Dan explained that they were trying to get in touch with the Resistance. As it didn't seem these particular people could help them in that regard, they thanked them for the food and went on their way rather than put anyone in unnecessary peril.

A few days later outside Toul they came across a farmhouse where they were taken in by a farmer and his wife. The other occupants of the house were the farmer's mother-in-law, his two small children, and a parrot that sat on the back of a kitchen chair swearing like a sailor.

During their brief stay, Dan's leg became badly infected. The cause couldn't be identified, but with gangrene looking likely to set in, a local doctor suggested amputation. Much to Dan's relief, the farmer's wife decided to try her own concoction of herbs and plants and Dan's leg began to miraculously heal.

The farmer and his wife also had a frequent visitor to the house, a well-dressed Englishman who spoke perfect French. He told Ben and Dan he'd escaped from a prison camp and had made his way to France where he'd found a safe haven with Pierre Mathy who owned the Café Croix de Lorraine. Mathy, along with Gregorie, was a chief supplier of men to Maquis 15.

146

Dan and Ben had just met Captain Williams. He introduced them to Pierre Mathy who hid them for a few days while identity papers were organized for them. In a departure from Jim's experience, they were enlisted to help on some clandestine night operations.

Danny Dunbar recalls, 'Dad played the part of the deaf-mute son of one of the families he stayed with. When the Germans came by, they were none the wiser. He actually lit a cigarette for a German officer then went out on a raid that night and killed the very same officer.'

Ben also passed himself off as a deaf mute. It's incredible to think that the number of deaf mutes of fighting or conscript age wandering around occupied France didn't arouse German suspicions.

As in Jim's case, Ben and Dan could not have evaded capture had it not been for the selfless people who had helped them. The quiet, unassuming heroics of these people were in no small way responsible for the ever-increasing number of evaders and escaped POWs drifting into maquis across France. And the maquis were causing the Germans all sorts of problems.

Chapter 25: Maquis

Having fled into the hills to avoid the forced labour draft, the maquisards lived rough in the mountains and hills of France and provided the Resistance with a valuable reservoir of manpower. They proved to be every bit as thorny and troublesome as the spiny Corsican brushwood after which they were named.

Most were still in their teens or early twenties and hadn't so much as picked up a rifle before let alone shot at anybody. However, their hatred of the German oppressors gave them an alacrity and enthusiasm that more than compensated for their inexperience.

Originally situated at Val de Plassey near the town of Choloy-Menillot, Maquis 15, to which Jim and his fellow evaders were sent, had been relocated to a plateau in the Jures Wood overlooking the locality 'Moulin Neuf' between Blenod-Les-Toul and Rigny-Saint-Martin. It had moved there on 12 July 1944 after an informant's betrayal had led to an unsuccessful German attack against its previous location. Under the authority of Colonel Grandval,[89] Head of Region C, they took the name Maquis 15 and saw their numbers gradually increase.

The truck carrying the evaders pulled over to the side of the Toul-Vanclouers road beside a wide, open field. About one hundred metres away on the far side of the field was a heavily wooded hill. The maquis was situated near the top of the hill, affording an excellent view of anything moving along the road or across the field. As the evaders alighted from the truck, they were handed large sugar sacks stuffed with food, tobacco and other supplies.

Gaining access to the camp required crossing the field and negotiating a creek at the bottom of the hill before tackling a stiff two hundred metre climb up through the trees and undergrowth, a task not made any easier by the heavy sugar sacks. As if the terrain didn't provide a good enough defense, a crude but effective alarm system of bottles, tins, spoons, and grenades attached to trip wires had been strung through the undergrowth around the camp perimeter.

The camp itself covered a small area with a heavy canopy of foliage camouflaging it from the air. There were no permanent structures. Make-shift shelters, each accommodating six or seven men, had been fashioned from branches, canvas sheets and a few pieces of scavenged corrugated iron. First impressions didn't bestow Jim with much confidence that he'd be kept warm or dry, but his assumption would prove to be well off the mark.

---

[89] Colonel Grandval (12 Feb 1904 - 29 November 1981) commanded the French Forces of the Interior (F.F.I) of eight departments of the East.

The new arrivals boosted the camp's contingent to about 60 men, which included thirty-three soldiers from the former French colony of Senegal. The Senegalese had initially helped control the unoccupied zone in the south of France where the Germans had installed the pro-German Vichy government. However, following the successful Allied invasion of North Africa in 1942, Senegal switched sides and aligned themselves with the Gaullists and the Allies. In retaliation, the Germans had rounded many of them up and thrown them into internment camps.

The Senegalese in camp had recently been rescued from a German hospital camp by maquis member Fernand Nedelec and other Resistance men, including Ugo. The operation to free them had been disrupted by the Germans, who had arrived unexpectedly with trucks and French drivers to take the prisoners to a prison camp in Commercy. The Resistance men took the German officer in charge to the camp office and neutralized him, while the French drivers and the remaining German soldiers fled.

When the evaders arrived at the maquis, they found some of the Senegalese still nursing the wounds that had put them in the hospital, while others were constructing more shelters. 'They were huge men, well over six feet tall and powerfully built,' Jim remembered. 'Because of their conspicuous physical appearance, they were restricted to nocturnal raids and charged with guarding the camp.'

While every able-bodied man was welcomed into the maquis, a feeling existed among the English speakers - Americans, Canadians, English, and Jim, the one New Zealander - that some of the French didn't think they were of much value because they didn't speak French. This irritated them because they considered themselves professionally trained military personnel while they saw the French, for the most part, as nothing more than exuberant amateurs.

Emile (Captain Williams) with his bi-lingual skills took charge of the English speakers which rubbed some of them up the wrong way, particularly Ben and Dan who were unaccustomed to what they perceived as the haughty pomposity of a prissy British officer. Emile may not have been Jim's favourite person, but it did make sense to have him as their liaison with the French.[90]

Upon arrival, they were greeted by the disturbing sight of a man sitting on the ground lashed to a tree. He looked a pitiful creature, and nobody paid him any attention whatsoever. When someone asked, 'What has he done to deserve such treatment?' Emile told them the man had passed information to the Germans which had resulted in another maquis being wiped out.

Two survivors of the attack had been delivered to the Gestapo. One had died under torture, but the second man had been rescued by the Resistance and was able to furnish the name of the traitor who, following a brief trial, had been sentenced to hang.

---

[90] See Author's notes, Chapter 25 - Maquis

On that somber note, Jim and Bill were introduced to the camp leader, a dark haired, no-nonsense looking man named Ledur Gaetan. Jim knew him by his alias, Gerin but always referred to him as the boss.

In accordance with his rank, Gaetan had his own shelter, but he wasn't much better off than his men, at least when he could be found in camp, as he often stayed in town with his wife, or was away organizing operations with other maquis leaders in the area.

In his memoir Gaetan recounted meeting two airmen who had been brought to the camp:

'I made the acquaintance of Johnny and Clarke, two airmen who had parachuted from their flaming Lancaster. It is after firing a final burst on their opponent that they jump with a parachute. A third airman was wounded and was in Pont-a-Mousson hospital under German guard.' [91]

Gaetan had their names wrong but Jim, Bill and Colin were certainly the men he referred to in his memoir. He told Jim and Bill that Colin had been taken in by a French family near Custines, but because of the severity of his wounds they had been left no choice but to hand him over to the Germans who now had him under guard in Pont-a-Mousson hospital. He would stay there until he had recovered sufficiently to be moved to a POW camp.

After introductions, Gaetan ordered the confiscation of all weapons from the new arrivals. Jim felt aggrieved at losing his knife, and the small automatic pistol Ugo had given him. But Gaetan assured everyone they would get their weapons back once he had verified they were all genuine evaders or escapers. They were then told to find themselves a shelter.

Jim found one with Bill and his two new American friends. None of them had joined the air force to sleep rough, but since this would be their home for the foreseeable future, they were determined to muck in and convince the skeptical French they could pull their weight.

Despite being portrayed by the Germans as nothing more than a bunch of unruly guerrillas, a myth often perpetuated by Hollywood, the maquis were in fact a disciplined military organization. Most of their operations were contrived and directed by the French Section of the Special Operations Executive (SOE) resident in London's Baker Street. Churchill's decree to the SOE to 'set Europe ablaze' saw agents and an ever-increasing number of arms and ammunition being dropped into France. In the first three months of 1944 the RAF dropped five times as many containers as they had during the last quarter of 1943.

Standard attire in the maquis consisted of a mishmash of military uniforms and civvies, with berets and leather jackets being very popular. Almost every

---

[91] Souvenirs De Combats, Et De Sabotages Du Groupe Franc, Les Voltigeurs De Lorraine Raconte, par le chef de groupe, Ledur Gaetan, Alias Gerin 2869-T 42, pg. 65.

man had a side arm permanently stuffed in his waistband and ladies from a nearby town had made armbands for them that incorporated a V for victory sign and the Cross of Lorraine. The cross was the symbol adopted by the F.F.I.[92] in response to the swastika. If not looking like one, the men at least felt like an elite outfit. Gaetan turned out to be as good as his word by returning everyone's weapons a couple of days later.

Strict discipline prevailed in camp. No fires were lit during the day and at night they were kept small and concealable. The men couldn't venture beyond the perimeter without permission, and a very good reason for going. Nobody went anywhere unaccompanied. Even something as mundane as going to the toilet required company.

Jim and the other new arrivals witnessed a demonstration of the strict discipline when they were ordered to fall in on parade during their first morning in camp. They had a moment of sickening realization as to what lay in store when they saw a noose hanging from a tree. Three old crates were stacked beneath it, with a fourth crate placed beside them as a step.

The parade snapped to attention and the informer came out, hands tied behind his back. Two guards led him to the tree and dragged him up onto the crates. They dropped the noose around his neck and tightened it. Jim didn't think the man would die quickly. A hanging required a lot of preparation and expertise, and he considered this a really poor show. The pitiable traitor listened silently to the charges being read out before sentence was passed. Then, without even giving the accused man an opportunity to speak, one of the guards kicked the middle box out from under him.

'They didn't hang the poor blighter,' Jim said. 'They strangled him. After they had cut him down, one of the Frenchmen said something to us Emile which translated as, 'A word to the wise.'

Capital punishment had been the only possible outcome for the informer because his betrayal had led to the death of loyal Frenchmen. However, collaboration with the enemy did not always mean such dire consequences. In circumstances where no lives were lost, the accused often had a choice - their money or their life. It would have taken someone of incredible conviction or utter stupidity to choose losing their life in favour of their savings.

Unnerving episodes aside, Jim found life not too far removed from that of the army, especially with the parades Gaetan held every morning to announce the latest news from the front. He also selected a number of men for clandestine operations most nights. For those not selected, guard duty and individual tasks awaited. On his second day in camp, Jim was approached by Emile who had a couple of Frenchmen in tow.

'As an air gunner, we've put you in charge of maintaining our weapons,' he said.

---

[92] French Forces of the Interior

He led Jim to a primitive arsenal stocked with a few shotguns and a variety of antiquated rifles, pistols and revolvers, most of which were completely foreign to Jim. 'Most likely World War One rejects that had been gifted,' he said.

'It's not a great cache,' Emile said. 'But beggars can't be choosers. I'd appreciate it if you could show these lads how to maintain them.'

Jim roped in Dan and Ben to help, because three air gunners were better than one. With their new French colleagues, they muddled through, sorting the cache and cleaning every weapon. Most hadn't seen oil in a month of Sundays.

Jim and Bill struck up a firm friendship with Dan and Ben, and they spent most of their time together, just as the other non-French speakers - the Canadians and English – established their own cliques. They knew the French thought they were of limited use, but just when they were thinking they might be relegated to greasing ancient firearms and peeling potatoes and carrots for the rest of the war, they were selected for a nocturnal operation. Now, they told each other, things were going to get exciting.

Chapter 26: Nocturnal Affairs

Thinking they were in for some hot action, Jim and his friends envisaged bullets whizzing around their heads and grenades exploding left, right and centre, but when they were briefed on the operation, they discovered it would be far less perilous than anything their vivid imaginations could conjure up. They were to do nothing more daring than 'capture' a few sacks of potatoes left out for them by one of the local farmers who was far more inclined to let the maquisards have his crop than the Germans.

Such operations provided the newcomers with an easy initiation into the marquis's nocturnal activities, so while they were disappointed to think they weren't going to see some real action they were also relieved not to be thrown in the deep end.

'Obviously, the French don't trust us yet,' Dan lamented.

Relieving farmers of their potatoes, while not a serious operation, helped guarantee the continued existence of the camp. A little Frenchman named Marcel,[93] who was responsible for the distribution of food and other essential supplies, organized a dozen men for the raid, including one of the giant Senegalese soldiers. As it would take two men to carry each sack of potatoes everyone paired up before they set out.

'How big are these sacks?' someone asked, gesturing with his arms.

A cherub-faced Frenchman with round tortoise shell glasses said, 'Pas petit. Tres grand.'

'From my limited schoolboy French, I think that means big,' Bill said.

Jim had intended teaming up with Bill, but before he could, the big Senegalese soldier tapped him on the shoulder and indicated that he would go with him. With the Senegalese man standing 6 feet 8 and Jim a diminutive 5 feet 3, they wouldn't have looked out of place in a vaudeville act. Bill ended up paired with one of the Canadians while Dan and Ben stuck together.

Shortly before setting off at eleven o'clock that night they were each given a pair of thick felt soles to tie to the bottom of their shoes. Jim had reservations about this novel approach to muffling their footsteps but his misgivings proved unfounded. The felt soles worked exceptionally well and they reached the farm without incident.

Behind one of the sheds they found six enormous sacks of potatoes awaiting liberation.

The Frenchman with the tortoise shell glasses grinned. 'Tres grand.'

The idea that it would take two men to carry one sack between them had been lost on Jim's Senegalese friend, because when Jim reached down to grab

---

[93] See Author's notes, Chapter 26 – Nocturnal Affairs. Note 1.

one, the giant nudged him aside with a shake of his head. 'Non,' he said, and poked himself in the chest. 'Moi.'

He lifted the sack of potatoes onto his head as effortlessly as putting on a hat, then waited uncomplainingly for the others to tackle the remaining sacks in stretcher-carrying-like fashion. When everyone was set, they headed back to camp with Jim embarrassingly unemployed as he trotted alongside his new friend. They stopped for regular breaks and everyone would plop down puffing and blowing except for the Senegalese giant who wore a big smile as he waited patiently for them to get their breath back.

Ben said, 'Gee, you're doing ok, Winkie.'

'He won't let me help,' Jim said. 'Watch ...'

He indicated to his giant friend that he would take the next leg, or at least help him, but the Senegalese man planted the palm of his enormous hand firmly in Jim's chest and shook his head.

Jim shrugged at Ben. 'What can I do?'

The big man then plonked the sack back on his head, waited for the others to get ready, then strode off without complaint with Jim trotting beside him all the way back to camp.

Sympathetic farmers weren't the only ones willing to help the maquis. Many people in the nearby villages and towns, including a number of shop keepers, knew the maquisards often lived a lonely existence. Knowing they were devoid of life's luxuries and often cut off from friends and family for weeks or months, many of the locals were happy to accommodate them in any small way they could.

Not long after the farm raid, Jim found himself recruited onto another raiding party. This time they would be going into one of the towns to relieve a shop proprietor of his precious supplies. Items such as tobacco, cigarettes and wine were always in demand.

The raiders left after dark, wearing their muffled shoes and armed with pistols and knives. Jim's Senegalese friend didn't go this time, which Jim found a shame because he liked having him around. The fact that the big soldier had appointed himself his personal body guard might have had something to do with that.

They reached the blacked-out town to find the curfew had left it shrouded in an eerie veil of clandestine furtiveness as they crept around to the rear of a particular shop and tapped on the backdoor. Similar to the farm raid, a selection of goods had been arranged for *theft*, although the maquisards certainly didn't consider themselves thieves. True, there had been the odd time when they had pinched a cow or pig from one of the outlaying farms, but they didn't make a habit of it for fear of getting offside with the farmers. After inspecting the goods, the shop keeper had set aside for them, the leader of the raiding party gave him what little money they had and a requisition note for any amount owing. If he wasn't paid the balance beforehand, then he would be reimbursed after the liberation.

Unlike a farm where the sacks of potatoes had been stacked out in a barn, where anyone could have stolen them, the Germans weren't going to believe a robbery had taken place if there was no supporting evidence, so while the shop keeper slipped away to hide the money and the requisition note, the raiders ransacked his shop as quietly as possible. When he returned, he sat himself in a chair to be tied up for the Germans to find in the morning.[94]

Back at camp the raiders sorted out the loot, including a few luxuries like cigarettes and bottles of wine. 'Not that we drank much in camp,' Jim said. 'Certainly nothing like the rowdy bashes that went on in the sergeant's mess or in the pubs around Mepal.'

Marcel rationed and distributed all the food and organized the collection of water from the creek at the bottom of the hill. That, too, was rationed. Not because there was a shortage, but because nobody liked collecting it.

'The job required two men carrying a barrel supported on a frame,' Jim recalled. 'And to get it back up the hill was a real bind, especially if it had been raining and the paths were muddy.'

Their diet didn't create any headaches for those cooking.

'One day it would be carrots and potatoes,' said Jim. 'Then the next day, just for a change, it would be potatoes and carrots.'

Meat didn't feature on the menu much at all because, as Jim said, 'We could hardly go around shooting up the countryside trying to get a rabbit,'

On one rare occasion some of the Senegalese killed a wild boar and dragged it back to camp for a moment of rear culinary extravagance. But neither the men who caught it, nor any of their comrades, got to enjoy it because they were Muslims and didn't eat meat. With big childish grins they sat watching the others enjoy the banquet while they supped on carrots and potatoes.

---

[94] See Author's notes, Chapter 26 – Nocturnal Affairs. Note2.

Chapter 27: Rendezvous

A few days later news came through that the US Third Army under the command of General George Patton was making rapid progress toward the northern French cities of Metz and Toul. To accelerate their progress, they requested that every maquis in the area do what it could to disrupt German reinforcements from reaching the frontline. To that end, the RAF were scheduled to make a series of supply drops. The members of Maquis 15 were told of these plans at one of their regular morning parades, and they were all very excited. As well as more guns, they would also get extra ammunition, grenades and plastic explosive, which the French lads had a particular love affair with. There would also be PIAT[95] anti-tank weapons in the consignment. The French were extremely keen to get their hands on those.

The English speakers had been kept out of harm's way to date, undertaking nothing more serious than the farm and shop raids, but now the leadership agreed the time had come to employ them in more meaningful work. A number of them, including Jim and his friends, were detailed to collect the cannisters from the supply drop.

Unfortunately, there were no meticulous plans for the operation. They were given the drop zone coordinates but no precise time, or even exactly which night, the drop would be made. They were simply ordered to make the rendezvous every night until the plane arrived. Having fought for years with whatever weapons they could lay their hands on, the thought of getting some decent weapons compensated somewhat for the poor planning.[96]

Emile assumed command of the operation, which took care of any potential language problems, and, as it would take a dozen men to haul the supply containers back to camp, Jim, Bill, Dan, Ben and a couple of the Canadian ex-POWs were joined by a number of exuberant Frenchmen.

The party set off after dark, using the moon and faint torch light to pick their way along the narrow paths of the densely wooded hill and across open country to the drop zone seven kilometers from camp.

They reached the rendezvous, a large clearing in a wood, two hours later and split into three groups to form the points of a triangle spaced thirty - fifty metres apart. When H-hour approached, each group lit a small fire and one of the Frenchmen went into the centre of the triangle to signal the aircraft when it approached.[97]

---

[95] Projector, Infantry, Anti-Tank (PIAT) – a one-man portable weapon capable of launching a two-and-a-half-pound projectile that resembled a dart with a long nose.

[96] See Author's notes, Chapter 27 – Rendezvous. Note 1.

[97] See Author's notes, Chapter 27 – Rendezvous. Note 2.

On the first night they waited until well past the appointed time, but no drop occurred. Complaining about the lack of organization, they had just finished dousing the fires when they were alarmed by noises coming from the trees. They fell flat in the high grass at the edge of the wood.

Ethereal voices drifted out of the tree line. With his face half buried in the grass, Jim reached down with agonizing deliberation into his jacket pocket for his automatic pistol, his palms sweaty and his breathing heavy. Out of the corner of his eye he saw the figures of two German soldiers silhouetted against the skyline. His heart thump worse than it had in the café. Again, he didn't think it possible that it wouldn't betray him. He smelt the heavy fragrance of tobacco in the air. The Germans' low chatter sounded like something in a dream. They were obviously just out for an innocent cigarette, and he prayed they would just walk away because he didn't fancy confronting death that night. Fortunately, the soldiers didn't stray from the tree line and trip over anyone.

'If they had have done', Jim recalled, 'it would have been bad for them.'

After an excruciating eternity the soldiers melted away into the night as peculiarly as they'd appeared. But where had they come from? It later came to light that the Germans had installed an anti-aircraft battery and a machine gun position on a hill overlooking the rendezvous. It may have been a coincidence, but suspicion lingered that they may have been alerted to the maquiards' plan. The hierarchy arranged another rendezvous at a different drop zone two nights later.

Unfortunately, things didn't work out much better. After lighting the fires, they hung around for a drop that might or might not happen. After an age the sound of an aircraft came out of the darkness and the Frenchman in the middle of the triangle pointed the beam of his torch vertically. Hopefully, the hefty containers would land bang in the middle of the triangle because nobody wanted to stumble through the bushes in the dark looking for them.

A pale moonlight meant they should have been able to see the aircraft silhouetted against the cloud, but when it sounded like it should have been directly overhead, they couldn't see a thing.

'The twit's flying far too high,' whispered Emile. 'He's above the cloud. How does he expect to see our light?'

As the tenor of the engine gradually began to fade, the Frenchman with the torch waved madly and spouted something rude about the RAF. The men were disconsolate. And then the low rumble of the engines returned. The aircraft sounded much lower this time and a few seconds later it flew into view, silhouetted against the clouds. It suddenly became obvious why it hadn't dropped any containers. At the same moment Jim recognized the distinct shape of a German JU88, someone shouted, 'Boche! Luftwaffe! Luftwaffe!'

The fires were hurriedly extinguished and the men bolted for the cover of the trees. They stumbled into the forest falling over each other in a panic to get away. Afterwards, they found their narrow escape rather comical but when they arrived back at camp the leadership weren't amused. Clandestine air drops were expensive, potentially dangerous operations, not only for the maquis but also for the RAF crews making the drops. The potential toll could be catastrophic. The drop was rescheduled for the following night at a different location and this time everything went to plan. The PIATs, the small bazooka-like anti-tank weapons, didn't look much, and in Jim's view they were never going to threaten a tank, but the French were desperate to see what they could do.

Chapter 28: Exit Strategy

With Gaetan often being away for a couple of days at time coordinating operations with other group commanders, periods of excitement tended to rise like monoliths on plateaus of boredom. The men were often left with mundane chores and had to find other ways of entertaining themselves.

One day without much to do, Dan asked if he could examine the knife that he saw Jim fastidiously sharpening with a wet stone. 'Do you mind?'

Jim handed him the knife and Dan balanced it across one finger, noting its perfect balance. He pointed out a suitable target.

'Think I can stick that tree?

'Be my guest,' Jim said.

Dan stood up and stepped out fifteen paces from the tree. He weighted the knife expertly in his hand, took a step backward, lifted his throwing arm, then stepped forward and sent the knife sailing through the air. The blade buried itself in the tree with a resounding thwack.

Jim was mightily impressed. Dan retrieved the knife and handed it to him. 'Have a go.'

Jim's first effort saw the knife hit the tree handle-first and bounce harmlessly to the ground. His second attempt didn't go much better.

'Let me have a go,' Ben said. He showed himself to be as spectacularly inept as Jim. Next, Bill stepped up. He produced a better effort with the blade hitting the tree but failing to penetrate.

Dan laughed, 'Don't worry you guys, a balanced knife like this is the most difficult to throw.'

He then demonstrated how to hold the knife correctly, and how to release it. 'To be effective you have to get a lot of power into the throw,' he explained. He illustrated his point by thumping the knife into the tree once more. 'But just remember, Winkie, if you throw your knife in combat you probably won't get it back.'

'Eventually we all got the hang of it,' recalled Jim. 'We were having quite a good competition until someone got it wrong. The knife hit the tree at such an angle that the blade snapped in half.'

'Well, I haven't seen that before,' Dan said.

Disheartened and irked, Jim picked up his broken knife. Dan examined the blade and gave the heartening prognosis that the patient could be save.

'Not much we can do here,' he said. 'But hang onto it. You can get it reshaped back in England. It won't have the same balance, but then you were never going to make it in the circus, were you?'

'Well, it was fun while it lasted,' Jim lamented.

Boredom loomed large, until one morning on parade they were delivered the stimulating news that in cooperation with the Resistance of Gonreville,

Fernand Nedelec had organized the sabotage of two sections of the Paris-Strasbourg railway line between Gonreville and Fontenoy-sur-Moselle with the aim of derailing a German supply train.

Two groups were organized to carry out the mission, one led by Emile, and the other by a Frenchman. Bill went with Emile's group while Ben and Dan joined Jim under the command of the Frenchman, their job being to act as lookouts while the French demolition experts laid the charges.

'Experts?' Jim exclaimed. 'I got the impression they knew only slightly more about it than we did, which was nothing.'

The stretch of railway line earmarked for sabotage ran parallel between two high embankments allowing Dan, Ben and Jim to perch themselves high above the line with a good view in both directions. A clear moonlit night made their job easier.

Down on the line, the French 'experts' dug the explosives in under the tracks. The charges were harmless until a detonator was inserted. After that, things could get a bit dicey, especially in the hands of an excited Frenchman. When they had finished placing the explosives, the experts ran a wire up the embankment to Jim's position and connected it to a plunger.

The fuse wires varied according to the job to be done, but the two most popular types were cortex, which burnt at 7 km per second, meaning instantaneous detonation, and Cordon Bickford dynamite cord which burnt much more slowly at 1 cm per second. On this occasion, they used a combination of Nobel 808 explosive and cortex.

The expert waved everyone to get our heads down then pushed the plunger. Nothing. The initial anticlimax quickly exploded into panic and annoyance. The sight of the French agitated over the failure didn't fill Jim with confidence. The man with the plunger frantically examined the connection, fiddled angrily with the terminals and rammed the plunger down again. Still nothing.

One of the other so-called experts jumped up with an extravagant French profanity and disappeared over the top of the embankment to check the charges. Busily trying to sort out the connections, the man with the detonator didn't notice the man's departure, and before anyone could stop him, he pushed the plunger again.

An almighty bone shaking explosion rocked the night. The men cowered, covering their heads as stones and debris showered down. With the dust settling, they scrambled to the top of the embankment to survey the damage and were aghast to see the man who had gone to check the charges stumble out of the smoke blurting a string of insults.

'Another few feet and the poor blighter would have been blown to pieces,' laughed Jim. 'Even then, he probably didn't hear anything for a month.'

Exciting as blowing up railway lines might have been, Jim's first priority had always been getting back to the UK. Also, camp life had started to wear thin. One morning when cleaning rifles with Ben and Dan, Ben held up an antiquated firearm that looked like it had survived the Battle of Waterloo.

'What are we supposed to do with this?' he moaned. 'Look at this piece of junk,'

'If you ask me, we need to get outta here,' Dan said. 'Try and get through to our lines. What do you think, Winkie?'

'It is our duty.'

'That's settled then.' Dan said.

They had no intention of simply walking out of camp and run the risk of being strung up or shot, so they asked Emile to arrange a meeting with Gaetan. Jim urged Bill to join them, but Emile wouldn't allow it. Their plan didn't impress him to start with, let alone having Bill be part of it. He did, however, agree to liaise and translate for them.

When the delegation walked into Gaetan's shelter, they found their boss sitting on an old chair behind a little table littered with maps. He had an automatic pistol within reach, and a silver alarm clock sat on the table ticking so hard Jim wondered how it hadn't attracted the Germans.

Gaetan listened in polite, solemn silence as Emile explained the situation. When Emile had finished, Gaetan lifted himself out of his chair and went to the entrance of his shelter. He stuck his head outside and barked out a stern order.

Two of his lieutenants arrived with Sten guns slung over their shoulders. As Gaetan spoke to them, the men slowly unslung their weapons. They obviously hadn't been invited to tea. Gaetan then spoke to Emile before retiring behind his table where he stood like an omnipotent schoolmaster.

'He has denied you permission to leave,' Emile said. 'If you attempt to do so, you will be shot. It's not personal, you understand. It's a matter of security. We can't afford to have you fall into German hands.'

This may have seemed rather draconian, but the Resistance had recently had a bad incident involving two disagreeable Yugoslavian airmen who had fled the camp unsupervised, throwing everyone into a state of high alert.

The Yugoslavians had been fighter pilots in their own national air force before escaping to England to join the RAF after their country was overrun by the Germans. In England, they thought they'd be flying Spitfires, but much to their chagrin they were put through aircrew training, one as an observer and the other as a gunner, and were then posted to a bomber squadron.

They didn't speak French, so Emile, who had just arrived on the scene, interrogated them in English. Why, the airmen wanted to know, should they be grilled by an Englishman instead of one of their own people? The fact that there weren't any of their countrymen within a thousand miles didn't appease them, and they demanded that they should be allowed to make their way to Yugoslavia to join Marshal Tito's forces.

Emile explained to them that it wasn't possible. The Resistance simply didn't have the resources to get them to Yugoslavia. The safest option would be to wait until the Allies liberated the region. But that didn't impress the Yugoslavians one iota. Afraid they would try to go it alone, despite being forbidden to do so, the Resistance bundled them off to the maquis. There, they did nothing but grumble and complain, until one night they vanished. While everyone assumed they had headed for Yugoslavia, it couldn't be assumed they would make it, and an anxious time ensued for everyone.

As the weeks passed with no dire reports concerning the Yugoslavians, things returned to normal. But the episode hardened Gaetan's resolve.

He spoke politely to Emile and then stood back, hands on hips.

'He wants your word that you won't take matters into your own hands,' Emile said.

In light of the aforementioned circumstance, Jim and his friends considered it a reasonable request, and agreed to remain in camp, especially as the lieutenants looked only too happy to use their Sten guns if necessary. When Emile gave Gaetan the news, the boss's face broke into an appreciative grin.

'Merci, comrades,' he beamed.

The two gun-toting lieutenants lowered their weapons. There were smiles and handshakes all round and Jim and his American friends went back to carrots and potatoes. Jim had felt badly about leaving Bill in the first place, so in that regard he didn't feel too perturbed at having to stay.

Chapter 29: The Dark Side of Life

Of course, life wasn't all potatoes and carrots. In between meals and routine camp chores other work needed to be done, some of it far from pleasant. The execution Jim had witnessed upon his arrival wasn't the last, and an Italian airman named Antonio became the next victim of maquis justice.

Antonio had been picked up by the Resistance in similar circumstances to Jim and Bill, but he had not endeared himself to anyone with his surly attitude and light-fingered inclinations. Not long after his arrival, he took part in a farm raid, but while everyone else collected the potatoes, he snuck into the farmhouse and helped himself to the farmer's valuables.

When the farmer reported the theft, suspicion immediately fell on Antonio. He was sent him on an errand to collect water while a couple of men searched his belongings and unearthed the stolen items. He protested his innocence, but to no avail, and everyone kept their distance from him. Disgusted at this pariah-like exclusion, he vowed to make the maquis pay, and went as far as threatening to report them to the German commander of the nearest town. It may have been bluster, but Gaetan and his lieutenants weren't taking any chances. They arrested him and tied him to a tree while they decided his fate.

Nobody was allowed to speak to him or give him any food or water. However, when it began to rain and he complained about a lack of shelter, one of the Senegalese soldiers produced a tarpaulin and cut a slit for him to stick his head through, allowing him to wear it like a poncho. It was a mistake, because it gave the Italian the opportunity to work his ropes loose. As soon as he had done so, he bolted. He might have made a better fist of things had he waited until dark, because they chased him down without difficulty. He wasn't necessarily a bad person, but to threaten the survival of the maquis courted severe retribution and it could only end in an inexorable consequence. They hanged him the next morning.

The taking of a life always weighed heavily on Jim's mind. While he assented that the loss of one man's life had to be measured against the possible demise of many others, and the partisan world in which he and his fellow evaders found themselves in operated in a far less scrupulous manner than to which they were accustomed, it didn't make the meting out of malevolent punishment any easier to accept. Antonio's execution wouldn't be the last.

A couple of days later Ben and Dan were surprised to find themselves recruited to accompany two of the French maquis members to an address in a nearby town.

'What's up?' Jim asked

Dan and Ben had no idea, but they dutifully left camp that night with the Frenchmen. When they returned a few hours later they had a dishevelled, weary looking man with them. Jim and Bill watched him being escorted into Gaetan's shelter, shadowed by Emile and a couple of Gaetan's lieutenants.

'Who do you think that is?' Bill asked.

'Let's ask the boys,' Jim said.

'Dunno who he is' Dan said. 'But I gather a good number of people have been deported or shot because of him.'

Dan and Ben weren't able to furnish any further information about the man, except to relate what had happened when they had arrived at his house.

'We were left on guard in the street while the two French guys went to the front door,' Dan said. 'This guy answers the door and the Frenchies drag him outside. He was absolutely terrified. They wouldn't let the poor bastard go back in for his coat, or even say goodbye to his family.'

Soon afterwards, raised voices, including Emile's, began to argue flamboyantly. Emile didn't sound at all happy. The quarrelling continued for ten minutes before Emile emerged to be confronted by a circle of onlookers.

'The man in there has just admitted giving information to the Gestapo,' he said. 'As a result, two Resistance men were arrested and executed. We've allowed him to write a letter to his wife, and sentenced him to death. The French lads want to hang him, but I don't think that's appropriate. I argued it would be militarily proper for him to face a firing squad.'

For once, Jim agreed with Emile. From what he'd seen, the French weren't particularly good at hangings.

'Anyway,' Emile said. 'We reached a compromise and let the fellow choose for himself. He wants the firing squad.'

That night they tied the man to a tree and posted a guard, giving him no chance of escape. Jim felt badly for him. Every time he looked at him, he felt a pang of sympathy. 'All the poor blighter could do was think about dying in the morning.'

The next morning the camp formed a tight parade. A firing squad of five men, including Dan, formed up. The execution didn't take long and once again it reminded Jim of the fragility of human life. And the way they treated the man's body after cutting him down disturbed him greatly. 'They simply left him crumpled at the bottom of the tree for the rest of the day and into the night.'

That night Jim sat on guard duty in the pitch darkness, with the dead man laying a few yards away in what had to be the loneliest, most nerve-racking experience of his life.

Suddenly out of the darkness rose the faint rattle of a tin. Despite the cool night, Jim felt perspiration trickle down his back. He released the safety catch on his rifle and felt the reassuring weight of the pistol in his jacket pocket. He waited with intense anticipation, but now he only heard the occasional muffled noise from the camp. He scanned the darkness. Listened. Waited. The woods in the dead of night, where the feeblest noise set him on edge, wasn't Jim's

164

favourite place to be. He would much rather have been in his turret looking for German night fighters.

No sooner had he consigned the noise to his imagination, when an alarming metallic sound rattled out of the darkness. His rifle and the hairs on the back of his neck came up at the same time. Then a strong hand gripped his shoulder and he nearly shot up into the branches of the nearest tree. Miraculously, his rifle didn't discharge.' As he caught his breath, he recognized his Senegalese friend from the farm raid sitting down beside him, his pearly white teeth grinning out of the darkness. He patted Jim reassuringly on the back and, without a word, settled down to keep him company throughout the rest of his shift.

Chapter 30: Ambush of Tigers

George Patton's Third Army was making steady progress toward the German Frontier in the face of increasing German resistance, prompting the Maquis to play an ever-increasing support role by disrupting the German supply lines and stalling their attempts to get reinforcements to the front. With orders flowing out from London to maquis leaders all over Northern France, rumours abounded that Maquis 15 would soon see more direct action. They had been hearing the dull krump and grumble of distant gunfire for the last couple of days and the French were especially keen to show they were capable of more than just blowing up railway lines and bridges. They really wanted to be shooting the filthy Bosch.

'The Polish boy was especially keen to shoot Germans,' Jim reflected. 'I don't know if the same could be said for us flyboys.'

But if anyone held any concerns about combating the enemy face to face, they weren't sharing them.

They paraded one morning in late August to be briefed by Gaetan. He had been absent for two days, meeting with other maquis and resistance leaders in the Toul area. An unaccustomed rigidity pervaded the ranks as the men waited for him. But when the canvas flap of his shelter flew open, the sense of anticipation and tension suddenly disintegrated into howls of laughter. Instead of seeing the solemn figure of their boss emerge, they were greeted by the sight of Emile, looking very dapper with a monocle stuck in his eye.[98]

The French contingent were especially amused. They thought it a most hysterical sight and thereafter, whenever any of them were relaying one of Emile's orders, they would make a circle with their thumb and forefinger and hold it in front of a squinted eye.

The hilarity dissolved when Gaetan emerged from his shelter to inform them that the time had come to take the fight to the enemy in a more challenging manner. Their mission was to stop, or at the very least delay, a German panzer column heading their way. This escalation in affairs caused tremendous excitement among the French who greeted the news with typical exuberance, cheering like idiots until they were called to order by Gaetan.

Jim didn't think they had much to cheer about. Stopping German armour? At best, they might cause a slight inconvenience, but knocking out tanks? Nevertheless, he spent the morning with Dan and Ben preparing their arsenal which had improved immensely thanks to the RAF drop. Their cache of weapons now included machine guns, grenades, Molotov cocktails, plastic

---

[98] See Author's notes, Chapter 30 – An Ambush of Tigers. Note 1.

explosive and PIAT anti-tank weapons, which Jim still had concerns about regarding their effectiveness.

The English speakers were denied use of a PIATs by the French who jealously declared they were more entitled to them. Their sense of prerogative didn't worry Jim. Not only did he think they would be no match for a Tiger tank, they were also a cumbersome weapon to use. Cocking one for the initial shot was difficult and time consuming. Only after firing the first shot did the weapon automatically re-cock itself, thereby making any following shots much quicker. It also proved to be a difficult weapon to employ when laying prone, which was the most desirable position to adopt if you wanted to avoid exposing yourself to the enemy.

But the most alarming aspect of the PIAT was how uncomfortably close the operator had to get to the target. Claims that it had an effective range of just over one hundred metres and could penetrate 4 inches of armour were somewhat exaggerated. In reality, it had a proficient range of only forty metres. With the unsettling realization that you had to get up close and personal with a German tank to use one effectively, Jim was happy to let the French have them.

The old-fashioned Molotov cocktail, a wine bottle filled with petrol and fused with a petrol-soaked rag, also meant the user had to get close to the action for it to be thrown against its target. The cocktail in itself lacked the capacity to put a tank out of commission, because even with its exterior engulfed in flames a tank could remain operational. The Molotov Cocktail's best quality lay in hindering the crew's escape if their tank was disabled. Life would become a little unpleasant for them if burning petrol seeped into the engine bay and caused smoke to enter the interior, but in most cases remaining trapped in their tank proved safer for a crew than risk getting picked off by rifle or machine gun fire.

The maquiards would be positioned among trees for the attack, so tossing grenades would require an underarm or round-arm throw, not the over-arm lob Jim had been taught during his army training, otherwise the grenade might rebound off a low hanging branch. One of the Frenchmen imparted some valuable advice before they set out:

'To act first is to win,' he said. 'To react is to lose.'

'In other words, shoot first and ask questions later,' Jim said.

They set off full of importance in the knowledge that they were going to make a meaningful contribution to the war. Jim had no extra ammunition for his Belgium-made pistol so he kept it stuffed in his waistband to be used as a last resort. Together with his broken knife in its sheath hanging on his hip, and an old rifle slung over his shoulder, he looked like some sort of cutthroat.

He fell into step with Bill. 'OK, mate?'

'Not quite what I expected when I joined up.' Bill slapped his rifle. 'And not sure about this. I've never shot at a man before.'

'Me either.'

'You shot down that Jerry.'

'Shooting at an aircraft is different. All I ever shot at on the ground were cardboard cut outs and clay pigeons.'

'You think the air force will pay us for this, Winkie?'

'Gee, Bill, as a flight engineer, I credited you with more intelligence than that.'

When they reached the ambush site, they found excellent cover in a rank of trees and bushes overlooking the narrow dirt road along which the German tank column would have to pass. Emile took charge of the English speakers, stationing them among the cover at twenty-metres intervals with Bill and Emile to Jim's right, and Dan and Ben to his left.

'The French chaps will kick things off,' Emile said. 'Nobody is to open fire until then. We'll try and knock out the lead and rear tanks and trap the rest of the column between them.

Burrowing themselves as low as possible they waited as the minutes ticked interminably by. Just as Jim began to wonder if it would turn out to be another botched operation, the first hint of trouble came with a low, distant rumble. It gradually developed into a haunting, ghoulish resonance. Then came the sound of clattering tank tracks and the groaning of metal. It sounded like death on the march, and it reached the men long before any tanks appeared. The ghastly sound only served to magnified their already heightened anticipation. They had no idea how many tanks to expect or what support they would have.

Jim's s hands sweated on his rifle. He looked across at Bill who squinted down the sights of his weapon. After what seemed an eternity, the first of several Tiger tanks lumbered into view. They came without supporting infantry, growling along like a pride of tyrannical beasts on the prowl. Dust mixed with black and grey exhaust fumes swirled around their flanks.

Suddenly the whomp of a PIAT split the air, followed almost instantaneously by the wallop of an explosion as a direct hit landed on the lead tank. One of its tracks buckled and it staggered like a wounded elephant. It limped a few agonizing metres then ground to a halt. A chorus of yelling and small arms fire broke out, and amid the commotion a couple of Molotov cocktails cartwheeled through the air with their petrol-soaked rag wicks aflame and smashed against the tank's armour plating, erupting in flames. The tank's gun traversed toward the primary threat, the man with the PIAT, who thankfully lay lower than what the gun could depress. Another PIAT round slammed into the second tank.

'Grenades,' called Emile.

Dan and Ben popped up and tossed a couple into the melee. One of them exploded in mid-air above a tank and the other rolled under it and exploded with little affect. The driver revved the tank to an angry pitch, trying to reverse, but found himself trapped by the following tank whose track had been ruptured. It immediately came under attack from Molotov cocktails that exploded against its thick armour.

Jim and Bill didn't have any grenades so they hit the tanks with suppressing rifle fire. The turret hatch on the lead tank swung open, received several hits for its trouble, and snapped shut again.

The plan to knock out the lead and rear tanks had worked well, with PIAT rounds exploding against their targets, causing a great deal of confusion, but it hadn't eliminated the threat, especially that of the unscathed tanks whose drivers began to manoeuvre for a counter attack. One of the tanks, with its hull a mess of flames, struggled into a position where it could employ its forward firing machine gun. A PIAT round bounced off its flank and machine gun fire strafed it from nose to tail. As bullets chipped and ricocheted off its sloping armour, Jim's biggest fear was being hit by a stray bullet.

Emile suddenly cried an order to pull back and the maquiards melted away into the bush and took stock. They had caused considerable damage and disruption without suffering a single casualty. It had been a victory of sorts.

Trekking back to camp they heard the sound of approaching aircraft.

'At times like that it was best to make ourselves scarce,' Jim recalled. 'British and American fighters had a habit of shooting up anything that moved'.

They ducked under cover as two American P-38 Lightnings came in low overhead and without any warning opened fire at something beyond the crest of the next hill. A krump of explosions followed, and columns of smoke rose tall over the tree line as the Lightnings wheeled away and vanished into the sun.

Over the hill, Jim got a good indication of the firepower the Germans faced when he saw what was left of a motorized column scattered along a stretch of road. Wrecked trucks, cars and motorcycles burned furiously and acrid black smoke belched into the air heavy with the stench of cordite and burnt flesh. 'It was a terrible smell,' Jim reluctantly recalled. 'One you never forget.'

Jim had never seen anything like it as he inspected the remnants of the column with a degree of incredulousness. Lifeless bodies littered the road in a scene that would haunt him many times thereafter.

The French appeared immune to the horror as they picked through the remains and scavenged whatever they could. One of them came up to Jim with a smile on his face and presented him with a brown leather map case he'd just taken from a dead German officer. Jim didn't really want it, but not wanting to offend the man, he tentatively accepted it.[99]

Apart from weapons and ammunition, there wasn't much left to loot so they were quickly on their way, much to Jim's relief. He feared German

---

[99] See Author's notes, Chapter 30 – Ambush of Tigers. Note 2.

reinforcements might show up, or the Lightnings would return. Either way he didn't want to be there

Chapter 31: Blenod-les-Toul

A couple of days later, against the distant krump of gunfire, the camp stood on morning parade being told that Patton's American Third Army had almost reached their doorstep. The American's continued advance would be greatly helped if all F.F.I. units in the area could make life as difficult as possible for the retreating Germans. Every enemy solider killed and every tank destroyed would be one less for the Third Army to deal with.

Maquis 15 received orders to deploy to the town of Toul 20 kilometres to the east, where they were to try and delay a number of retreating German troops. Everyone knew they were likely to face some hot action.

On 30 August 1944, they organized themselves for the trek to Toul. Dan and Ben helped Jim make sure the camp's stocks of weapons and ammunition were sufficient for the task. The French took possession of the PIATS again, being reluctant to give them up after their recent success against the Tigers. The Polish boy decided he would carry their only heavy machine gun, a relic from World War One that came with a limited supply of ammunition.

The French contingent were full of enthusiasm for what lay ahead. The evaders were more pragmatic but equally determined to make a significant contribution as they set off for Toul. En route, they held up for the night in the village of Blenod-les-Toul where they established themselves in both the inhabited and uninhabited houses in town.[100] The previous German occupiers had left the village, but there were reports that some retreating Wehrmacht and Panzer units were still in the area. Much to their chagrin, the F.F.I. received orders not to engage the enemy unless they were attacked first. The French were particularly irritated by this because it went against their every instinct, and they couldn't fathom why such a restraint should be imposed upon them. To fire only in self-defense? They did not fight that way.

In the morning they were to rendezvous with another F.F.I. unit at a crossroad on the highway just outside Toul where they planned to ambush any retreating German troops. In the meantime, they settled in for a quiet, uneventful night.

Jim took up a post with Dan, Ben, Bill and the Polish boy on the ground floor of an abandoned two-story house situated on a bend at the top of a narrow road, and a handful of Frenchmen stationed themselves on the upper floor. The house might have given them a good view of anything coming up the road, but it also put them in a direct line of fire. Most of them only had a rifle or a pistol, but Bill, who had volunteered to help the Polish boy with the ancient machine gun, also had an old grenade which Jim thought looked capable of exploding if Bill so much as looked at it the wrong way.

---

[100] See Author's notes, Chapter 31 – Blenod-les-Toul.

The next morning jubilation and excitement pervaded the air, with many believing that this would be the first day of liberation. The Americans were not far away and the general consensus seemed to be that they could possibly make contact with them some time that day, an especially enticing thought for Jim and his fellow evaders. After many weeks spent living a restricted existence, they would finally be able to step out of the shadows of prevarication.

The morning started with routine work in preparation for their hike to Toul, and everything seemed calm, but on the western approach to the village side things had turned dark.

'Germans!'

The shout went from house to house, carried from every man with a vantage point to see the first of a retreating enemy convoy approaching from the west. Shots rang out. Nobody knew who had fired them, but as the villagers retreated inside their homes, the F.F.I. put themselves in shooting positions behind houses, in the gardens, and on the roof tops.

The first Germans troops to appear came in cars, and they were immediately fired upon. Bullets spat up the dirt and thwacked into the vehicles, and a smattering of infantrymen scattered behind whatever cover they could find. Following the cars came something the F.F.I. weren't equipped to deal with - a column of 40 Tiger tanks.

'Someone had opened fire without realizing the danger he was putting us in,' Fernand Nedelec explained. 'Now we were in a terrible situation'.

The Tigers prowled ominously into the village, the grinding, groaning and clattering of their caterpillar tracks making a terrible, haunting din as they pulverized the road beneath their 50-ton weight. Their guns traversed left and right, ready to obliterate anything in their path. Fernand Nedelec expressed what everyone thought.

'What can we do against these steel monsters?'

A young boy of Blenod, aged 13, whose account was recorded by Nedelec, witnessed the scene:

'Two small cars approach. As soon as they [the Germans] arrive in the village the shooting starts; in fact, the F.F.I. are in the village and accommodate the German cars with grapeshot. The tanks arrive. We expect a battle between the F.F.I. and the Germans.

As the shooting starts, one of the tanks camps across the road and launches a shell below the café. The SS go into houses sprinkling them with gasoline, or with grenades. The guns thunder continuously. A shell hits a house. It breaks the door down and a woman runs for her life, hiding herself in a trench. In the middle of the shooting and blows of the guns, the incendiaries are unleashed and the roofs of the houses crush heavily in the earth. All the village is in agitation.'

From Jim's position, the approaching danger hadn't been immediately obvious, but it didn't take long to be realized as a convoy of cars and trucks appeared at the far end of the long road that Jim looked down from his ground floor window. Some of the vehicles were being towed, which told on the German's dire gasoline shortages, and they were accompanied by rag-tag infantry. Most were on foot, but some rode bicycles.

As small arms fire erupted. Jim rested his rifle on the sill of the open window and started shooting. Dispatching cardboard targets at Burnham army camp seemed a million years ago. Beside him, the Polish boy jammed the butt of the old machine gun into his shoulder and squeezed the trigger, while Bill fed the ammunition. The gun jammed after half a dozen rounds, and the boy cursed as he cleared the blockage. He fired a few more rounds, but experiencing the same result he abandoned the temperamental machine gun and picked up his rifle.

Those Germans who were armed, returned spasmodic fire. Those who weren't, ran for cover. The number of unarmed men highlighted the appalling state of the German army. Drivers abandoned their vehicles, and infantry, both armed and unarmed, sought the protection of abandoned vehicles or doorways along the narrow street.

'Not that the French cared whether or not they were armed,' Jim reflected. 'They were shooting at anything that moved.'

A number of Germans were shot off their bicycles before they had a chance to ditch them. The Polish boy shouted at Jim and Bill.

'The shoulder! The shoulder! Shoot for shoulder! Look, I show you!'

He took careful aim and fired at an unarmed retreating German. A single bullet caught the fleeing man in the right shoulder, spinning him around and flinging him to the ground in an explosion of dust.

'You see,' the boy cried enthusiastically. 'They spin. Funny, funny.' He would have killed the German had he not spent his ammunition. He frantically searched for more, and at the same time yelled at Jim, 'You kill that Nazi. Kaput, kaput! You kill him!'

Jim looked at Bill, whose moral compass aligned with his own. Neither of them had the inclination to shoot a wounded man.

'Had it been 'him or me' it would have been different,' Jim admitted. 'But many of the Germans weren't armed. They were just scared young men - like us.'

By the time the Pole had reloaded his rifle, his victim had struggled behind the cover of a stalled vehicle. He cursed again, flung Jim and Bill a look of disapproval, and then began hunting for another victim.

Smoke billowed inside and out, and the stench of gunpowder filled the room. Men fired and reloaded as fast as they could in order to keep the Germans pinned down. Then events developed a more sinister complexion with the appearance of a Tiger tank. It rumbled around the bend at the top end of the street and headed straight toward the house. A second tank appeared and then a third.

With no room to manoeuvre around the abandoned and incapacitated vehicles clogging the narrow street, the Tigers bulldozed them out of the way or simply crushed over the top of them. The Tiger in the van came to a halt and trained its gun on a house from where F.F.I. fire streamed, and within seconds the building was torn apart by two 88mm shells.

The Tiger then lurched forward towards Jim's house where the Polish boy had grabbed the old machine gun again. Amazingly, the ancient weapon managed to fire a sustained burst, but the boy might as well have been using a pea-shooter. As the bullets sparked and ricocheted harmlessly off the Tiger's armour plating, it stopped and traversed its gun around to swat away the nuisance.

Jim jumped up and grabbed Bill by the collar. 'Let's get the heck out of here, now!'

Everyone in the room made a hectic scramble to save their lives, bursting out of doors and windows. Jim and Bill darted across the room to an open window overlooking the back garden. Jim leapt out, rifle in hand, with Bill hard on his heels. He stumbled, regained his balance, then ran as fast as he could, his legs pumping furiously.

'It was like being in a dream,' he recalled. 'My legs were going flat out, but I didn't seem to be getting anywhere.'

He heard the shrill screech of an 88-mm shell followed by a deafening krump and turned instinctively to see the upper part of the house torn apart in a cloud of smoke, dust and flame. The concussion from the explosion threw him to the ground as masonry, mortar and wood whistled over his head, and dust, plaster and macerated brick rained down. With smoke and dust mushrooming from the house, men clambered out of the rubble, dazed and confounded to have survived. Jim looked back with incredulous horror, unable to fathom how any of them had escaped without serious injury. It would have been comical if it hadn't been so serious. A moment later a second shell walloped into the house, destroying the ground room where he had been moments earlier. More debris hurtled toward him and the house vanished in a huge cloud of smoke and dust.

Jim and Bill picked themselves up and ran for cover with the whomp-whomp of exploding shells behind them. The Germans might have been retreating, but they were doing some serious damage in the process. It wasn't the Wehrmacht carrying out the assault, it was the SS units who followed up, systematically razing everything in their wake. The sound of engines and caterpillar tracks cranking up higher could be heard above the carnage as the panzers sought to outflank the defenders. The F.F.I. had no way of holding them with their limited supply of small arms and the order to retreat to the hills filtered through their ranks.

Fernand Nedelec recalled how a member of their maquis, Rene Fourriere, knowing the Germans would burn the F.F.I. flag, tried in vain to recover it from where it had been wedged in the entrance of the Town hall. Nedelec made no mention of Fourriere's fate.

Nedelec and a small group of men, including Emile, escaped hurriedly up a hill toward Ford Blenod. They bolted through gardens and vineyards in complete disorder as German tracer bullets tore through the air and kicked up the ground all around them. Miraculously, everyone got to the top of the hill, exhausted and gasping for breath.

From their vantage point they watched helplessly with angry hearts as the houses in Blenod-les-Toul spewed pungent clouds of black smoke and crackled in blazing infernos. The cries of the inhabitants, many of whom were struggling up the hill behind them, left them feeling impotent in the face of the innate revenge being displayed by the SS.

A young witness to the carnage later reported, 'The people whose houses are on fire are forced to save linen and their clothing. The guns in the east begin to calm down. The last tanks start to pull out leaving a lieutenant, who is concealed, and two soldiers. Some blows of rifles still bore the air but we don't pay much attention, one is so much occupied extinguishing incendiaries and has to protect the other houses from disaster. Seventeen dwellings are on fire. The men use buckets of water to stop the fire, but in vain. The roofs and the walls collapse. What a disaster. A large farm at the bottom of the village is burnt. However, firemen arrive and save the body of the building. All day one occupies oneself extinguishing fires.'

In the chaos, the order to retreat up the hill to the old fort had never reached Jim and Bill, and in the ensuing confusion of running and dodging of shells and bullets it had become every man for himself. There was so much confusion that Jim suddenly found himself separated from Bill who was nowhere to be seen. It was like he had just vanished. Jim was searching for him when he ran into Ben and Dan who'd escaped the house unscathed. They looked for Bill without success before deciding to move onto their next objective, the crossroad where the F.F.I. had planned to ambush any retreating Germans. When they arrived at the location, they found themselves alone.

'The plans must have changed,' Dan said, looking around the deserted intersection.

'Or they were thrown away altogether,' Ben suspected.

'Let's hang about and see if anyone turns up,' Jim said.

When nobody came, they voted to make the long hike back to camp.

They didn't encounter anyone on their trek but they could hear gunfire the entire time. They arrived a few hours later on the brink of nightfall. The only people in camp were the Senegalese soldiers, and a wounded man resting on a homemade cot nursing a bandaged leg. He hadn't been injured in the battle but had slipped on steep ground and got entangled with an old branch that had skewered him in the groin.

Men straggled back into camp throughout the night, including Emile. Jim had expected to see Bill with him.

'Sorry,' Emile said. 'I haven't seen hide nor hair of him. I thought he was with you chaps?'

'We got separated when our house got hit,' Jim explained. 'That was the last we saw of him.'

'I'm sure he'll be fine.'

Jim spent the night on guard duty with Dan and Ben. They listened to the boom of the American guns and stewed over Bill's absence.

'I don't understand where he got to,' Jim said. 'He was right behind me getting away from the house.'

'The way that house went up, I'm surprised any of us got out,' Dan said.

Throughout the night, the krump of gunfire rumbled like distant thunder, accompanied by the low, guttural moans of the wounded man. Without the proper medical know-how, his comrades could only apply basic first aid, which they feared wouldn't be enough, and they faced the very real danger of gangrene setting in if they didn't get him proper attention. Fortunately, they didn't have to wait long.

Chapter 32: Liberation

By the next morning, the wounded man had a raging fever. When they peeled back the bandage, they found his wound swollen, blistered and red.

'What the hell do we do?' Ben asked. 'This guy could die.'

But before anyone could say anything, their concerns were pushed to one side when one of the French lads rushed into the camp, yelling and waving his arms frantically. 'Tanks! Tanks!'

Everyone's immediate concern was that another retreating German column had arrived in the area, and they raced to a place where they could survey the main road. In the distance a couple of half-tracks, an armoured vehicle, and a jeep churned up clouds of yellow dust. As they drew closer, white stars on the vehicles became visible.

'Americans!' Emile cried. 'Advanced party probably. Reconnaissance.'

'Let's get outta here,' Dan said.

In that moment, Jim felt a bizarre rush of exhilaration and panic.

'We were right on the doorstep of the American front line. So close to getting home and yet fearful we might miss the boat.'

They flew around the camp gathering up what few personal belongings they had, and just for good measure, Jim souvenired Gaetan's alarm clock before chasing the others down the hill to intercept the American column. He left in such a hurry he forgot to say goodbye to his Senegalese friend.

They scrambled down through the bush and plunged through the creek at the bottom of the hill. With the armoured vehicles now only a hundred metres away, they tore across the field, yelling and waving like mad men. As they got closer to the column the lead vehicle, a Greyhound, which Jim later described as looking like an oversized jeep, jolted to a halt, and a G.I. manning a .50 machine gun, swung round on them. Despite wearing their F.F.I. armbands, they stopped and flung their hands in the air.

Dan called out, 'God, are we glad to see you guys.'

The surprised gunner replied, 'You speak mighty good English.'

'I should,' Dan said, 'I come from the same place you do.'

The gunner waved them closer. 'Identify yourselves.'

At that moment, a jeep screamed up in a cloud of dust and a colonel jumped out with a lieutenant in tow.

'What's going on here? Who are you people?'

Emile took immediate command of the ragtag quartet. 'Captain Williams, sir. British Army.'

'And these other men?' the colonel demanded.

Emile pointed out Dan and Ben. 'United States Army Air Force. And,' he added, pointing at Jim, 'Royal New Zealand Air Force.'

'You're all a long way from home.'

'We've been with the F.F.I.'

The colonel listened with hands on hips as the men rattled off abridged versions of their stories.[101] 'Are there any more of you?'

'Possibly,' Emile said. 'We had a skirmish with a panzer column yesterday and some of our men have yet to show up.'

'Where is your camp?'

Emile pointed toward the top of the hill. 'There are some Frenchmen and Senegalese soldiers still there. You'd better send a medic as there's a wounded man in need of immediate attention.'

'Well, this is just a recce party,' the colonel said. 'But I'll get on the radio and organize some transport to take you back to HQ. And we'll get some help for your man up the hill.'

They waited until after noon before a jeep arrived carrying an American Captain and Lieutenant, and everyone crammed in. At the American's temporary HQ, tents had been erected along with a P.O.W. compound secured by nothing more elaborate than ropes slung around a few iron standards. Disheveled German prisoners milled about dressed in rag tag blends of assorted uniforms. They smoked and chatted and seemed in surprisingly blithe spirits.

The minimal security surprised Jim until one of the G.I.s explained, 'They don't want to escape, buddy. Why would they? They're away from the fighting, and they're sure as hell away from the Russians. They ain't causing us no problems.'

Jim and his friends ate royally in the officer's mess tent. 'The Americans baked their own bread,' Jim recalled. 'It was the best I'd ever tasted. But after weeks of carrots and potatoes, anything would have tasted good.'

After their meal they were taken to the quartermaster, who was in a large tent sorting through several piles of clothes. Jim believed quartermasters were the same no matter what army they were in, and this guy seemed no different - brusque, diligent, and master of his little domain.

'What ranks are you guys?' he demanded.

He had no trouble finding uniforms for Dan and Ben, who were both sergeants, and after a brief rummage he dragged out a tunic displaying captain's bars for Emile. Jim, however, posed something of a quandary.

'Flight sergeant?' he asked. 'What's that? A sergeant-major or something?'

'Not really,' Jim said.

'Warrant officer?'

'Not quite.'

'Well buddy, I got no idea what our equivalent of a flight sergeant is, so you better have this.'

---

[101] See Author's notes, Chapter 32 – Liberation. Note 1.

He threw Jim a master sergeant's tunic displaying three stripes up and three down. It was terribly oversized.

'Because they didn't have many small fellas like me in their army,' Jim laughed.

It fitted comfortably enough with the cuffs turned up and the belt tightened, but Jim may not have felt quite so good had he realized he'd been given a hand-me-down from a man either killed or wounded in combat.

'For a while I was a master sergeant in the United States Army,' he said. 'Unpaid, I might add.'

The quartermaster gave them combs and toiletries and sent them off for hot showers in the ablutions tent. After weeks washing in a cold creek, they now found themselves in relative luxury, and that night they slept soundly in decent cots. The next morning after a slap-up breakfast, the colonel took them to his tent where they were introduced to a two-star Major-General whom Jim remembered as General White[102]

The general, a plain-speaking man, interrogated all four men in depth. He wanted to know every detail about the places they'd been and the people they'd had contact with.

'It's important that we know, he said. 'Because we've had reports that some of the French people have been taking matters into their own hands, taking reprisal against suspected collaborators who were in fact helping men like yourselves.'

Jim's story didn't take long, but Dan and Ben, who had been in Germany and France longer, and had been in contact with more people, had much more to report. Emile, who had been with the Resistance longer than any of them, spent considerable time providing the general with information.

The one burning question they had - could the general get them back to England?

'The best I can do is Paris,' he said.

Fantastic.

'But only if you're prepared to guard four truck-loads of German prisoners. We're transporting them to a camp at Troyes, which is on the way.'

By that stage Jim and his friends were prepared to go by horse and cart.

'Ok,' the general said. 'Go see the logistics officer. He'll fix you up.'

They found a captain in charge of logistics and he appreciated the extra help loading the prisoners. He issued them with carbines, a couple of clips of ammunition each, and a quick briefing about their weapons, as none of them had had the pleasure of handling one before. Jim liked the fact that it didn't have a bolt action like the old heavy .303. Once cocked, the American carbine could fire as fast as you could pull the trigger.

---

[102] See Author's notes, Chapter 32 – Liberation. Note 2.

'Right, let's get these Krauts aboard,' the captain ordered. 'Don't worry, they won't give you any trouble'

The prisoners took only a fleeting interest in their new guards as they were marched out of their compound, searched, and lined up behind four trucks, with officers in one truck and the lower ranks in the other three. The logistics captain handed one of the truck drivers a clipboard with his inventory and said to his new recruits, 'Sit yourselves up top and keep an eye on 'em.'

Jim and Emile clambered onto the roofs of separate trucks, while Dan and Ben sat together on another, with a regular G.I. on the fourth. Despite reassurances that there wouldn't be any trouble, no chances were being taken and the truck decks were left uncovered. Jim certainly wouldn't have felt comfortable being hidden under a canopy with the prisoners as he would have been hard-pressed to contain a revolt. But the prisoners had no mind for conflict as the trucks rolled out for Troyes, a good two-day journey away.

A number of the prisoners on Jim's truck had a reasonable grasp of English and were happy to discuss the war and its effect on them and their families. Things were cordial as they shared their opinions about Hitler, and some, without any fear of repercussion, admitted they thought him a mad man and wished him dead, sooner rather than later. Others argued that he'd done a lot of good for the German people by rebuilding the economy and giving them jobs and a semblance of hope, before the power had gone to his head. Whatever their personal opinions of Hitler they all agreed, that as ordinary soldiers, they should not be tarnished with the accusation of fighting in his name. They had, they argued, been guilty of nothing more than fighting for their country. Jim couldn't help but agree, but he wondered how he would have been treated had there been a reversal of fortune.

Things continued in a genial mood until the convoy arrived at the first of a number of villages en route to Troyes. Word of their arrival had preceded them and they were confronted by angry mobs lining the streets, hurling abuse and running up to the trucks, jeering, spitting and hitting out at any German prisoner within reach.

On two occasions, Jim and the others had to fire warning shots to drive off the baying throngs. One prisoner thanked him profusely for saving his life after a French woman jumped up on the side of the truck and grabbed a handful of his hair. She fell off the truck after Jim fired a shot into the air, and they left her sitting on the ground cursing and screaming. Similar scenes were encountered at every village and town they drove through. Rather hair-raising stuff for a butcher boy from New Zealand.

The trucks travelled on until early evening when they pulled over in a field for the night. The guards did a head count as they ushered the prisoners into another makeshift compound and posted guards. Jim thought the guards must have slept the entire night because when they conducted a head count the next morning, they discovered they had more prisoners than the night before.

'What the hell is this?' Dan exclaimed. 'Where did they come from?'

'God only knows, Buddy' one of the G.I.s said. 'The Krauts are in such a mess, a crap load of their guys got cut off in the chaos of their retreat. Rather than wander around the countryside and risk falling into French hands, they sneak into our compounds.'

On one hand Jim considered this a real drag, because it meant all the prisoners had to be searched again, but on the other hand the new prisoners were happy to surrender thousands of French Francs in the hope of buying themselves better treatment. Jim happily pocketed the money, the first he'd had since handing over his escape funds to Maurice.

Late on the second day, they rolled into Troyes where they delivered the prisoners unscathed to a large POW camp on the outskirts of town. Jim, along with Ben, Dan and Emile carried on to a US air base outside Paris where they were interrogated by an American officer and given some spending money - two thousand francs apiece - to stuff into their already bulging pockets. Then they were taken by car into Paris where Jim and Emile reported to Brigadier Cathew-Yorstoun, head of British Military Staff in Paris. Dan and Ben were taken to the American authorities. After an exhausting day of travel and interrogation, all four men were delivered to the Hotel Meurice where they were put up in opulent suites until a flight to England could be arranged.

It hadn't been too long ago that the Hotel Meurice had been the haunt of German officers and high-ranking officials. Now it had become a haven for dishevelled evaders and escaped POWs who, after weeks or months of deprivation and living hand to mouth, found themselves enjoying the hotel's plush dining room, wallowing in magnificent suites, and indulging in the luxury of a descent bath, even if hot water remained somewhat limited. Space came at a premium at the hotel, which meant bunking three or four men to a room. Jim, Ben and Dan roomed together, while Emile went off in search of company more in keeping with his rank. They all retired to a good night sleep in real beds.

The next morning, they woke late, but nobody cared. Jim made some inquiries after Bill, hoping his friend had found his way to the hotel, but nobody had heard of him. This didn't surprise Jim, considering the number of men passing through, but he did begin to harbour a few unpleasant thoughts about Bill and his grenade. Next, he went to the British Embassy and sent a telegram home. Later, his mother told him that his telegram had reached her before the official one from the Air Ministry.

Back at the hotel the men discovered they could buy champagne for 300 francs a bottle, or two bottles for 500 francs. With a wad of cash to spend, they bought two bottles each and went back to their room to celebrate their survival and toast their friendship.

Later that night, despite being advised to stay indoors because of a number of Vichy and German snipers running around the sewers and popping up to shoot indiscriminately, they went out to see Paris. In a champagne-induced haze, all Jim remembered was floating across the hotel lobby and down the magnificent marble steps to the pavement where a young boy ran up to him and tugged at his sleeve.

'Monsieur, monsieur,' the boy cried, as he tried thrusting a water pistol into Jim's hand and pointed down the road to an overturned car. 'I find there.'

'What do I want with a water pistol?' Jim declared. He gestured at Dan. 'Give it to him.'

The boy shoved the water pistol into Dan's hand and ran off. Dan briefly examined it then slipped it into his pocket. The next morning, he showed Jim the water pistol which turned out to be a rather handsome German Luger.

'So much for champagne,' Jim lamented.

With all that cheap plonk, it's little wonder Jim remained sketchy about their night out in Paris. Daniel Dunbar, however, offered slightly more insight.

We tried one of the French cafes, most of the people wouldn't let us pay. The women were friendly. Two of the French girls living with their Mom and Pop took us home with them. They could speak some English. The girls were sisters and the family wanted to hear our stories and where we were from. This family wasn't poor nor were they rich but they fed us and showed us parts of Paris not everyone got to see.

On the third day, Jim and his American buddies learnt that a flight to England had been organized for them. They were driven to Le Bourgent airport a few kilometres outside Paris. Following a heavy bombardment during the liberation, much of the airport lay in ruins, but nothing significant enough to delay them boarding a DC-3 transport plane with other repatriated men.

'The basic seating arrangements had us on the floor so they could squeeze in as many as possible,' Jim said. 'Hardly luxury travel, but nobody cared. We were going home.'

The DC-3 took off for England without incident. It would be 40 years before Jim set foot in France again.

Chapter 33: Late Arrival

After an uneventful flight, devoid of the fear and trepidation of combat, Jim touched down at Hendon with the landing resurrecting the elation of returning unscathed from an operation. It seemed like a lifetime since he had been on friendly soil.

He found a British reception committee waiting for him, and Dan and Ben found a similar American on hand to greet them. The three of them arranged to meet in London the next day for a drink and a proper farewell. They had only known each other for a few short weeks, but they had experienced more in that brief period than most people would in a lifetime.

The reception committee whisked Jim away to the Air Ministry building in Bond Street where he received a thorough grilling by an MI9 officer who wanted to know everything about his time in France.

Where had he been shot down? How long he had been in France.? Who had helped him? What escape line had assisted him? Jim did his best to provide the officer with what he wanted, but as most of the people he'd met had used aliases he wasn't sure how useful his information would be.

'That's all right,' the officer said. 'Just tell me anything you can remember. We actually know a great deal about the Resistance activity in the Lorraine region. I'm not surprised you ended up fighting with the F.F.I. How did you find that?'

'Different,' Jim said.

'Yes, they are a rather colourful bunch by all accounts. Tell me about bailing out.'

'Our aircraft was at 9,000 feet[103] when we were attacked by a night fighter. All four of our engines were shot out. The aircraft was blazing and out of control, but Ian pulled us out of the dive long enough to enable our navigator, flight engineer and myself to get out.'

'Do you know what became of your crew?'

'Bill and I were in the maquis together. I lost contact with him. Colin is a prisoner of war.'

'The others?

'I believe our mid-upper gunner and wireless operator were killed during the fighter attack. The skipper and our bomb aimer were killed in the crash. They're buried in a village called Millery, I believe. North west of Nancy. I'd like it put on record that it was due to our skipper's heroism -'

'Pilot Officer Blance, correct?'

'Yes. It was due to his heroism that Bill, Colin and myself survived.'

---

[103] German records state the aircraft was at 14,000 ft. when attacked.

Like many other skippers, Ian had remained at the controls for the sake of his crew. And, like many other skippers, he had made the ultimate sacrifice. Yet, in Jim's opinion, Ian and many men like him never received the appropriate recognition.

When the intelligence officer had gleaned as much as he could, he said, 'Well, you've certainly earned a spot of leave.'

'And after that?' Jim asked. 'I'd like to rejoin my squadron.'

The intelligence officer shook his head. 'Not possible. Standard policy I'm afraid. You've been with the Resistance, and the F.F.I. That could get you in trouble if you were shot down over that region again. The Germans would be very interested in what you know.'

The fact that most of France was back into Allied hands didn't sway the officer. 'You'll probably get a posting somewhere as a gunnery instructor,' he said. 'We need chaps of your ilk to pass on your knowledge to the new boys.'

'You mean I'll be one of those 'screened' chaps?'

'You make it sound terribly tiresome. Remember, those 'screened' chaps, as you call them, have earned the privilege of their position, and so have you.'

'If I recall, most of them wanted to be back on ops.'

'Patience is a virtue, Flight Sergeant. You'll get your chance in due course.'

In due course. Where had Jim heard that before?

'In the meantime, you'll be staying at the London District Transit Camp.'

The officer read Jim's disappointment.

'It sounds dreadful, I know, but it's really quite a charming place.'

The Transit Camp turned out to be the Great Central Hotel next to Marylebone train station, one of the many elegant establishments The Air Ministry had commandeered. Jim took a room and received a fresh uniform. He could never remember what happened to his American one.

'I'm sure I must have kept it. After all, the Americans had given it to me and they never said they wanted it back.'

The next day, he met Dan and Ben in a pub not far from the Air Ministry building. They had been given leave prior to their next posting, and they too, were prevented from flying in the European theatre again. Jim swapped addresses with them and promised to keep in touch, but alas, as in so many cases, they went separate ways and Jim never heard from either of his American friends again.

After the pub, he visited a little shop around the corner from the Air Ministry where he had heard he could get a small embroidered winged flying boot to represent his newly entitled membership into the Late Arrivals club.

Bearing the motto, 'It is never too late to come back', the Late Arrivals club had been established during the North African campaign by aircrew who had returned to their own lines after being shot down. The idea of exclusive clubs tended to be frowned upon in the upper echelons of the RAF, but they remained popular with the aircrews. Fellow aircrew usually presented the fortunate recipient with the award in a very light-hearted manner, but it in no way diminished the appreciation and admiration for the wearer's efforts in getting home. As an unauthorized award, recipients usually wore the winged boot on the left breast of their flying suit or the underside of a lapel.[104]

Jim had barely settled into the transit camp before being shipped off to an Aircrew Allocation Centre at Morecombe on the the east coast of Lancashire. Morecombe was a seaside town that would later become known for producing comedians like Eric Morecombe and Victoria Wood, but when Jim got off the train there at the beginning of a month long wait at the Aircrew Allocation Centre, he found the pre-war vibrancy and carnival atmosphere for which seaside towns were so famous, had been shelved for the duration of the war.[105].

He had been in Morecombe for two weeks when one morning Bill Hyde showed up. The last time they had seen each was when they were running for their lives in Blenod-les-Toul. Once again, they shared a happy and emotional reunion. 'We have to stop meeting like this,' Jim said. 'What happened?'

Bill confessed that in all the confusion he had lost contact with everyone. 'I was wandering around the village looking for you chaps when the Americans showed up.'

'What did you do with that grenade?' Jim asked. 'Did you get a chance to use it?'

'No,' Bill laughed. 'I was afraid to in case it blew up in my hand, so I buried it.'

'Very wise,' Jim said.

They both had leave due, and with Morecombe being a little more than an hour from Bill's home town of Manchester, he invited Jim home for a couple of days. Jim had no idea how they got to Bill's house because they had to walk through thick, sooty fog akin to an old London pea-souper.

'Terrible,' Jim complained. 'It put me off wanting to live in England, I can tell you.'

After spending a couple of relaxing days at Bill's place, and with a few days still left up his sleeve, Jim made his way down to Mepal to catch up with his old squadron and see his mates Jock and Paddy. The C.O. congratulated him on a successful evasion and he received a great welcome from his mates who hadn't expected to see him again. He also had a reunion with his crew's old bomb aimer from OTU, Mac Maaka, who had been posted to 75 Squadron.

Before Jim had been shot down, Jock and Paddy had yet to fly an operation, but by the time he returned, they were both well into their tours. Jim's late arrival culminated in homecoming drinks in the mess, and a boisterous night at *The Chequers*.

---

[104] See Author's notes, Chapter 33 – Late Arrival. Note 1.
[105] See Author's notes, Chapter 33 – Late Arrival. Note 2.

Jock announced he had leave starting that Friday, so Jim invited him up to Aberdeen to spend a few days with him and his friend Ma Jamieson and her daughter Anne. When he told Ma, she said, 'He's welcome. It will be bit of a squash, but who cares?'

Jim arranged to meet Jock off the midnight train at Aberdeen station on the Friday night, but fate conspired to make sure things didn't turn out that way. Walking to the station just before midnight, Jim had the portentous feeling that Jock wouldn't be on the train. He wasn't. The Hadley crew were posted FTR and Jock and Paddy were both missing. It had been Paddy's 17th op and Jock's 20th.

Not knowing the fate of his friends left Jim struggling with a peculiar mixture of pessimism and optimism. Fearing the worst, but praying for the best, he wrote to RNZAF Headquarters in London. In late November 1944, he received their reply.

Dear Kirk

I am in receipt of your letter of 7th November, 1944 and following is the only available information concerning NZ.426041 Pilot Officer W.C. Hadley and the remaining members of his crew.

One New Zealander, namely Flight Sergeant D.S.R. Wilcox, is a Prisoner of War, and the only Royal Air Force member, namely Flight Sergeant C.R. Fowler, has returned safely to the United Kingdom.

Flight Sergeant Fowler has stated that the aircraft crashed at Orsley, Zeeland, and that at the time he left the aircraft all the remaining members of the crew, with the exception of Wilcox, were still in the plane, and that they may have been killed by enemy action, but, so far, no confirmation has been received to this effect.

Arrangements have been made to inform you of any further news received concerning Flight Sergeant Biggar and Flight Sergeant Giles, and immediately further details come to hand you will be notified.

Yours faithfully.
(A.H.A. MacLean)
Flying Officer,
For/Air Commodore, R.N.Z.A.F
AIR OFFICER COMMANDING

On 27 July 1945, Jim received a second letter from RNZAF Headquarters in the Strand which regretted that in view of the complete lack of evidence, and owing to the period of time which had elapsed, it had become necessary to presume, for official purposes, that Jock and Paddy and lost their lives on 12 September 1944.[106]

[106] See Author's notes, Chapter 33 – Late Arrival. Note 3.

Chapter 34: Final Days

Following the loss of his good friends, Jim received an air gunnery instructor's posting, and at the end of October 1944 he arrived at No.3 Air Gunnery School at Castle Kennedy in Scotland, newly promoted to Warrant Officer Kirk. And to think, at gunnery school he hadn't been considered instructor material,

Five miles east of Stranraer, Castle Kennedy sat in an area of relatively low laying ground on a gravel outwash deposited by ancient glaciers that had retreated up the Firth of Clyde. The aircraft equipping the school were Avro Ansons for gunnery and Miles Martinets for target towing. Jim spent a month there before being transferred to No.2 Air Gunnery School at Dalcross near Inverness in the Scottish Highlands.

Flying at Dalcross usually took the trainees over the Firth of Moray where strong winds were the norm. Even taxying the aircraft could be fraught with disaster. Fortunately, Jim didn't do much flying. The bulk of his responsibilities were carried out with his feet firmly on the ground.

He spent ten somewhat frustrating months at Dalcross. Despite his previous escapades he wanted to get back on ops. However, any return to flying operationally wouldn't happen in Europe, because the war there ended on 8 May 1945 before he had a chance to get back into action. Jim heard the news with profound sense of relief tinged with a degree of melancholy. He had survived when some of his closest friends hadn't. Unfortunately, most personnel weren't permitted to leave the station to join the celebrations in Inverness.

'It would have been fantastic to get out, but we had a great knees-up all the same. A really wonderful, joyous time, even if we were snubbed by Churchill.'[107]

When the VE Day celebrations subsided two or three days later, there came the realization that Bomber Command still had work to do. Once the deliverers of high explosive and destruction to hundreds of European cities, they now began Operation Manna, a multitude of humanitarian food drops to millions of starving civilians across the continent. Dropping food instead of bombs brought a great deal of satisfaction to the crews who relished doing something constructive rather than destructive, and it was a relief not to be flying into flak and fighter infested skies.

The Operation Manna flights also gave the ground crews an opportunity to fly with the crews as sightseers. The unsung heroes of Bomber Command, they often worked in atrocious conditions without the praise or accolades bestowed

---

[107] See Author's notes, Chapter 34 – Final Days.

upon the aircrews. Nothing would have been possible without them. Jim held the firm opinion that the ground crews never got the credit they deserved.

'They were always there to wave us off, and they were always the first to greet us when we returned. They actually cared more about *their* aircraft if the truth be told.'

Operation Exodus, the repatriation of thousands of allied prisoners of war, also swung into effect, bringing home men from POW camps from all over Europe. Soon after the end of hostilities, Jim had a happy reunion with Colin, who visited him at Dalcross after being repatriated during the early part of Exodus.

Badly wounded in the legs during the night fighter attack, and with Ian struggling to keep the burning Lancaster level, Colin had dragged himself to the forward escape hatch. After Bill Hyde had fallen though the hatch, Oscar, should have been next to exit, but he selflessly forfeited his chance of escape to make sure his wounded navigator got out first. Colin left the aircraft just seconds before it broke in two. The terrible G-forces made it impossible for Ian and Oscar to escape.

A French family took Colin in, but his wounds were too severe for them to treat and they were left with no choice but to hand him over to the Germans. He convalesced under twenty-four-hour guard in the Pont-a-Mousson hospital until pronounced fit enough to be moved to a POW camp.

His first stop, as for most captured allied fliers, had been Dulag Luft[108] where he spent a couple of weeks recuperating before being interrogated by a senior Luftwaffe officer. The officer had been educated at Cambridge University before the war and spoke impeccable English.

At one point he took Colin into a room where an H2S set had been set up, and he asked Colin to explain the intricacies of it. But Colin could only shrug. "I can't help you, mate.'

'But I understand your aircraft was equipped with such a set.'

'Was it?'

'You won't be imparting any secrets.'

Colin wasn't swayed by the officer's geniality 'I don't know how it works. I used a slide rule and a compass.'

'You really cannot tell me anything?'

'I'm afraid not. Every time I touched it, the bloody knobs fell off.'

'In that case, Flight Sergeant' the affable German said, 'Let *me* show *you* how it works.' Which he did, much to Colin's bemusement.

Following his brief stay at Dulag Luft, which later became an American army base, Colin went to Stalag Luft VII at Bankua, near Silesia, where he became the camp's 588th prisoner.

---

[108] Dulag Luft was the abbreviated name for Durchgangslager der Luftwaffe, the name given to Prisoner of War transit camps for Air Force prisoners.

Stalag Luft VII had opened on 6 June 1944, to accommodate a growing contingent of downed allied airmen. It also accommodated a number of glider pilots captured at Arnhem following the ill-fated, Operation Market Garden.

If Colin's first impressions of the camp were anything like those of fellow POW, Flight Sergeant Norman Oates, who had arrived at the camp shortly after Colin in August 1944, Stalag Luft VII was far from being the Ritz of POW camps.

Oats described being *'marched into a large compound surrounded by a high double-wire fence and watch towers; but even more surprising was the realization that the "dog-kennels" were for us to live in!'*

These dog-kennels were small, wooden huts sleeping four, later six men. The POWs were issued with two blankets and a palliasse filled with wood wool which rapidly disintegrated. The camp lacked the creature comforts often found in more established camps and the accommodation would not improve until October that year. During this period, there was no electric light, and only one water pump for 800 men.[109]

Conditions were not only tough but also dreary, with not much to entertain the prisoners. Life was so boring at times, Colin took up smoking a pipe to relieve the tedium.

Jim found some of Colin's stories about camp life disturbing. Like when Colin told him about a man in his hut who often woke up screaming from nightmares. After being shot down, the man had been helped by a sympathetic family before his eventual capture. After being tortured by the Gestapo into giving up the family, he was taken back to the family's home and made to watch as they marched the family into the backyard and shot them in front of him.

On 19 January 1945, the Germans evacuated Stalag Luft VII in the face of the approaching Soviet army and forced 1,565 NCOs to make a marathon trek west to Stalag IIIA at Luckenwalde.

Each man received two and half days rations for the arduous journey. With no transport for the prisoners or their guards, they set out in sub-zero temperatures. Following his stint in hospital, Colin found the going excruciatingly difficult. The appalling conditions are highlighted in Oliver Clutton-Brock's excellent, 'Footprints on The Sands of Time.'

'As the day wore on, so the kriegies'[110] *strength gradually diminished and they were forced to shed excess baggage. After 28 kilometres they arrived at Winterfield, where some spent the first night on the floorboards of an unheated schoolhouse. Others were billeted in barns where they were so densely packed that it was impossible to lie down. Sleep proved elusive as the freezing wind whipped through cracks in the walls, and with it came the snow.'*

---

[109] Oliver Clutton-Brock, Footprints on The Sands of Time, Pg.124
[110] Prisoners of war.

The next day after a 12 kilometre journey that took more than five hours, the prisoners were allowed to rest in a disused brick factory. At 8 o'clock that night they were back on the road. The German guards sprayed the dark interior corners of the building with automatic fire before leaving. Nobody would be left behind, at least not alive.

A number of airmen did manage to hide well enough to avoid the next stage of the march in -13-degree weather. A bitter wind cut through the prisoners' threadbare clothing and whipped up the falling snow at regular intervals. Prisoners who collapsed were forced to carry on or face certain death. After a brutal 30 kilometre march in the atrocious conditions they reached the bridge across the Oder River. They were just in time. The next day German engineers destroyed it.

On the 5 February the prisoners reached Goldberg marshalling yards where they were piled into cattle cars, fifty-five men or more in each, with no food, sanitation or room to lie down for three days. The conditions were appalling. Excrement covered the floor and walls, and men had to urinate through the sides of the wooden cars.

When they arrived at Luckenwalde, on 8 February, 1945, they were starved and suffering from a number of illnesses including dysentery, bronchitis, septic feet and diarrhea. The Soviets eventually liberated Luckenwalde on 22 April 1945.

Jim maintained the utmost respect for Colin. 'I don't know if I could have survived what he did. He was a tough nut.'

For the crews not involved in the Manna and Exodus operations, the days following the victory celebrations were something of an anticlimax. With the cessation of air operations, surplus aircrew had to be dealt with somehow, and many men were relegated to ground duties, and demoted into the bargain.

A man who had been a Flight Sergeant air gunner, or a Flight Sergeant bomb aimer suddenly found himself driving a truck as a Leading Aircraftman. Ranks for volunteer aircrew had only ever been temporary appointments that could be rescinded at any time.

To avoid such a fate, Jim requested a transfer to 2nd Tactical Air force, operating B-25 Mitchell bombers in the Pacific Theatre. His request met with a favourable response, but before he could pack his bags, the Japanese surrendered on 15 August 1945.

'I didn't have to go up against the Japanese after all, but at least I didn't have to paint latrines either.'

With the war over, he requested a transfer back to New Zealand, which came through at the end of September 1945. He went to an aircrew holding unit (ACHU) and stayed there until early October 1945 before being posted to No.12 PDRC, his last overseas posting before heading home. Later, he regretted not getting hold of Bill and going back to France to pay their respects to their friends.

'It would have been nice to see all those people who had helped me, but at the time I didn't have much money for travelling to France, and I'd reached the point where I just wanted to get home. I'd been gone too long.'

He boarded a ship called the Vulcan for the long uneventful voyage home. After stops en route in Freemantle and Auckland, he sailed into Lyttleton Harbour. From there he took a train crammed with returning servicemen into Christchurch where his mother, grandmother and siblings were waiting to welcome him home. The bedlam at Christchurch station reminded him of the underground platforms in London, but he didn't care. He had made it home when so many others hadn't.

Therese Vuillemin Photo: Zane Kirk   *M.Hardy, whose father hid Bill Hyde.*

Charles Francois (middle).   *Melle Francois. Photo: Gerard Lebel*
Photo courtesy of Gerard Lebel

193

Maurice Schwartz
Photo Courtesy of Jean-Claude Schwartz

France Schwartz with Jean-Claude
Photo courtesy of Jean-Claude Schwartz

Home of Maurice and France Schwartz. Jim's first safe house. Photo: Gerard Lebel

The boot shop in Frouard.   *The house of Charles Francois.* Photos: Zane Kirk

With my brother Leroy and sister Deborah in front of the Francois house with local Pont-a-Mousson historian Jean Magne. Photo: Gerard Lebel

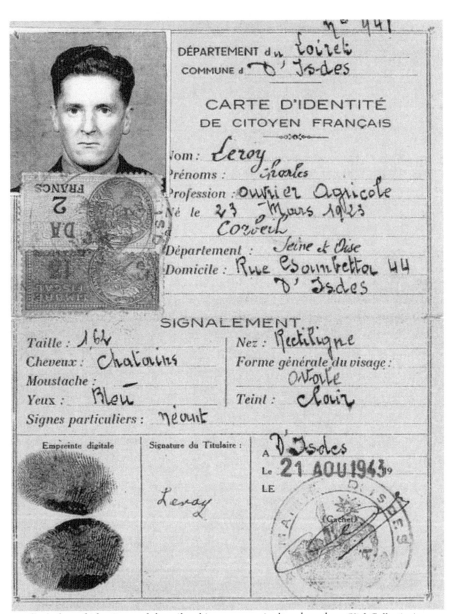

Jim's forged identity card describes him as an agricultural worker. (Kirk Collection).

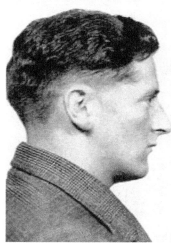

Additional escape photos carried by Jim, and a certificate exempting him from forced labour. (Kirk Collection).

COMMISSARIAT GÉNÉRAL
AU SERVICE
DU TRAVAIL OBLIGATOIRE

CERTIFICAT DE RECENSEMENT

M. *Leroy Charles*

Domicilié à *D'C Jadres* _____ Départ : *Loiret*

Rue : *Gambetta* _____ N° *44*

Hameau ou lieudit : _____

a satisfait aux obligations de la loi du 4 septembre 1942, en ce qui concerne le recensement de la main-d'œuvre.

Bulletin de recensement N° *85*

A Jargeau, le *24* _____ 1943.

Cachet
de la
Mairie.

Le Maire

The card reads: French State Office of the Compulsory Labour Service Certificate of Census. The certificate states that Charles Leroy has fulfilled the obligations of the law of September 1943, with regard to the census of manpower. (Kirk Collection).

CERTIFICAT DE TRAVAIL   Mod. 1

délivré sous la responsabilité de:

Monsieur   Gérôme

Qualité :   Jardinier

(l'Employeur indiquera son titre, la raison sociale et l'adresse de son Établissement)

Rue des Roses n° 23

A   Isdes   , le 15/4   1943

Signature et cachet du Responsable :

J. 37280-43. (8)   T. S. V. P.

Jim's travel certificate naming Gerome Jardinier as his employer. (Kirk Collection).

IDENTITÉ DU TITULAIRE

Nom et Prénoms : Leroy   Charles

Né le 23 Mars 1923

Adresse : 44 Rue Gambetta   à Isdes

Nationalité :

exerçant (dans l'Établissement) moins de 30 heures
        (à son compte   ) plus de 30 heures

(rayer les deux mentions inutiles)

le métier de ouvrier agricole

depuis le 15 Mars 1941

Inscrit dans la catégorie   2

sous le N° 474   Le Titulaire :

Leroy

57/124-2

Travel certificate (reverse) – Identity of holder – Charles Leroy. (Kirk Collection).

198

Captain Chester Williams's POW identity card. Williams (Emile) had a prickly relationship with Jim, but his numerous escapes from P.O.W. camps were Boy's Own stuff. Courtesy of Kate Beaumont.

The Herrick crew with Daniel Dunbar sitting front row left and Ben Norris standing back row second from right. Photo courtesy of Edouard Reniere

Dan and Ben's B-17 after crash landing in Germany. Photo courtesy of Edouard Reniere

Jim (second from left) with fellow instructors and Colin Greig (far right) at Dalcross, Scotland following Colin's repatriation from Germany. (Kirk Collection).

Jim's membership card for the Caterpillar Club, having had his life saved by an Irvine parachute. (Kirk Collection).

Jim beside the type of rear turret he jumped from in 1944. (Kirk Collection).

Chapter 35: Heroes

Jim had survived the war and arrived home physically unscathed, but what about the people who played important and memorable parts in his story? Heroes, all of them.

Colin Grieg returned to New Zealand on 23 September 1945 and lived in Taupiri. He never fully recovered from the effects of the atrocious conditions he confronted during his imprisonment, but nonetheless he began a new life as a builder. He remained good friends with Mac Maaker, and Mac asked him to be best man at his wedding. In 1963, Mac and his wife, June, stopped by to visit Colin and were surprised to find his little builder's truck parked up with cobwebs growing in the windows.

'We thought it a bit strange,' June said. 'Later we found out he had been ill for some time, but we didn't realize just how bad he was.'

Colin was diagnosed with leukemia and died aged 41 on 23 September 1963, something Jim was unaware of when he wrote him a letter in June 1965.

Dear Colin
This letter will come as a surprise to you (that's if it finds you)
It was not until the other week I found your old address in my wartime autograph book, and after being to an aircrew reunion for the South Island I thought it would be interesting to find out how things have been going for you since the war.

Colin, this letter is only a line to see if I can contact you and if successful, I will write you a longer one next time giving you a bit of gen about what's happened since we last met in Scotland, and maybe we could arrange to go to the New Zealand aircrew reunion in Auckland Jan 29th 1966.

I close now hoping to hear from you soon.
Your old rear gunner
Winkie

It wasn't until the following year that Jim found out about the death of his old navigator.

Inia 'Mac' Maaka went through his second period of operational training with Harry Yates, DFC and completed 30 operations with 75 Squadron. He received a commission and ended the war as a Pilot Officer. He eventually married June, the girl he had left behind when he went overseas. According to June, 'It was a few years after the war when I was walking down the street in Napier that I bumped into him. We started to chat and that was that. Bishop Bennett married us in 1947.'

Mac worked for the Maori affairs department for many years. He attended regular reunions with his crew, including a trip back to Germany. He died in 1996.

'He went out after dinner one evening to sweep up some leaves in the backyard,' recalled June. 'He was wearing his favourite straw hat which we all would rather have burned, but he loved it. He had a heart attack. I found him laying peacefully on his back with his rake still in his hand and his hat beside him. He could just as well have been asleep.'

Bill Hyde received his discharge from the Royal Air Force in 1946. Regrettably, he and Jim lived for many years without ever making contact. In the 1990s, Jim received a letter from John Thorpe in Western Australia. John, Bill's son-in-law, had spent considerable time tracking Jim down after being told stories about the crew by Bill. He recalled taking Bill to a museum in Perth where there was a Lancaster on display.

'Bill showed me the front hatch where he bailed out on the night they were shot down. I remember him telling me about his time with the maquis and always talking about his friend Winkie, with whom he shared many adventures. He knew Winkie came from New Zealand, but wasn't sure where exactly. It would have been fantastic if I could have found out and arranged for them to meet after so many years. He always had a story about the crew.'

After the war, Bill went back to the Manchester Fire Brigade and continued to care for his mother. He returned to France a couple of times to visit the people who had helped him. In later life, he moved into a retirement village where he met a woman named Annie, and at the age of sixty-eight he married for the first time.

John: 'I only wish I'd asked Bill a lot more about his wartime experiences. He showed me his gold caterpillar badge and membership card for the Caterpillar Club and his yarns always fascinated me. It's just a shame I didn't do more research much earlier.'

When Annie died, Bill's health and will to live died with her, and he passed away in 1985.

In 1993, Jim met Frank Jenkins' sister, Elva. She had a treasure trove of stories about Frank, painting him as an irascible rouge, but Jim could tell she loved him dearly. Elva stayed in touch with Jim until her death.[111]

Captain Chester Williams returned to England where he died at the comparatively young age of fifty-nine.

Daniel Dunbar and Ben Norris returned to the States after the war. Although they never saw Jim again, they did mention him as their Kiwi friend when recounting stories of their time in the maquis.

Ugo, the man Jim spoke of so highly, remains something of an enigma. After the war, a Frenchman named Andre Hugot provided the Missing Persons

---

[111] See Author's Note, Chapter 35 – Heroes.

Research Unit with a detailed account of the crash of Jim's Lancaster. In an account to the Air Ministry in 1947, No.2 M.R. & E unit reported: *Mr. Hugot is most anxious to communicate with Flt/Sgt. Kirk and it would be greatly appreciated if you were to furnish this office with this NCO's address so it may be passed on to this gentleman.*

Jean-Claude Schwartz, who lives in Corsica, knew the man Jim called Ugo as his uncle Andre Hugot. He recalled how the only person to call his father Maurice, was his uncle. Everyone else in the village addressed him as Mr. Schwartz. Unfortunately, Andre Hugot never talked about his wartime exploits, being satisfied to let such things rest in the past. He worked as a mechanic after the war and died in 1998.

Jean-Claude's father, Maurice Schwartz, the man to whom Jim owed so much, continued as mine manager at Marbache. He died in 1978. His wife, France, died at a young age in 1947. One of Jim's greatest regrets was not ever seeing these wonderful people again.

Jean Claude believed that Marie, the young women willing to accommodate Jim on his first night at Maurice's house, may have been his mother's younger cousin, but he could not glean any further information from his family.

Epilogue

Ahead of Jim lay an uncertain future. Like so many other returning servicemen it took him some time to readjust to civilian life. After his discharge he enlisted in the Southern Reserve Wing as a gunnery instructor with the rank of Warrant Officer.

He never completed his butcher's apprenticeship and over the course of the following two years he held fourteen different jobs, including working as a machinist for the Singer Sewing Company and as a tram driver in Christchurch. He didn't last long at the latter because he would let people ride for half price, or for free if they couldn't afford a ticket.

While working at the Marathon Rubber Footwear Company, a friend told him there were lineman jobs going at the P & T (Postal and Telegraph) department. It meant working outdoors, which he found more appealing than being cooped up in a hot factory, and it also provided the security of a government job. He signed up and remained there for the next 40 years.

Jim married in 1959 at the age of thirty-six, being something of a late bloomer in that regard. Children arrived at regular intervals thereafter. Vikki came first in 1961, followed thirteen months later by Zane. Leroy, christened with the name Jim had been given by the Resistance twenty years earlier, came along two years later. By the time his youngest child Deborah arrived in 1967, Jim had reached the ripe old of forty-four, twice the age of most of his friends when they died.

Jim counted himself fortunate to have survived the war when many others hadn't. He went on to live an active life, while many of his closest friends remained buried in foreign cemeteries. Only in later years did he become more reflective about his past and sought to reestablish his connection to it through membership in various associations. Perhaps the business of raising a family had left him little time to indulge in such reminisces, but in the last 20 years of his life he became a very active member of the Christchurch Returned Servicemen's Association and the Christchurch Brevet Club. He also joined the Royal Air Force Escaping Society, and the Air Gunners Association.

At the RSA and Brevet Club, Jim and his aging colleagues shared many a drink and yarn about their war years. After a few beers they would regress to younger versions of themselves, a time when they were naïve airman living in the moment. Their war stories, stretched a little over time, competed for attention, but the toasts to old friends and long-lost comrades were held in a reverence befitting those young men who had sacrificed everything in the struggle to free the world of tyranny.

Jim's story is that of an ordinary man, one of millions of stories to have risen from the ashes of a devastating war now long past but never forgotten.

Many of those who had volunteered for war service couldn't wait to get involved, afraid they would miss out on the adventure of a lifetime. The naivety of youth often led them down bleak and dangerous paths; paths to unknown fates; paths with unforeseen twists and turns; paths lit by beacons of comradeship, duty, friendship, and selfless acts of daring and fortitude. Many were never to return. For others, like Jim Kirk, whose life had once hung by a silken threat, it had not been too late to come back, even if it had been something of a late arrival.

Millery Communal cemetery, 2009. Photo: Zane Kirk

Honouring Ian Blance, Ronald Spencer, Fred Climo and Frank Jenkins. Photo: Zane Kirk

With dignitaries and the mayor of Millery, Denis Bergerot (with sash) VE Day 2009 Photo: Gerard Lebel

Gerard Lebel meets the local press on our behalf. Photo: Zane Kirk

Author's Notes

Chapter 1 – The Naivety of Youth

Situated 22 km west of Palmerston North, Ohakea was first proposed as an air base as far back as 1927, being selected as the site for a mooring mast to accommodate airships of the British Imperial Airship Service. However, when the Australian government of the day would not commit to establishing similar moorings in Australia, the idea of an airship service across both countries died.

Ohakea air base opened in 1939, the intended home of 30 Wellington bombers on order to the RNZAF. Two arched hangars, each spanning 61 metres with a height of 18 meters and costing £76,750 each, were built to accommodate the Wellingtons which never arrived. They were donated to Britain to form C Flight, which in turn became 75 (NZ) Squadron. Ohakea became New Zealand's main training base for operational conversion on fighters as well as the training of air gunners and observer/navigators for medium bombers.

Chapter 2 – The Making of an Airman

The following article from the Independent describes life for a typical recruit at an ITW:

'Training makes you one step better than the enemy,' was an axiom learned at the first lecture. There is so much study in the air force that men are relieved of most fatigues. The course is intensive. Men must keep their uniforms clean, and modern facilities including a drying room are available for personal washing. But there are no cook-house fatigues, nor are recruits expected to clean up the camp grounds - he has quite enough to do with his studies, varied by some early morning exercise and breaks between lectures. Most of the men go to bed by 9pm.

Every man has a wardrobe and sleeps on a spring mattress. He must be tidy. In the morning, the bed clothes have to be folded into a neat pile like a sandwich at the foot of the stretcher. The men come to the mess with their own cups and cutlery; they line up to be served and find the tables laid.

Diet is planned to include raw and cooked fruit and fresh vegetables such as lettuce. The men represented on the messing committee, with the camp officers, include the doctor. The dietary scale is decided periodically.

Chapter 3 – Dots and Dashes

Note 1.

Living in Christchurch throughout the 70's and 80's, the noise of RNZAF Harvards from Wigram airbase circling the city became a common anthem. At night, I loved being kept awake by their raucous night flights. While I found their nightly symphony melodiously comforting, many others did not and consequently the Royal New Zealand Air Force were obliged to cease their nocturnal activities.

Note 2.

In the 1980s, completely out of the blue, my father received a letter from Margaret O'Neil, who had tracked him down through the RSA. He visited her a couple of times in Canada, but any flames of passion that may have burned in 1943 were, forty years later, reduced to the glowing embers of friendship.

Note 3.

In 2012, I wrote a speculative letter to the Calgary Herald seeking anyone who might have known my father during the war. It was a long shot, of course, but sometimes even long shots pay dividends. A reply came from a man named Barry Marks in Calgary.

My wife first read your letter on Nov. 10, 2012 in our Calgary Herald newspaper. Intrigued by what she read about a New Zealand Air Force man who was stationed here in Calgary during the Second World War, she pointed the letter out to me. I was amazed to read about your Dad, Aubrey Kirk, who also went by the nickname of "Winkie". I was amazed because I recognized the name "Winkie" as belonging to a picture of a gentleman my Dad had put into a photo album of New Zealand and Australian Air Force personnel who were stationed at the RCAF Wireless Training School in Calgary during the War.

During the War, local people in the surrounding communities were asked to invite these men over to their homes in order to give them a sort of 'home away from home', for a visit, a meal, a picnic, a drive in the country, etc. My parents, Marjorie and Lewis Marks, were two people who had many of these men over to our home. I was born in 1939 so was very young during the War and these visits. I do not remember any of them.

In Dad's album of photos there must be 30 – 40 Air Force personnel pictures mounted. As well as individual pictures of these men there are numerous pictures of these men with me and my parents, at home for a visit, for a meal, on picnic or a drive, etc.

Of course, what caught my attention was your reference to your Dad as "Winkie". But there he is with my Dad's printing under the picture identifying him as "Winkie", the picture being taken in our living room. It looks like your Dad may also be in some other photos because there is a man in those photos that looks very much like him. Unfortunately, my Dad did not identify who was in those pictures so it is difficult to tell.

What was the RCAF Wireless Training School is now known as SAIT, the Southern Alberta Institute of Technology, which is a poly-technical degree granting institution now with a strong emphasis on all the Trades and Digital Technology professions. It is a world-renowned School, drawing students from all around the world. So, it has been a centre of world-wide training for many years!

I'm so glad we are in touch and it is such an interesting connection for me to have and to be able to give you some information about your Dad (also to honour my Mom and Dad).

Chapter 4 – Taking Up Arms

In January 1943, Arthur Harris, the C-in-C of Bomber Command, became exasperated by the incidences of venereal disease among his aircrews. He construed that capitulating to such frailties showed a premeditated attempt to escape attacking Germany. He decreed that any man who contracted VD during his tour of 30 operations would have to begin his tour over again. The order was promptly rescinded after the Air Ministry and parliament heard about it.

Chapter 5 – A Strange Sort of Marriage.

Some critics within the Air Ministry, and even within Bomber Command itself, thought air gunners were totally unnecessary. Frank Musgrove, a navigator with 149 Squadron, adamantly held the nonconformist view that gunners in their tiny Perspex fish bowls were obsolete. He argued, 'They should have been long redundant and their turrets removed, making the Lancaster more streamlined, adding 50 mph to its speed.'[112]

Fortunately for the gunners, Bomber Command's determined, single minded commander, Arthur Harris, decreed that the Lancaster's turrets were to be retained, as they encouraged a positive psychological effect on the crew. Also, the two main gunners acted as rearward lookouts for the aircraft, 'a role that could not be performed either by technology or other crew members.'

---

[112] Leo McKinstry, Lancaster, The Second World War's Greatest Bomber, pg. 158.

Chapter 6 - A Hazardous Environment.

Some years ago, I visited a military antique shop with my friend Bruce Fittock. We often frequented the shop, and Bruce had made a habit of searching through some old, scruffy shoeboxes stuffed with tarnished buttons, picking out all the brass air force buttons and giving them a shake. One day, during his routine rummage, the shop owner laughed, 'You won't get anything out of that box, mate, except grubby fingers.'

A couple of minutes later Bruce picked out an air force button and gave it a shake. His eyes lit up when he heard it give a rattle. With mild nonchalance, he asked, 'How much for the button?'

'Fifty cents,' the owner replied.

Outside the shop, Bruce grinned. 'I reckon I just found a compass button.'

His attempt at unscrewing the button met stiff resistance.

'Are you sure that's a compass?' I asked.

He rattled it again, 'Has to be.' Then he tried unscrewing it clockwise.

Bingo!

That's when we discovered that compass buttons employed a reverse thread in an effort to make them more difficult to detect. I bought the button from Bruce for $50, to match one that my father had brought home from the war. Later, I sold it to a collector for $375. Not a bad return for a set of grubby fingers.

Chapter 7 – Onto the Heavies.

1651 HCU came under the sphere of 31 Base which had been formed on 26 April 1943 with its headquarters at Stradishall. Bomber Command bases were originally identified by the name of the Base Station and its role, e.g. Mildenhall Operational Base. From September 1943 each base had a two-number identifier designated to it. The first number (e.g. '3') indicated the group to which a particular base belonged and the second number (e.g. '1') identified the function of that base within the group. '1' denoted a training base. Hence, 31 denoted the training base for 3 Group.

Stradishall, itself home to 1657 HCU, had a number of satellite stations - Chedburgh, Feltwell until 7 August 1944, Ridgewell until 1 June 1943, Waterbeach until 25 August 1943, Wratting Common from April 1943, Shepard's grove from May 1944, Birch from 31 July 1944 and Gosfield and Matching from October 1944.

Chapter 8 - Lancaster Finishing School, Feltwell.

Note 1.

I was five years old the first time I got up close to a Lancaster at the Museum of Transport and Technology (MOTAT) in Auckland. My father had taken the family there to see a Lancaster that had been gifted to the people of New Zealand by the French government in recognition of the 'goodwill, friendship and comradeship in two World Wars.'

At that age, I had no understanding of the significance of the Lancaster to my father, but as I grew older, the importance of his association with the Lancaster became more obvious and, nurtured in the shadow of his heroics, I found it easy to claim an affinity, if a somewhat fraudulent one, with this incredible aircraft.

Since that visit to MOTAT, much of which I don't remember, except being dwarfed by one of the Lancaster's gigantic black wheels, I've been up close to Lancasters in museums in Canberra, Duxford, and Calgary. My biggest thrill had been seeing the Lancaster of the Battle of Britain Memorial Flight performing a display at Biggin Hill.

Until recently, my examinations of this famous aircraft had been limited to exterior views, with an appreciation of the interior only being available through watching documentaries or having the good fortune to get close enough for a peak into the rear turret of a static example.

This changed during my second visit to MOTAT, forty-eight years after my first, when Peter Wheeler, the New Zealand Bomber Command Association Administrations Officer agreed to give me and my partner Daphne a tour of their restored Lancaster, a privilege generally reserved for veterans and their families.

We met Peter outside the Sir Keith Park Memorial hangar just before opening time. Inside, we found the Lancaster looming over us. It's often said that when an aircraft looks good, it is good. The Lancaster looks better than good. To be up close to this amazing aircraft is to be in the presence of incomparable omnipotence, supremacy and beauty. I wanted to climb aboard straight away, but Peter annoyingly delayed the privilege by starting with a tour of the Bomber Command exhibition which in itself was fascinating, but rather difficult to get enthusiastic about when you're in the shadow of a Lancaster.

We finally moved to the aircraft where Peter gave an exterior tour whilst detailing its history. Built by Austin Motors in early 1945, MOTAT's Lancaster MKVII started service life as NX685, destined for the Far East. It was one of several produced without a mid-upper turret. At the end of the war it went into storage before being sold as part of a batch of 54 Lancasters to France under the Western Union Defense Scheme. It went to the French Aeronvale, carrying out maritime duties in New Caledonia as MU13.

In 1963, the French government decided the Lancasters had reached their use-by date and decided to scrap them. Fortunately, Bob McGarry, an alert young Leading Aircraftsman, proposed to save one of the airframes. Mervyn Sterling, a MOTAT foundation member, sent an official request to the French Embassy in Wellington, and in 1964 WU13 arrived at Whenuapai to be presented to the people of New Zealand.

Sitting outside for years, exposed to the elements, with the cockpit broken and covered by a piece of old canvas, WU13 fell into disrepair and nothing happened with her until 1982 when members of the Pathfinder Association, and latterly volunteers from the NZ Bomber Command Association, started a restoration project to return NX685 to its former glory. Well over a hundred volunteers, not all ex-aircrew, gave their time and skills to restore NX685 as a Lancaster MKIII in the colours of a 75 (NZ) Squadron aircraft complete with a mid-upper turret rescued from Canada.[113]

Peter escorted us to a small set of spiral stairs leading up to the Lancaster's main entrance door. My excitement ramped up as we ducked through the door and down a step to find ourselves in a green painted fuselage tinged with an aroma of paint and oil, and much narrower than what it appeared from the outside. Helped by strategically placed electric lights we could move around freely, a far cry from a blacked-out aircraft being bumped around in the night skies.

Peter handed us each a cap that had been hanging on the flare chute. 'For when you hit your head on something,' he chuckled. 'And you will, trust me. We've had Governor Generals, Prime Ministers and other dignitaries come through here and there's been blood on more than one occasion.'

He pointed toward the open rear turret situated beyond the anti-draught doors which the rear gunner would close behind him before sliding into his cocoon. Shutting himself off from the rest of the crew, he would stay there, alone and vulnerable, until the aircraft returned to base.

The MOTAT Lancaster was fitted with a Rose turret armed with twin .50 caliber guns as opposed to the Fraser Nash turret with the four .303s my father had operated. The Rose turret, produced later in the war, had been fitted to only 180 Lancasters, MU13 being one of them.

Entering the turret took some dexterity. First, I had to climb over the tail spar. During the war, the rear gunner would use the elsan, a small toilet that looked like a rubbish bin, to step up onto the spar. To make life easier for visitors, a small platform had been installed over the elsan. Even so, it took a degree of suppleness to get into the turret.

---

[113] There was an element of opposition regarding the fitting of the mid-upper turret by a few 'no' men, but the NZ Bomber Command Association members insisted that the mid-upper gunner would not be forgotten on the memorial. The turret is the only one known to be a fully rotational in twelve museums in three continents.

'You'll have to slide feet first,' Peter said. 'Use the handle above your head to pull yourself in.'

I crawled onto the spar and spun myself around to point my feet toward the open turret. I'm sure it wasn't the nimblest entry ever made, and certainly a lot less accomplished than that of the rear gunners I'd seen in old film footage. But as Daphne rightly pointed out, they were thirty years younger than me. As if to make me feel even less adequate, Peter happily reminded me that gunners had to get in under the weight of their bulky flying gear. No wonder my father had perspired so much getting into his turret.

'Slide the doors shut behind you,' Peter said. 'You can't leave them open during an op.'

Reaching back to pull the door sliding doors shut required something of contortionist act, and I could imagine a gunner having some difficulty trying to open them in an emergency. With the doors shut, I found myself enclosed in a tiny bubble, surrounded by the mechanics of a fighting machine with nothing but the sound of my own breathing to keep me company.

Marginally roomier than the Fraser-Nash turret, the Rose turret didn't precisely represent what my father had faced, but it still gave me a great insight to what it must have been like. Facing backwards, with my feet jammed into the foot rests, I wrapped my hands around the trigger handles and manipulated the column while examining every inch of the tightly engineered turret. There was nothing surplus to requirement, except perhaps the front Perspex panel which most gunners removed to improve visibility at the expense of comfort.

I had heard stories about gunners bailing out of their turrets by throwing themselves forward where the panel had been removed. This seemed plausible if the metal arm holding the gun sight could be lifted up, but even then it would have taken a considerable effort, especially if the aircraft was going down out of control. The gravitational force would have trapped the gunner in his turret. Sitting in a stationary aircraft in the safe haven of a warm hangar was far removed from being in the frigid night skies over Germany, so I could only wonder at what my father, and men like him, had voluntarily put themselves through.

Getting out of the turret proved more difficult than getting in, a feat accomplished by twisting, sliding, and grabbing whatever I could. More than once my father told me he could never have served in a tank or a submarine during the war. 'Death traps,' he said. 'No chance of escape.' And yet he had volunteered to operate in one of the most dangerous environments imaginable. The idea of trying to escape the turret in an emergency lay beyond the bounds of my imagination.

Back in the fuselage I stood up with a few inches of headspace to spare. With little room to manoeuvre we made our way along the cramped fuselage, past the main door, a much more inviting option for bailing out, and ducked around the mid-upper turret, another formidable obstacle. By all accounts NX685 is the only example of a non-flying Lancaster with a fully rotational mid-upper turret.

For gunners, climbing into the turret required a bit of dexterity, with only a small fold-down step to give them a boost up. Once inside, they clipped a canvas sling under their backside and settled in for the duration of the flight. Hardly the most comfortable seating arrangement. As with the rear turret, it's difficult to contemplate a speedy exit in an emergency, especially with the aircraft in trouble.

Beneath the mid-upper turret, we side-stepped the circular covering for the H2S housing and made our way forward along the claustrophobic fuselage with the aid of sympathetically placed handrails, something unavailable to the young airmen flying their hazardous operations. Running along the sides of the fuselage were the ammunition ducts that transported ammunition from the magazines to the rear turret. At this stage, we were also standing on top of the Lancaster's massive 33-foot long bomb bay, the second longest of any British aircraft. The Stirling had the longest, but being divided into sections it couldn't accommodate anything bigger than a 4,000-pound bomb. The Lancaster with its uninterrupted bomb bay had the capability of carrying the heaviest bomb load of any bomber during World War Two, including the massive American B-29 Super Fortress.

Continuing forward, we passed two shelves of electronic equipment on our left before reaching a wing spar that rose to knee height. 'Ah, the dreaded main spar,' I thought as I clambered over it with contemptuous ease. Daphne followed. Having heard stories about how difficult aircrew had found the main spar, I felt some smug self-congratulations coming on. However, it didn't last long because there were in fact two spars - the small one we'd just negotiated, and then the main one. Between the two spars Peter sat down on the rest bed provided for injured crew and politely ushered us toward to main spar.

Higher and wider than the first smaller spar, the main spar was indeed a difficult looking proposition. Peter showed no interest in demonstrating how it should be done, leaving us to our own devices. 'Not at my age,' he quipped. 'There's no proper or right way. Every man for himself.'

Not until you are standing inside a Lancaster do you have any idea just how difficult it is to get over the spar. Or maybe I'm making excuses because I embarrassed myself. Conquering the height of the spar wasn't the problem, thanks to a small step placed in front of it, but contorting myself over it proved a different kettle of fish thanks to a pole in the center of the fuselage reaching from the floor to roof that left a space 28 inches wide by 28 inches high to squeeze through. Daphne opted not to try.

I avoided clobbering the arched fuselage frame a few inches above my head, but in doing so I warped myself into an awkward position that left me straddling the spar with one foot on the floor next to the wireless operator's seat and the other jammed at an awkward angle between the back of the seat and the spar. I untangled myself without damaging anything except my ego. Unbelievably, aircrew had to negotiate this challenging hurdle in full flying kit.

Next, I came to the wireless operator's compartment with its assorted pieces of radio equipment and early warning systems which, although rudimentary by modern standards, were state of the art technology in 1944. The compartment was situated just in front of the main spar on the left side of the fuselage, and as I slipped into the wireless operator's seat and scanned the array of dials, knobs and switches on the various sets, I came to the immediate conclusion that if I'd been in my father's shoes, I would have opted for life as a gunner, too. The wireless operator had a small space in which to work, with his equipment occupying most of it. His work bench had a fold-down lip about four inches wide to accommodate his Morse set. There was, however, the luxury of a small window, a padded cushion for his left arm to rest on, and the privilege of having the hot air duct next to his leg.

After the wireless operator's station, I came to the navigator's 'office' with its table and a padded bench long enough to accommodate two people - the navigator and often the bomb aimer, who might assist with the H2S. The 'office' could be curtained off from the cockpit, leaving the navigator to operate by the light of a small table lamp. Many navigators preferred to cocoon themselves in their little office and remain oblivious to the fireworks going on outside as they approached the target.

I slid passed the navigator's bench to the cockpit. Peter encouraged me to climb into the pilot's seat. I struggled to get my left foot around the control column and onto the rudder pedal. How on earth pilots were supposed to extract themselves in a hurry was beyond me. Sitting in the most important seat in the house, with the only piece of armour plating in the entire aircraft behind my head, I could sense the immense responsibility placed upon the shoulders of those young pilots who flew these aircraft into battle, and my admiration for them increased immensely.

I scanned the well laid out instrument panel. Not an inch of wasted space. Most of the instruments appeared vaguely familiar thanks to a few flying lessons I took many years ago, but it looked a lot for one man to deal with. Hence, the need for a flight engineer to help monitor things. The control column had a rugged appearance in keeping with the massive weight managed through its manipulation. Extension arms for a second control column and rudders could be fitted for training purposes, but very few operational Lancasters were equipped for two pilot operation.

To the right of the pilot's position, the flight engineer's jump seat was hinged upward and flat against the fuselage just beneath the canopy. The flight engineer's panel on the starboard side included oil and fuel gauges, fuel tank selector cocks, booster pump switches, fuel pressure gauges, and emergency air control and oil dilution buttons. It's easy to appreciate why flight engineers were kept constantly busy during a flight.

I extracted myself from the pilot's seat without mishap and moved down into the bomb aimer's office in the nose of the aircraft. As a rule, Bomb aimers weren't supposed to be in the nose during take-off, but many flouted the regulation as they found it difficult to squeeze under the flight engineer's seat to return to the front compartment. While the outlook must have been marvellous (apparently, the Lancaster gave the bomb aimer the best view of any bomber) bomb aimers themselves must have felt rather vulnerable, and I wondered how many feared that the forward escape hatch cover, on top of which they lay prone, might drop out at any moment. A thought as irrational as Frank's fear of his mid-upper turret unscrewing itself, but a remote possibility all the same.

Scrutinizing the bomb aimer's panel made me aware that dropping bombs wasn't as simple as just pushing a button and shouting, 'Bombs gone!' On the top left of the panel were sixteen selector switches and below them a timing-device for stick-bombing. Another dial was used for selecting the timing interval between bombs. In the center of the panel the selector box controlled the order in which bombs departed the bomb bay. It was essential to keep the aircraft balanced during release.

A Master switch, camera controls and photo flare release were situated on a separate, smaller panel below the main panel. On the top right-hand side of the main panel was the 4,000lb bomb slip heater which prevented bomb hang-ups due to freezing. No crew wanted to carry a 4,000lb bomb home and have to land with it. The bomb release switch had a cover guard to prevent accidental depressions.

Above the bomb aimer's compartment, the front turret was equipped with two .303 Browning machine guns, which were rarely used in combat. I didn't try standing in the turret because it looked a tight fit, and I'd already proved I wasn't as agile as I had been twenty years ago. I went back to the cockpit where Daphne, who had braved the main spar against her better judgement, waited for me. She had no ambition to get down into the bomb aimer's blister. We tackled the main spar again without mishap and rejoined Peter who said, 'I'll switch off the lighting to give you a better idea of what it was like for the crews flying at night.'

He headed to the main door and a moment later we were plunged into an isolating darkness. While providing only a sliver of the hazardous ambience the crews faced on a night raid, we certainly got a sound appreciation of what they had endured, especially the gunners who were detached from the rest of the crew.

On exiting the Lancaster, we left behind a paradox; an aircraft flaunting grace and elegance, yet oozing intimidation and supremacy; an aircraft designed for only one purpose - to drop bombs - at which it proved omnipotent.

It represented a world of seventy years ago, a world of fear, anxiety and peril. A world of heroes.

Self-imposed modesty prevents the men who operated these aircraft from considering themselves heroes. They were young, often naive, caught up in a wild adventure. Like my father, most wouldn't claim to be fighting for king and country, but rather for each other. For them it meant not letting their mates down, and in pursuit of that intent they had an aircraft that seldom let them down.

Note 2.

I drove into Feltwell on a January morning in 2018 en route from Leicester to London. You'll see from a map that en route actually meant going somewhat out of my way, but I didn't know when I'd get a chance to get there again, so I didn't mind.

A blue sky and robust sun belied a frigid air as I slowed down to pass RAF Feltwell. What had once been home to 75 Squadron and 3 LFS, RAF Feltwell is now disposed to housing United States Air Force personnel stationed at the 100th Air Refueling Wing at nearby RAF Mildenhall and the 48th Fighter Wing at RAF Larkenheath. Armed guards and razor wire fences suggested no possibility of a closer inspection.

There wasn't much happening when I parked outside *The Wellington* pub whose sign pictured a Wellington bomber. I was curious to learn the story behind the pub sign. Hopefully there would be some wartime memorabilia inside. With 15 minutes to wait until opening time at noon, I went for a leisurely mooch around the village, visualizing young men ambling about in air force clobber proudly displaying brevets on their chests and sharing their far-flung origins - Australia, New Zealand, Canada, Rhodesia - by way of their shoulder flashes. I felt privileged to walk in their footsteps as I trod the pavements of an ancient village that wore its past like a treasured mantle.

Back at *The Wellington* a few locals had drifted in. Some were leaning on the bar beneath the ancient exposed beams that had been there since 1730, while others were settled in a snug beside an old Inglenook fireplace resplendent with a modern stove.

It didn't take long to figure out that the pub had been named after the twin engine bomber of the same name. Kitset models and paintings of the famous Vickers Wellington were placed devotedly about the pub. It looked like a school boy's obsession run amuck. I loved it.

I bought a beer and met the owner, Stuart Samuels, who found it amusing when I told him I had come to Feltwell on holiday.

'My father was here in 1944,' I explained. 'With the Lancaster Finishing School.'

'That makes sense,' he said. 'Nobody comes to Feltwell just for a holiday.' He took pause then asked, 'Do you have any ID on you? Passport?'

221

'Only my driver's licence,' I replied. 'Why?'

'I thought I might be able to get you onto the base. Give you a look around. The parade ground and some of the buildings would have been familiar to your father. How long are you here?'

'Not long,' I said. 'Just stopped in on my way to London.'

'Too bad. If you were staying a couple of days, I could have arranged a visit.'

'I'd love to,' I said, 'but I have to get back to London. I'm leaving the country in a couple of days.'

He handed me his business card. 'If you're coming back give me a ring. With a few days' notice I'll be able to arrange a visit to the base for you. In the meantime, grab your beer and come with me.'

With a frosty Fosters in hand, I followed him through a narrow door and up a claustrophobic wooden staircase. The walls were embellished with paintings and photographs of Wellington Bombers, famous RAF pilots, including 75 Squadron's only VC winner, James Allen Ward, and scenes of Feltwell.

'Quite a collection,' I marveled. 'Who gets to see these?'

'Only the people I invite.' he replied. 'I have plenty more still in storage, which will come out eventually.'

Stuart gave me a brief history of RAF Feltwell, enlightening me to the fact that between 1958-1963 it had been a base for Thor missiles, and between 1989 – 2003 it had been home to the US Air Force's 5th Space Surveillance Squadron.

We came downstairs to the pub. 'Of course, Feltwell itself has stayed pretty much the same,' he said. 'This however,' he added, sweeping his hand around the pub that had by now enticed a few more patrons through the doors with its quaint warmth and unaffected friendliness, 'is not something your father would have known as a pub. Back then it was the village store.'

He led me out to the beer garden to show me a recent addition - a mural wall showcasing 75 Squadron and in particular, Jimmy Ward, V.C. I cursed that my camera battery had died and I couldn't get a photograph, because I thought the whole thing quite splendid.

'I'll send you a picture,' Stuart said.

'And I'll see if I have anything that might befit the pub and send it to you,' I said.

'Anything would be welcome if it helps tell the story of Feltwell, and especially 75 Squadron or the Wellington.'

I let Stuart go to attend to some lunch guests who were patiently waiting for him next to the fire place, and I finished my beer in a leisurely fashion as I inspected the souvenirs and wartime artifacts tucked in the crooks and crannies around the ancient pub. Somewhat reluctantly, I bid Stuart and the boys behind the bar farewell and went back to my car. As I drove slowly out of the village, I reflected that 73 years earlier, on 28 June 1944, my father and his crew had arrived in this unassuming Norfolk village, designated crew 12 on course 39, to be introduced to arguably the greatest heavy bomber of the Second World War.

Chapter 9 - Mepal 2009

I visited Mepal on a balmy Saturday morning in July 2009. Although the village itself had probably not changed much since 1944, there was little evidence to suggest that one of Bomber Command's most famous squadrons and once been stationed there.

I found an ugly industrial estate blotting the landscape, and the A42 cutting a swath right through the middle of where the airfield had once been. The only indication that men had once flown from there toward the dark heart of Nazi Germany, and possible oblivion, was a monument at the entrance to the estate dedicated to their memory.

The old control tower would have been a more fitting memorial, but in 1988, in the face of a huge public outcry, the farmer who owned the land threw a chain around the tower's decaying façade and pulled it down with his tractor - or so the story went. The surrounding buildings, like the machine shop and the Nissan huts where the crews had once slept and attended briefings, were nefariously bulldozed in the middle of the night and left stacked like corrugated flat-pack furniture.

My father had been visiting friends in Cambridgeshire at the time of the demolition and had had the foresight to get what may well be the last pictures taken of the tower the day before it was destroyed. He also cut off a pair of Bakelite door knobs from the control tower door and took a piece of slate from the roof, cherished morsels of history now sitting in my cabinet at home.

In a nearby paddock, I found part of the old perimeter track, cracked and weed-infested but still capable of conjuring up images of a line of Lancasters snaking their way toward their take off point with the thunderous roar of their Rolls Royce Merlin engines reverberating across the countryside and nearby villages.

I walked for a while, letting my mind wander into an ethereal world of Lancasters parked at their dispersals as the ground crews, the unsung heroes of the RAF, worked on their charges, maintaining engines, cleaning canopies, arming the gun turrets, and bombing up. I could almost hear the crackle of the tannoy calling the crews to briefing. It had once been a place of real people and vanquished lives. However, no matter how intricate or vivid my imagination was, it didn't hold a candle to the veracity of the real thing.

The scene as 25 Lancasters crawled nose to tail around the perimeter track amid a hurricane of prop wash was something I could only experience through old film footage, but Bernard Leighton, who I met in 2009, and whose father had been the flight engineer on Keith Whitehouse's crew, got to witness the scene first-hand.

'It was a fantastic,' he said. 'I stood at the perimeter fence watching the Lancasters thunder down the runway and climb into the night at 30 - 60 second intervals. 'I was only a lad, but that was something I'll never forget.'

His mother had taken him to Mepal to see his father. With no accommodation available in the village they slept in a cell at the police station. Bernard remembered the camaraderie of his father's crew and what a tight-knit bunch they were.

'You could see they were great mates and they were all so friendly to me, a little sprog in shorts, letting me climb inside their aircraft and hang around.'

The pace of life in Mepal had shrivelled since 1944. After driving twice around the village and seeing nothing more exciting than a man painting his fence, and a couple working in their garden, I decided to hunt out the pubs where the crews had spent many boisterous evenings.

The Three Pickerels, situated down by the river, didn't open until 11 o'clock. With time to kill, I followed a gravel path toward a little stone church surrounded by long grass and crooked headstones, browsing for any connection to 75 Squadron, but I found nothing. I wandered back to the pub but it was still closed, so I got in the car and drove off in search of *The Chequers, The White Horse* and *The Ship,* where according to Ron Mayhill in his book, *Bombs on Target,* the crews had sung themselves hoarse.[114]

I didn't find *The White Horse* or *The Ship* but I came across *The Chequers* in neighbouring Sutton, a small village situated a couple of miles away on what would have been the eastern boundary of the airfield.

Things hadn't changed much since my father and his crew had first walked through the door of *The Chequers* 65 years earlier. The exterior had been painted and there were neat, colourful gardens in full bloom out the front, but things would have been comfortably familiar for any old aircrew returning to the place after so many years.

Inside, there were plenty of old 75 Squadron photographs on the walls but neither my father nor any of his crew featured among them. The only people in the pub were two workmen on their lunch break and a woman serving behind the bar. Unfortunately, the workmen propping up the bar did not provide the same animated atmosphere as a roomful of exuberant young airmen with a life expectancy measured in days rather than years. When I returned to *The Three Pickerels,* I found it still closed so I left.

In 2014, I revisited Mepal with Daphne. We walked into to *The Three Pickerels* only to be let down with the almost non-existent salute to the young men who had frequented the pub during the war. It smacked a bit of irreverence, but that's only because I knew what a big part the establishment

---

[114]   Ron Mayhill, Bombs on Target, Pg. 71.

had played in the lives of so many young men during the war. They would have saluted lost comrades over a beer, and many would have had their last drink there. We stayed the night in very comfortable accommodation above the pub. Through the old floorboards, we listened to a raucous rugby team drinking well into the night. Laying in the dark, listening to the hum of chatter, punctuated by regular explosions of laughter, my imagination transported me back to the heady days of 1944, and I fancied my father and his mates living it up down in the bar, making the most of every precious moment available to them.

Chapter 10 – Ake Ake Kia Kaha.

My visit to the MOTAT Lancaster had emphasized my father's reservations about the mid-upper turret. It certainly offered a great 360-degree panorama and was the best position to appreciate the size and majestic proportions of the aircraft, but it also felt like a very exposed position. An apron of armour gave the gunner some protection from the waist down, but it didn't dissuade from the disconcerting feeling of having one's head poking above the parapet.

Chapter 11 – Prepped for Flight.

My father told me the story of the blanket in the parachute pack a few times over the years, and it always struck me as a little far-fetched. It wasn't until reading Ron Mayhill's *Bombs on Target,* that I discovered the incident had really happened. Apparently an Irk, disgruntled at being transferred off the base for some misdemeanour or other, decided to get his own back in the cruellest way possible. It made me wonder if there had been other misguided acts of revenge that had never been discovered.

Chapter 12 – Night Flight.

A 1941 report conducted by David Bensusan-Butt, a civil servant in the War Cabinet Secretariat, highlighted a contradiction in Bomber Command's claims that with 4,000 bombers it could destroy forty-three German towns with populations over 100,000 and finish the war in six months. The Butt report, as it became known, showed what many within Bomber Command already knew, that crews were failing to navigate to, identify, and put bombs on the target, with only one in three aircraft getting within 5 miles of its objective. Accuracy improved over the French ports where two of three reached the target, but over

Germany itself only a quarter of an attacking force managed to reach the target. Over the heavily defended Ruhr only one in ten found the target.

On moonlit nights, the lack of accuracy proved even more disturbing. With a full moon, only two in five bombers reached the target and during a new moon it plummeted to a paltry one in every fifteen. With an absence of haze over the target, half of the attacking force could expect to hit it. With haze, it dropped to one in fifteen. Intense anti-aircraft fire also reduced the number of aircraft reaching the target.

During a one-year period between May 1940 and May 1941 more than half of Bomber Command's bombs were falling in open country. Accuracy improved with the introduction of bombing aids such as H2S and the creation of pathfinder squadrons, but precise bombing remained a difficult proposition in the face of night fighters, searchlights and radar predicted flak.

Chapter 14 - The Fires of Hell

My father often remarked how he would like to have met the pilot who'd shot him down. But finding out who that was proved rather difficult, and not something that would be achieved in his lifetime.

Researching the Luftwaffe's World War Two activities is notoriously difficult because only about 10% of their records survived the war. A large portion were either destroyed by the Allied bombings or put to the torch by Luftwaffe units before their airfields were overrun in the closing months of the war.

Despite these difficulties, I thought I had learnt the identity of the German pilot responsible for the demise of my father's Lancaster when I discovered that the only JU88 reportedly shot down over France on the night of 28/29 July 1944 had been 4R+KT piloted by Hptm. August Speckmann who had been operating with 9/NJG2 and had crashed 20 km south-west of Toul, not far from where my father's aircraft came down. Three of the night fighter's four-man crew, including Speckmann, were killed. Only the radio operator, Arthur Boos, survived[115]

1,523 aerial victories were claimed by NJG2 during the war, including 23 on the night of 28/29 July 1944, but Hpmt. Speckmann does not appear among the list of claimants. This isn't surprising considering Speckmann had been killed on the night in question. With nothing to refute the circumstantial evidence I'd unearthed, I felt confident I had found out who had shot down my father's Lancaster.

I didn't give the matter anymore thought until 2009. I lived in England at the time, not far from Tunbridge Wells. One day I stopped at the Aviation

---

[115] Killed were Hptm. August Speckmann, Ofw. Wilhelm Berg & Uffz Otto Bruggenkamp.

Bookshop, a place I'd been meaning to visit for a while, but had always put off. Prominently displayed just inside the door was a newly published book by Theo Boiten and Roderick J. MacKenzie called 'Nachtjagd War Diaries, An Operational History of The German Night Fighter Force in The West, Volume Two April 1944 - May 1945'.

The staggering amount of information in the book included entries for German night fighter claims for almost every night between April 1944 and May 1945. Taken from surviving Luftwaffe records, the details of each claim included the name of the German pilot, his unit, the type of bomber he had claimed, plus the location and time the bomber had been shot down. Occasionally the serial number of the downed British bomber and the squadron to which it belonged, augmented an entry

The night of 28/29 July listed 84 night fighter claims, many of them accounting for British bombers lost on the Stuttgart raid. One entry leapt off the page at me:

Oblt. Martin Becker: 34, 2/NJG6, Lancaster, N. Luneville 4,500m, 01.25. 75 Sqn Lancaster ND756.

I experienced a strange mixture of triumph and frustration. With little other evidence, I had assumed August Speckmann had shot my father down, but now I held contrary evidence in my hands. I purchased the book and raced home to see what I could find out about Martin Becker.

Becker was born in 1916 at Weisbaden in Hesse, and started his Luftwaffe career in 1940, flying 27 missions with an unknown Reconnaissance unit before transferring to the Nachtjagd in early 1943, about the same time my father was beginning his training in Canada. Becker went to 11/NJG 4, which was re-designated 2/NJG6 on 4 August 1943. He scored his first night victory on September 22/23 1943. Promotion to Staffelkapitian of that unit soon followed.

Known as Tino, Becker became a proficient night fighter pilot. On the night of 30/31 March 1944, he and his crew shot down three Lancasters and four Halifax bombers. He received the Ritterkreuz (Knight's Cross) on April 20 1944 after achieving 26 victories. He continued his habit of multiple victories by shooting down three four engine bombers on 26/27 April and another three on the night of 27/28 April.

The award of the Oak Leaves to the Knights Cross came on 20 March the following year, and he also received the German Cross in Gold, or the fried egg as Luftwaffe crews drolly dubbed it. Becker flew 83 night fighting missions, mainly operating an Me110, and shot down 58 enemy aircraft, the majority being four engine bombers. He ranked eleventh on the list of most success German night fighter aces and held the record of shooting down the greatest number (9) in a single night. If you were going to go for a Burton it

227

might have been some small consolation that it came at the hands of a Nachtjagd expert.

It's one of my great regrets that I only found out about Martin Becker after my father's death. Becker himself died in 2006 at the age of 92, and in 2009 his radio operator Karl-Ludwig Johanssen also passed away. Johanssen received the Knight's Cross for shooting down 3 four engine bombers in a single night using his rearward firing machine gun. I will always wonder what might have been had I managed to track down either man before my father died. It is unlikely any of them would have travelled halfway around the world for a meeting, but I know my father would have been delighted to have corresponded with them in some way.

The information in Boiten and MacKenzie's book, and further research, revealed that Becker operated an Me110, which reconciles with my father's suspicion that the aircraft he shot down had not been the one that had attacked his Lancaster. To confirm that suspicion, I contacted Rod MacKenzie who explained that following an accurate line of investigation so long after the event can be difficult at the best of times, and anything to do with the Luftwaffe is often near impossible. Rod said:

'The official records that survived often provide no circumstances of loss. It is important to understand that an estimated 90% of Luftwaffe operational records were successfully put to the torch in the closing weeks of the war. This means that any detailed account or reconstruction of any night's battles must be constituted from a range of fragmentary documentary sources.

'With regard to the specific combat that your father was involved in, it may remain a mystery. From my research, I've found that events at night could be perceived inaccurately by the various witnesses - this is especially true of aircraft seen going down. Without knowing ALL of the Luftwaffe loss data for this night, no conclusion can be reached - there are simply too many variables and possibilities. Night fighters did not intentionally operate in pairs - that would simply be too dangerous and difficult. It was, however, possible for two independent night fighters to attack the same aircraft at around the same time purely by chance.

'Anyway, I hope this provides some sort of satisfactory answer. Sadly, in this game, x rarely marks the spot because of lack of solid and complete documentary evidence.'

Rod went on to explain that the two principle surviving sources on German losses were Personnel loss returns and Material (i.e. aircraft) loss returns. The Personnel loss returns only applied to air crew killed, missing or wounded and not to losses where crews were unharmed. The Luftwaffe General Quartermaster's Material Loss returns only applied to aircraft attrition and practically all of the returns for the whole of 1944 are still missing, or did not survive the war.

The Official History of New Zealanders with the Royal Air Force states that 'bomber and fighter eventually crashed within half a mile of each other'.[116] However, this is uncorroborated, and in the light of the preceding evidence it would appear to be wrong. An unsubstantiated report of a JU88 crashing between Leminol and Chermoit some distance to the north of Toul also surfaced, but I had learnt to grow sceptical of unsubstantiated reports.

So, while it appears Martin Becker had shot down my father's Lancaster, I remain certain it was August Speckmann whom my father shot down in those last desperate minutes before he escaped his blazing Lancaster.

Chapter 15 – Into the Silk.

I once naively asked my father if he had found parachuting into the night exciting. 'I wouldn't say that,' he reflected. 'Not when you're watching your aircraft going down in flames.

Chapter 16 – Evasion.

Note 1.
Except for my father's name and his aircrew trade, the letter from Wing Commander Lesley is, word for word, the same as those received by the next of kin of all his crewmates. While this seems lazy and insincere on Leslie's part, it is understandable as he could not possibly have known every man under his command on a personal level.

Dear Mrs Carey
I deeply regret the necessity for a letter of this sad description. During the time your son was with us, he had proven himself to be a skillful Air Gunner, carrying out his duties with keenness and determination. He had made many friends, too, on account of his cheerful and willing disposition. His loss, a temporary one I pray, is a grievous blow to yourself and he will be sadly missed by us all.
On this particular night, your son and his fellow crew members of that fine team, had been detailed to attack a heavily defended target in Germany. As to the cause of their failure to return, I regret I hold no clue, for after leaving Base no further signal was received from their aircraft. There is, of course, the

---

[116] Thompson, Official History of New Zealanders In the Second World War, New Zealanders With the Royal Air Force, pg 410.

possibility that they were forced down and may be in enemy hands. Any news forthcoming will be forwarded to you without delay.

Meanwhile, all your son's personal effects have been gathered together for dispatch to the R.A.F Central Depository for safe custody, pending completion of all necessary formalities. If you wish to obtain any information regarding your son's affairs generally, I suggest that you write direct to the Air Department in Wellington, where I am sure, you will be given every assistance.

It is desired to explain that the request in the telegram notifying you of the casualty to your son was included with the object of avoiding his chance of escape being prejudiced by undue publicity in case he was still at large. This is not to say that any information about him is available, but is a precaution adopted in case of all personnel reported missing.

Please accept the deepest sympathy of all ranks of my squadron and of myself during this time of sorrow and anxious waiting. We pray with you for his safety and well-being.

Yours sincerely
(signed Wing Commander Leslie)[117]

Note 2.

In an official report made to MI9 after his return to the UK, my father stated that he weighed down his parachute harness and Mae West life jacket with iron and threw them in a river. It's hard to argue with a report filed a matter of months after the event rather than when jotting down his memoirs more than 60 years later. It would not be the last time his recollections differed from the official reports.

Note 3.

I used to own a pair of 1941 pattern fleece lined flying boots. Having listened to my father's story, it seemed sensible to take a walk in my boots to get a small idea of what he had experienced. Burwood Plantation, a sprawling forest on the edge of Christchurch, provided a reasonable substitute for the type of terrain and conditions he would have faced.

I had chosen a warm day and it didn't take long before the fleece lined boots were causing me some prickly discomfort. It felt like I had warming pads strapped to my legs. To add some authenticity to my experiment, I had taken my father's knife, the one he had actually had with him. Jammed in my boot, it rubbed aggravatingly against my leg the entire time. The boot's crepe, gummy soles made for reasonably good protection from anything underfoot but they weren't designed for a long walk. Thank goodness I had had the forethought to take my Nike running shoes with me, because I don't believe I

---

[117]Letter from Wing Commander Leslie to my grandmother, dated 29/07/1944.

even managed two kilometres before my feet were barking for a rest. I don't know how my father had managed for three days.

Chapter 17 - Roll of the Dice

Note 1.

I had difficulty establishing with any certainty in which cemetery my father had been when he found help. Not that it really mattered, except I wanted to be as accurate as possible in retracing his steps. He never said which cemetery it had been because either he had not known, or his memory had deserted him.

Leroy, Deborah and myself did find a cemetery that overlooked Pompey. An orchard bordered it on one side, just as our father had described, so we were confident we'd found the right one, especially as our father had said he'd been taken to Pompey. Gerard Lebel, however, believed the cemetery in question would more likely be the one at Marbache further to the north. We never went to Marbache three kilometres north west of Custines, but looking at it on Google maps, I had to concede that Gerard might have been right. And Marbache isn't far from Saizerais where Maurice managed the iron works.

Note 2.

After the war, a report from No.1 Missing Research and Enquiry Unit, Royal Air force, British Forces in France, dated 9 January 1947, reported: *At 0.1.30 hrs. on the 29.7.44, a Lancaster aircraft crashed at a spot known locally as "Au Dessous de la Falaise". Four members of the crew were killed and later buried in the Communal Cemetery of Millery. One of the members of the crew was made a prisoner by the Germans and the other two were aided by the Resistance Movement in their evasion.*

The four killed were: - 421469 P/O Blance
1575186 F/Sgt. Spencer
4310148 F/Sgt. Climo
423845 F/Sgt. Jenkins
They were all identified by their identity discs, bar F/Sgt. Jenkins who is buried as Unknown. In his pocket, however, was found a small envelope bearing some photographs of the "Escape Type". The envelope bears the inscription "F/S Jenkins. B Flight." Inside the envelope was a negative bearing the inscription "F/S Jenkins" and the date 17.7.44.

The Initial report that Frank Jenkins was buried as an unknown, because his body was too badly burnt to identify, was amended by a secondary report by No.2 Missing Research & Enquiries Unit, RAF. 'F/Sgt. Jenkins was not buried as "Unknown" because although his body was badly calcinated, he was identified by an envelope which was found in his pocket, and also two small photographs.'

The graves do not bear a G.R.U (Graves Registration Unit) marking, and so it is presumed that they have not yet been registered.

As there seems to be no doubt that these graves are indeed those of the four missing airmen, it is requested that permission may be granted to consider this case closed.

Note 3.

I visited Millery for the first time in 2008. Nestled on the east bank of the Moselle River amid verdant countryside, the village is consecrated by an air of serene ambience that pervades its narrow streets and swathes it in a wraithlike stillness and shabby charm that's difficult to ignore.

On the outskirts of Millery, on the road to Nomeny, I found the small communal cemetery hidden behind high walls. I recognised it from an old wartime photo my father had been given, and also from some photos he taken during a trip there in 1984.

An old wrought iron gate gave a protesting squeal as it opened to let me in, and then closed again behind me with a metallic click. The cemetery was deserted. Rendering had fallen from parts of the walls to expose yellow brickwork to the elements, but the graves of my father's crew were in excellent condition. The Commonwealth War Graves Commission does a remarkable job maintaining the cemeteries and individual graves of fallen Commonwealth servicemen across Europe. Almost all of them are upheld to a standard befitting the sacrifice made by those who lay beneath the ground.

I took plenty of photos in case I never returned, then left a note for my sister Deborah, who I knew would be visiting Millery later in the year. I stole a piece of stone from the cemetery wall before I left.

When Deborah visited the cemetery later in the year, a lady approached her wanting to know why she had an interest in the graves of the four airmen. Deborah spoke no French, but tried her best to explain that her father had jumped from the stricken aircraft before it had crashed. With plenty of hand gestures and a few words of English, the woman explained that she had been a little girl at the time of the crash. She had heard the plane coming in low and indicated to a spot on the hill just beyond the cemetery where it had crashed. She then called over a man who had been tidying a nearby grave. He introduced himself as Gerard Lebel, and showed a great deal of interest in what Deborah had told the lady. He said his mother, who still lived in the village, had photographs of the funeral held for the four airmen. At the end of their conversation, he promised Deborah he would send her copies of the photos. She learnt some months later that the woman she had met in the cemetery had been Gerard's cousin Michelle.

Gerard's mother had been a teenager at the time of the crash, and she had gone around the village with her cousin collecting donations for flowers to put on the graves of the dead airmen. They raised so much money that two rooms in the village hall overflowed with wreaths and flowers.

Despite the Germans forbidding the local population from attending the funeral, 1500 people from Millery and the surrounding villages turned up. The most conspicuous absence turned out to be that of the local priest. Fearful of what the German response to this outpouring of respect and solidarity might produce, he refused to officiate, and a priest from nearby Custines had to be called. Despite the huge attendance, there were no reprisals by the Germans, and there was actually a suggestion they had filmed the funeral, but there was no way of substantiating that.

One Air Ministry intelligence document claimed my father had attended the funeral, but he had still been on the run at the time and it wasn't until he met Maurice Schwartz three days later that he learnt the fate of his crew.

Not long after their initial meeting, Maurice gave Jim a photograph of the crew's graves, the only photograph my father had ever seen of the graves prior to his visit to Millery in 1984. The prospect of showing him the photographs which Gerard had promised to send, made Deborah very excited, but sadly our father passed away a matter of days before she arrived home with her wonderful news.

Gerard remained true to his word, and the photographs he sent a few weeks later depicted the respect and gratitude the people of Millery had shown for their fallen allies. They show the graves swamped in flowers and wreaths, with ornate wooden crosses erected in front of each one. A propeller from the crashed Lancaster was inscribed with the men's names and positioned over the graves.

During their initial conversation, and in a subsequent e-mail, Gerard told Deborah that the residents of Millery held a commemoration ceremony for the crew every 8 May in conjunction with their VE Day celebrations. Deborah, myself, and our brother Leroy (our sister Vikki couldn't make it) decided to attend the 2009 commemoration.

A year later, we found ourselves at a roadside caravan outside Verdun eating burgers and fries when Gerard Lebel rang. With his marginal English and our almost non-existent French, we cobbled together enough of an understanding to agree on a rendezvous at the Millery communal cemetery.

We arrived at the cemetery moments after Gerard. He possessed a thoughtful, erudite demeanour and a broad smile. After exchanging pleasantries as best we could, he explained that Millery's mayor, Denis Bergerot, would be joining us.

We waited in the warm May sun for what we supposed would be some grizzled old geezer swamped in black cloaks and weighed down by a gold or silver mayoral chain, but instead it was a middle-aged wearing a casual V-necked sweater, jeans and black cashmere coat who came through the old wrought iron gates. With his handsome olive skin face and swept back greying hair, he looked more like someone who'd lost his way to a movie set than a mayor.

He welcomed us enthusiastically in excellent English then fell into fervent conversation with Gerard. Every now and then he let us in on their conversation, telling us that he had finalised arrangements for the next day's commemoration ceremony which would start at 10 a.m. He invited us to be at the mayor's office at 9.30 a.m. From there we would join Millery's residents at the local war memorial.

About this time Gerard handed us a newspaper clipping. The headline read: *Le crash du Lancaster,* and the sub-heading read: *Le 29 juillet 1944 un avion de la Royal Air Force etait abattu dans la vallee de la Moselle. Le 8 Mai, Millery rendra homage aux soldats disparus, en presence d'une des familles.*

As best that I could make out, it translated as: The crash of the Lancaster. On 29 July 1944, an aircraft of the Royal Air Force was shot down in the Moselle Valley. On 8 May, Millery will make homage to the fallen, in the presence of one of the families.

We were punctual for our meeting at the Mayor's office the next morning. Denis Bergerot arrived accompanied by two petite young ladies, Mallaury and Camille Dechaseaux, no older than 14 or 15. Mallaury wore a red, white and blue sash which denoted her position as Young Person's mayor.

We were wondering why we had been invited to the office when a young woman carrying a note pad, a tape recorder, and a rather intimidating looking microphone turned up accompanied by a photographer. Denis Bergerot had thought it a great idea to waylay us with radio and newspaper interviews. It was an ambush worthy of the Maquis. When he asked which of us would like to be interviewed, you would have thought he had asked for volunteers to embark on a suicide mission. Leroy and Deborah beat a hasty retreat, leaving me with the young woman reporter. Fortunately, after giving her a brief explanation as to why we were there, I managed to direct her to Gerard, whose contribution to her story would have been far more valuable than my miserable effort.

Soon after, we all headed across the road to the war memorial where a sizable crowd had already gathered. We would have been quite happy to loiter in the background, but Denis Bergerot had other ideas and presented us front and centre. Local school children sang La Marseilles and Mallaury read, in English, the story of our father's last flight, with Denis Bergerot translating it into French. She spoke very well and could in no way be blamed for a number of inaccuracies in the story.

There had been the belief that our father's crew had been flying a B-17 Flying Fortress, that the pilot had been a Canadian, and that there had ten crew members instead of seven. The mistakes were easier to understand when we were made aware that at least one B-17 crew had also been shot down in the area. A post-war report from the Missing Enquiries Unit suggested some of its crew were buried in the same Communal cemetery as our father's crew, which could have contributed to the confusion, but after a thorough search of the cemetery we found the report to be inaccurate.

After the ceremony at the War Memorial, we made our way to the communal cemetery, where an intimate and moving commemoration for our father's crew took place within sight of where their Lancaster had crashed over 60 years earlier. In a surreal moment, as we stood at the graves of these men of whom our father had always spoken of so highly, a lone trumpeter played the Last Post a few hundred metres from a small clump of trees on an overlooking hillside where our father's friends had died.[118]

At the conclusion of the ceremony everyone went for wine and food and celebration at the village hall. We felt sure they had put it on for our benefit. Yet another humbling reminder of the gratitude they harboured for those who had fought for their liberation.

We were introduced to Marie-Therese Vuillemin, an elderly lady with silver hair, and a countenance creased by 84 years of living. A triple string of pearls adorned her neck, but the real pearls were her memories of the night my father's Lancaster had crashed.

Twenty-one years old at the time, she had heard the crash and hurried to the site of the disaster. She later regretted her curiosity and lamented her impetuosity. 'The silliest thing I've ever done,' she reflected through an interpreter. 'But I knew no better. The pilot was still sitting in his seat at the controls and there were bits of other men laying around. They looked like burnt chickens. It still haunts my memory.'

Gerard showed her one of the 1944 cortege photos and she pointed herself out as an attractive young woman cradling a bouquet of flowers at the front of the cortege. With a mixture of pride and sadness she said, 'That is me. I was much younger then.' She remembered the funeral with all the clarity of something that had happened only last week. 'Many people came,' she explained. 'The village hall was filled with flowers. We were grateful to the British for what they were doing. We wanted to honour those young men who had died. They will be here with us forever.'

Chapter 19 - The House of Maurice

Hearing the story about Maurice and France trying to wake my father always made me laugh. I knew from personal experience what an unenviable task it could be. As children, we certainly preferred to be well out of earshot when our mother called for someone to wake him for his night job.

---

[118] The belief that one of the crew had been Canadian encouraged the locals to mount a Canadian flag over the grave alongside the New Zealand and British flags.

Whoever drew the short straw would have to creep into our parents darkened bedroom to the sound of our father's thunderous snoring. You would start by giving him a tentative prod at arm's length. Of course, this never worked, and you would have to get closer and give him a firm shake on the arm or shoulder. If you were brave enough you would stand your ground, but none of us were, and the general rule was to leap six feet backwards as soon as you'd shaken him, because he'd invariably wake up in something akin to a blind panic, ready to karate chop anything within reach. At the time I found it terrifying, and in later years rather hilarious, but now when I think back on it, I wonder what sort of dreams might have tortured him in his sleep? If he had nightmares, or ever relived horrific moments from the war, of which I'm sure there were plenty, he never mentioned it.

Chapter 20 - Burying the Old Life

Note 1.

I was always confident that the shop where my father's possessions were buried would still be there, because when my father visited Pompey in the 1980's, he'd taken photos and remarked how little the shop had changed. I'd scrutinized his photographs to the point the shop was etched indelibly in my mind. But when I visited Pompey for the first time in the Spring of 2008, I found no sign of it. I drove all around the little town, but on every street, I met frustration and disappointment. Later that year, my sister Deborah met with similar dismay.

Early in 2009 we asked Gerard Lebel for help. He came to the rescue for what would not be the last time, and after some brief inquiries he wrote to say he'd found the shop across the river from Pompey in the neighbouring town of Frouard.

Believing the shop had been in Pompey would have been an easy error for my father to make. Separated by the Moselle, the two small towns of Pompey and Frouard could easily be mistaken for a large town with a river coursing through the middle. Only a small sign on the main bridge indicated that we were leaving Pompey on the north bank and entering Frouard on the south.

Gerard spoke with the owners of the boot shop on our behalf, but with frank disappointment they told him they knew nothing about the building's history or that of any of its previous owners.

Note 2.

For years, I clung to the far-fetched idea that the tin containing my father's effects might still be buried in the garden at the back of the shop, and I harboured the idea of one day digging it up. But really, what were the chances?

236

My father's belongings appeared to have been lost forever and no amount of wishful yearning could change that. All thoughts of the tin and its precious contents were shelved until one morning in early December 2009, not long after I'd arrived back in New Zealand from the UK, I received an email from Gerard:

Hi Zane

This morning Mr. Jean-Claude Schwartz (6 years in 1944) phone me he is in possession of various objects from a New Zealand airman [sic]:
- the packaging of a box of rations (food).
- stripe with three chevrons.
- a list of English words and French
- maps in English and German
- and a bracelet that bears the following inscription: NZ425844 A.C. KIRK, Kia ora to Winkie love Phyl[119], November 6, 1943.

The father of Jean-Claude SCHWARTZ (6 years in 1944) was Maurice SCHWARTZ who lived near Custines bridge.
He was mine manager of Saizerais and he had no left hand. He died in 1978 and his son lives in Corsica since 30 years. I had many difficulties to find him.
Regards
Gerard

I never fully learnt how Gerard had pulled off this astonishing coup. Nevertheless, it must have been a remarkable piece of detective work. When I wrote to Jean-Claude to express my gratitude for keeping my father's possessions safe for so many years, he promised to return the items as soon as he could. As the days became weeks it seemed he had forgotten, until one day a small white courier package bearing a French post mark arrived. When I opened it, the jewels of my father's past tumbled out. My father would have been amazed to see them, and I have to admit, I found it a little bit emotional to handle such treasures. They weren't valuable in a monetary sense, but for what they meant to our family they were priceless.

Chapter 21 - Up Close with the Enemy

In writing his story from a distance of nearly 60 years, my father wrote that he had been taken to a large house in Pont-a-Mousson belonging to a veterinary surgeon named Maurice who spoke excellent English. But this turned out to be incorrect. In fact, on more than one occasion my father's

---

[119] Phyllis Hunter, one of my father's lady friends in Calgary, Canada during his time at wireless school.

memory of events didn't reconcile with what I later learnt. I couldn't blame him. After all, how many of us can recall events in perfect chronological order six or sixteen years later let alone sixty?

The house in question belonged to Charles Francois. This came to light for Deborah, Leroy and myself the day after the commemoration ceremony when Gerard met us in Pont-a-Mousson and introduced us to Jean Magne, a small, slightly hunched little man with a school master's face and thinning grey hair. He had lived in Pont-a-Mousson all his life and as a sixteen-year old in 1944, he had been a member of the Red Cross. In later years, he'd taken on the role of town historian.

While sifting through some old photos, he asked us if our father had mentioned his kayaking trip down the Moselle River. This startled us. Our father had never recalled such a venture. However, it didn't take long for us to figure out it was Bill Hyde, who had been the paddler in question. It left me to wonder if Bill had ever mentioned his kayaking jaunt to my father. Perhaps he had, and my father had simply forgotten about it after so many years.

When recounting the kayak trip, Jean Mange gave us the impression that Bill had made a simple river crossing - not that such a venture would have been safe in occupied France with the Germans patrolling the waterways and river banks - when in fact Bill and his guide had paddled 15 kilometers from Millery to Pont-a-Mousson.

Jean led us down to the river where there were people sitting on park benches enjoying the warm summer day. There were a few recreational kayakers on the water as we followed a wide path along the shore line to a two- storey boat shed, home of the Nautical Club where Bill had come ashore with his guide and had been astounded to be approached by the German soldier offering to help them stow their kayak. Jean then escorted us into town through a series of cobbled back streets and dusty alleyways.

'Bill would have come through these streets,' he said, as we followed him down a narrow street and stopped in front of an ornate arched entrance in a high rendered wall. Behind the wall, visible through a wrought iron gate, stood a three-storey L-shaped house. It reflected a past opulence but now, with flaking paint and chipped rendering, it looked more like an advertisement for faded decadence. Some of the windows were protected by shutters or, like the window above the front door, by wrought iron bars. The garden was overgrown, and behind a broken pane in an upper window I noticed a 'for sale' sign.

'This,' Jean said, 'was where Bill came. And your father also stayed here.'

The gate opened with a protesting squeal and in a surreal moment we treaded up the same path our father had walked all those years ago. The only real difference was our father had been oblivious to the fact that the house had belonged to Charles Francois, Colonel-In-Chief of the Pont-a-Mousson sector

238

of the Resistance, or the Union of The French Forces of The Interior, a fact now highlighted by a commemoration plaque above the front door.

Gerard showed us a photograph of Charles Francois, a small man with swept back black hair and an erudite, no-nonsense countenance. I would have been hard pressed to have picked him out of a line up as a Colonel-In-Chief of the Resistance.

At this point someone needed to fill in the blanks in our father's story, and that someone turned out to Melle Francois, the daughter of Charles Francois. Gerard had tracked her down through another remarkable piece of detective work, the details of which were lost in translation. He arranged for Leroy, Deborah and I to meet Melle at her retirement village in Pont-a-Mousson.

A little silver haired lady, well into her seventies, Melle Francois had a permanent smile, and plenty to say. She had been twelve years old in August 1944, she said, as she reminisced with enthusiasm and emotion, remembering our father with a great deal of fondness. Gerard showed her a photograph of our father's crew and she immediately recognized not only our father, but also Bill Hyde, who had arrived at the house about the same time our father was waking up in the cemetery.

We spent an entertaining afternoon with Melle. The years rolled back as she talked rapidly and continuously, and we were glad to have Gerard and Jean Magne to translate for us, although I'm not sure even they managed to glean everything she told us.

Melle had no hesitation in bringing out the champagne to honour the occasion, and she took the opportunity to recall how our father had been introduced to Mirabelle wine.

'I do not believe he knew it was alcohol,' she laughed. 'He drank and drank, and we kept filling his glass. I do not know how he got up the stairs to bed that night.'

This story fits with an account my father told me about a dinner he'd had with a lovely family. He admitted not remembering the entire evening because, as he described it, 'I was given some lovely sweet red wine which I really enjoyed. My hosts noticed this and kept filling my glass.'

Our father stayed at the house for two days, and Melle Francois remembered him as '...a cheerful, jovial young man.' Of course, that might have had something to do with the Mirabelle wine.

Chapter 22 – Bill's Story

Note 1.

In a letter he later wrote to Ian Blance's mother, Bill sheds a slightly different light on the calamity.

Dear Mrs Blance,

It is with deep regret that I have to write this letter to you.

I am Bill Hyde, the Engineer on the Lancaster Bomber of which your son Ian was my skipper, pilot, and good comrade.

I am sorry that I have been so long in writing to you, but I have only recently obtained your address from "Winkie" Kirk, our rear gunner, as the Air Ministry refused to let me have the relatives' addresses.

I don't know whether you have been informed of the disaster which happened to us on July 28th on our bombing mission to Stuttgart, but I think you will be anxious to know a little more from one who was there at the time. I should dearly have loved to have been nearer to you, and been able to talk with you for a little while, but I shall have to try my best in writing instead.

All I can tell you, Mrs Blance, is that we were attacked by a German fighter aircraft near the German border at about 1.30am on the 29th July, and our aircraft was set on fire immediately about halfway along the fuselage, and believe me when I say it was well away from your son.

Ian called to me, quite calmly, and I went to him from where I was working in the nose if the aircraft; I knew that he was going to order me to fight the fire, but the damage was greater than we were then aware, for 2 engines were also on fire and the other 2 engines stopped very soon afterwards. Well, when I reached Ian's side he shouted: 'The controls have gone; bail out!'

He was not wounded by the attack, and manfully struggled to gain control while I went back to the Bomb-aimer's compartment to open the escape hatch. The hatch jammed and it was a few minutes before it opened with the assistance of "Oscar", the Bomb-aimer.

Oscar and I stood each side of the escape exit when something happened and I was knocked unconscious by a blow to the head (I was told by the French people later that our Lancaster broke in two pieces in mid-air) and I recovered consciousness to find myself floating down on my parachute - that was surely a miracle, wasn't it Mrs Blance?

I think that when I was knocked unconscious the same thing must have happened to the other boys, as Oscar, who should have escaped, did not get out, and the French people found Ian still sat at the controls.

We might be able to learn a little more from Colin Greig, the navigator who escaped [the aircraft] and is now a prisoner of war in Stalag Luft VII, Germany.

I hid for two days in a ditch, and then found a cottage which proved to be French. I knocked at the door of the cottage and slipped inside, and from then on, I was in good hands. The good people gave me clothing and food, and hid me in different houses...Young Winkie also escaped from the rear turret, and we met after a few days in France. It was grand to see him as I thought I was the only survivor. The French people informed us that Greig was wounded and *in a French cottage, but the Germans must have found him as he is now a prisoner.*

...Winkie shot down the JU88 German fighter which set us on fire, so that is some little consolation, isn't it Mrs Blance.

The French people gave our 4 boys a very nice funeral, with hundreds of people to pay homage - the church and outside was packed, they told me; and scores of beautiful flowers. Later a cross was made from one of the propellers, with the four names inscribed on it.

They are resting at a village named;
POMPEY[120]
MEURTHE-ET-MOSELLE
FRANCE
and I am going back as soon as I can when this is all over, to pay my respects to some wonderful lads.

Dear Mrs Blance, I would like you know how very much I sympathize with your great loss, and hope you understand how much I would like to be with you, as I miss the boys very deeply.

If there is anything I can do for you, in this part of the world, at any time, I should be honoured if you should ask me,

In the meantime, God bless and comfort you, are the thoughts from my mother and myself.[121]

Note 2.
H.L. Thompson, in his Official History of New Zealanders With the Royal Air Force, described the fate of the Blance crew on the night of 28/29 July, 1944.

The second crew had bombed and were flying back across France when an enemy fighter attacked. Its first burst put all four engines out of action; then it raked the fuselage with bullets, killing both wireless operator and mid-upper gunner and wounding the navigator. Closing in for a second attack, the fighter met determined fire from the Lancasters rear guns and down it went. But it was too late to save the bomber. Blazing furiously, it also began to go down out of control. By a supreme effort, the pilot, Pilot Officer Blance, succeeded in arresting the downward plunge just long enough to allow three of his crew to bail out safely but he and his bomb aimer were unable to leave. Bomber and fighter eventually crashed within half a mile of each other. Of the survivors, only the rear gunner, Flight Sergeant Kirk, managed to evade capture.[122]

---

[120] In fact, the cemetery was in Millery.

[121] Letter from Bill Hyde to Mrs Ivy Blance, 30/11/44.

[122] H.L. Thompson, Official History of New Zealand In the Second World War, New Zealanders With the Royal Air Force, Volume II: European Theatre January 1943 - May 1945, pg. 410.

Official histories are not always accurate.

Chapter 23 – A Shot in the Dark

My father never knew the extent of Captain Williams' escape record. A War Office Report dated 25 March 1945 recommended Williams be awarded the Military Cross. The citation stated:

This officer was captured in the action of 3 Indian Motor Brigade at MECHILE (Africa) in April 1941 and was taken as a prisoner of war to North Italy. He twice escaped captivity but was recaptured on both occasions and on collapse of Italy was removed to Germany. While in transit he escaped for the third time but was recaptured a few days afterwards. On a fourth occasion, he got away from a prison camp in Germany only to be recaptured again. Owing to his intransigent attitude while in captivity and to his continued attempts to escape, he was placed in special punishment camps both in Italy and Germany.

At the end of April 1944, he made a fifth and successful attempt to escape from the camp at LANSDORF in Eastern Germany, he made his way across Germany and reached occupied France on 17 May 1944. Here he joined up with the F.F.I. (Maquis) in the Toul area and fought with them until the arrival of 2 American Cavalry Division of 3 American Army. By reason of his contacts with the F.F.I. and his knowledge of local conditions he was able to afford much valuable information to the American command.

He was dispatched to PARIS where he reported to BRIG. CARTHEW YOURSTOUN.[123] Because of the fact that he possessed important information with regard to possible bombing targets he was flown to England so that the information might be available to R.A.F. Bomber Command.

This officer showed courage perseverance of the highest order in during more than three years of captivity he made five attempts to escape which were finally crowned with success. During this period, his one object was to make his escape so that he might take part in the war. I strongly recommend that his conduct should be recognized by the award of the Military Cross.

Major General G.W. Symes.

At the end of April 1944, Captain Williams swapped identities with Signalman A. Beaumont of the Royal Signals to make his successful escape, getting away from the camp at Lansdorf in Eastern Germany. He trekked across Germany and reached occupied France on 17 May 1944 where he joined up with the F.F.I. in the Toul area.

---

[123] Brigadier M.A. Carthew Yorstoun, CBE, DSO, Black Watch. Born 13 Sept 1897. Head of British Army Staff in Paris, 1944.

Signalman Beaumont's family received a letter from the War Office in which they were informed that their son had switched identities with Captain Williams without the German authority's knowledge. The department couldn't say for what precise reason the exchange had been made and although it wasn't thought the swap should be cause for any uneasiness, they considered, in the interests of both individuals, that the enemy should not become aware of the position. If, therefore, their son wrote to them as Captain Williams, and in the absence of any instructions from him to the contrary, the Beaumont family were requested to address letters to Beaumont as Captain Williams. The War Office stated that in matters of this kind the greatest discretion should be observed, and suggested that the facts should not be discussed, even among their friends.

Chapter 24 - Dan and Ben's Escape

As my father rarely told a story about his time in the maquis without mentioning his American friends Dan and Ben, I decided I needed to find out more about them. My father had never mentioned their surnames, so the task of tracking them down seemed nigh impossible. Where on earth to start?

Dan and Ben said they had walked out of Germany after their B-17 had crash landed, but I had no idea what squadron or bomb group they had belonged to. Having the serial number, or even the nickname of their aircraft, would have been a huge help, but I had nothing. Compared to tracking down information on these guys, finding the proverbial needle in a haystack would have been a piece of cake!

I avoided the issue for a few weeks because the enormity of the task gave me a headache, and it was only after pretty much giving up did things start to happen.

One night, while surfing a few military websites for something completely unrelated to my 'mission impossible', I stumbled on a site called Conscript Heroes, the brainchild of Keith Janes, an Englishman to whom I shall remain deeply indebted. As part of his site, Keith had not only put together a list of British escapers and evaders, along with the file numbers of their MI9 Escape and Evasion reports (Aubrey Kirk and Bill Hyde were on the list), he had also compiled a list of American evaders. I started trawling through the list looking for any airmen named Dan or Ben.

After scanning a few hundred names, and nearing the brink of abjection, two entries suddenly jumped off the screen at me:

#1503 Sgt. Benjamin Norris 305BG/365BS (B-17) 42-39878 FTR May 44 Crash landed in Germany.

#1504 Sgt. Daniel E. Dunbar 305BG/365BS (B-17) 42-39878 FTR May 44
Crash landed in Germany.

Here were a Dan and Ben who had been aboard the same aircraft when it had crash landed in Germany in May 1944. This ringed them as likely candidates. True, they had crash landed a couple of months previous to my father being shot down, but their walk out of Germany would have accounted for much of the time that passed before meeting my father.

Without confirmation that these were the men I was looking for, I had to temper my excitement. Nonetheless, with surnames, a squadron, a bomb group, and an aircraft serial number, it now felt like I was now digging through a haystack for a broomstick rather than a needle.

I started by Googling the 305th Bomb Group and found they had a Bomb Group Association. I immediately emailed them, explaining my situation.[124] At the same time, it dawned on me that perhaps the Americans had something similar to the now defunct Royal Air Force Escaping Society. I went back to the internet and lo and behold I found the AFEES (Air Forces Escape and Evasion Society). I emailed the association president, Larry Grauerhol, who replied within 24 hours.

Larry could not find Benjamin Norris on the AFEES membership roll, but there had been a Daniel E. Dunbar whose name had last appeared on the 1997 roll, which suggested he may now be deceased. However, Larry gave me the last known address for Daniel Dunbar in Tucker, Georgia.

When I checked the Georgia White Pages, I found a Daniel T. Dunbar who, while not currently residing in Tucker, had lived there previously. Hoping that he may be related to Daniel E. Dunbar, I wrote an old-fashioned letter pleading for information. A response arrived a couple of weeks later via email.

Danny T. Dunbar turned out to be Daniel E. Dunbar's son.

Excited to have found each other, he promised to dig out whatever he could relating to his father's time in France. He thought his father's memoirs were floating around the house somewhere, and there were also some letters which he had received after the war from the French families he had stayed with. I emailed him all the relevant information about my father and we promised to stay in touch.

Next, I had to find Ben Norris or, should he have died, any living relatives. Ben hadn't been on the register of AFEES, so finding him seemed more daunting. I went as far as trolling through U.S. Army enlistment records as far back as 1941, looking for anyone called Norris and came up with half a dozen likely candidates. One, who resided in California, seemed like a promising candidate.

---

[124] I never did get a reply from the 305 BG Association.

Before I got any further, my investigation received a dramatic shot in the arm by an unexpected email from a man named Edouard Reniere who lived in Belgium. He had information about Daniel Dunbar and Benjamin Norris. He gave me their dates of birth, names of their wives, dates they had died, plus the names and addresses of their surviving sons. I don't know how he tracked down this material, but he did say that he belonged to a group of people who investigated such things, and that he had read my message on the Conscript Heroes message board. The message I posted would later bring further information to light. Never let it be said that the internet hasn't made the world a fraction of the size it used to be.

I wrote letters to Benjamin Norris's sons, Kevin and Ben, and received replies in short order. They wondered how I had managed to find them so long after the events that had brought our fathers together. I couldn't tell them much because Edouard had found them, although the Ben Norris I'd ringed as my most likely candidate during my own research (a man born in 1916 and who had resided in Los Angeles, California at the time of his enlistment) turned out to be the Ben Norris I had been looking for.

Kevin and Ben were just as thrilled as Danny Dunbar that I had found them. I gave them Danny's email and hoped we would all stay in contact.

I then switched my focus to the aircraft on which Dan and Ben had flown their ill-fated mission. Armed with the ship's serial number, I discovered the aircraft's date of manufacture, its nickname - War Eagle - and the date of its demise.

Then one day, out of the blue, Edouard Reniere sent me an excited email telling me that he had been working with a man in Germany whose grandfather had served with a Luftwaffe flak unit in the area where Ben and Dan's B-17 had come down. Edouard's work colleague related how his grandfather's flak crew had raced to the site of a crash-landed B-17. As most of the American flyers had been captured by the time they arrived, the flak crew was able to loiter and take souvenir photos of the crippled aircraft. Edouard had attached a couple of these photos to his email.

The pictures show a B-17 bearing the name War Eagle, and is in remarkably good condition. The starboard outer propeller is bent out of shape but the inner propeller exhibits a perfectly straight upright blade in the feathered position, suggesting the aircraft had suffered an engine failure and the propeller had stopped spinning before it hit the dirt. Later research confirmed that Dan and Ben's aircraft had indeed suffered engine failure and the starboard outer propeller had been feathered prior to crash landing.

I forwarded the photos to Ben, Kevin and Danny. A few weeks later Danny sent me a copy of his father's brief wartime memoir which gave a more in-depth account of Daniel Dunbar and Ben Norris's adventures.

Chapter 25 - Maquis

In his memoirs, Fernand Nedelec made note of the new arrivals: *'The resistance numbers went up again; we received a dozen English speakers sent by the Kimmel Toul group. Among them the English captain Chester, who was designated as responsible for the group because he is the only one who understands and speaks our language.'*

Chapter 26 - Nocturnal Affairs

Note 1.

In his memoirs, Fernand Nedelec paid particular homage to Marcel, saying he showed courage and resolution at every turn.

'Marcel was also responsibility for the Senegalese soldiers, containing their recriminations and distributing equally between them the insufficient food supplies. Furthermore, poor Marcel's feet were constantly ravaged by incurable blisters. Not that it stopped him undertaking dangerously long walks if necessary.

'He organised life in the maquis very well. He retained responsibility for daily duties, that's to say the supply needs, food rationing, and the security guards.

According to Nedelec, the job of guarding the camp was essentially done by the Senegalese. They couldn't be used for other services, apart from farm raids, because they were far too noticeable.

Note 2.

Fernand Nedelec adds: *'Regarding cigarettes, we go directly to the tobacco shops to take the reserve, leaving them the main stock to sell. In this way, the population can always buy their tobacco ration.'*

Chapter 27 - Rendezvous.

Note 1.

Fernand Nedelec wrote about the airdrop in his memoir stating, *'Finally, the British think about us and we'll soon possess weapons in quantity. That's what we need most over here, because we are now some 60 strong with a couple of guns, a machine gun and a shot-gun... It is thin. We are running out of rifles. We are capable and daring so we agree that every night we will go to the ground on Mont Blenod high above the vineyard 7 - 8 kilometers from the maquis.*[125]

Note 2.
An account of an airdrop operation flown by 75 Squadron is given by Wing Commander H.L. Thompson. *'…These were interesting if rather uneventful missions. 'The target was reached just after midnight,' says a typical report. 'The area was identified near a wood at the intersection of a road and railway. The reception was good, consisting of three bonfires and a faint flashing light from a man holding a torch. Twelve containers were dropped from about 500 feet. On the return flight two packages of leaflets were also dropped …'*

Chapter 30 - Ambush of Tigers.

Note 1.
According to Charlotte James, the great niece of Chester Williams, her great uncle got into the habit of wearing a monocle because the man with whom he'd exchanged identities before making his escape, Signalman Beaumont, had been a jeweller before the war and had often worn a monocle.

Note 2.
My father gave the map case to his brother, Frank, who kept it in his garage for many years before returning it. It now sits in my curio cabinet surrounded by my father's other wartime memorabilia.

Chapter 31 – Blenod-les-Toul

Maquis member Fernand Nedelec recalled: *'We organized our short stay here, waiting for our imminent departure for Toul. Some young people of the village, ages 14 or 15 years old, joined us.'*
Some of the maquiards suggested the youngsters run along, but the boys were having none of it.
Nedelec continued: *'Our flag had the honour to fly above the door of the Town hall and sentries were placed at each entry to the village which had been deserted by the previous German occupiers.'*

---

[125] Fernand Nedelec, Toul 1940-1945 Forbach, Souvenirs De Resistance Et De Combats, pg.99.

Chapter 32 - Liberation

Note 1.

Daniel Dunbar's narrative corroborated what my father had told me, but it didn't offer much more about their meeting with the American column.

The colonel had the lieutenant radio back to base in code about transportation for us. The colonel was told of the German tanks, trucks and cars headed in the direction of Toul. The names of each underground member and their families were given. This was to help those men and women who had given help to us. The colonel told us we would not be able to serve in the European theatre any more. Should we be captured we risked being be shot as spies.

I told the colonel how the moral of the Germans was. Where the German soldiers had once saluted their officers with a 'heil' they got to just saluting them. Then it got so as the soldiers would pass an officer and not pay any mind to him.

The colonel's [radio] call was answered in short order. Stay with these men, transportation on the way. It was late in the afternoon when a jeep arrived with a captain and lieutenant. The colonel introduced everyone and then got back in his jeep and disappeared back down the road.

Later, in their E&E reports my father, Dan and Ben were succinct to say the least about their liberation. Ben Norris reported '…we were picked up by the 2 Cavalry of the 4th Armoured Division, 20 kilometres west of Toul, France.' My father's stated report stated, 'Americans arrived near Toul and took Captain Williams and me to their H.Q.' Daniel Dunbar didn't mention anything at all in his evasion report about being picked up by the Americans.

Note 2.

None of my research could unearthed a Major-General White commanding any American forces in the Lorraine province in 1944.

I believe my father simply got the general's name wrong. This is quite understandable given the length of time that had passed. The 4th Armoured Division, which liberated the region in which maquis 15 had operated in September 1944, was commanded by Major-General John Shirley Wood. To my mind, my father and Ben and Dan had been interrogated by General Wood. Wood took the attitude that a general needed be at the front with his men, and therefore he could always be found in the vanguard of his division's advance. He also believed a commanding officer needed to lead by example, which meant living under the same conditions as his men. To that end, he could be critical of his superior, General Omar Bradley, for living in a special panel van instead of using a tent like his men. Wood had been given the nickname 'Tiger

Jack' because whenever General Patton yelled at him, he would pace like a caged Tiger and argue back.[126]

Chapter 33 - Late Arrival

Note 1.

On the matter of exclusive clubs, my father earned eligibility to the Caterpillar Club, a club established in 1922 by Leslie Irvin, the founder of the Irvin Airchute Company of Canada. Their motto: 'Life depends on a silken thread.' Membership is restricted to those who have had their life saved by an Irvin parachute. On becoming a member, my father received a club membership card, a certificate confirming his membership, and a small gold caterpillar pin, which he wore with great pride. As an aside, the caterpillar pin displayed amethyst eyes, not ruby as many people believe.

Among my father's souvenirs I found two letters from Leslie Irvin. The first responds to his application to join the Caterpillar Club.

Dear F/Sgt. Kirk

Many thanks for your letter in the first instance, and I am sorry that I have not had a previous opportunity of replying.

I am indeed glad that you were able to save your life with an Irvin chute, and have much pleasure in welcoming you as a member of the club. Did you land in enemy territory? If so, please accept our hearty congratulations on your return to this country.

Your membership card and Caterpillar Pin are on order, and I will send them to you as soon as received. I regret however, that as far as the pin is concerned this may not be for several months, due to restrictions.

Wishing you the best of luck, I am.

Yours sincerely

Leslie L. Irvin

The second letter received at the end of February 1945, reads:

Dear F/Sgt. Kirk,

I am terribly sorry for the delay in sending you your Caterpillar, but it has only just been received.

I have much pleasure in enclosing it herewith, with our compliments and the hope that it brings you Good Luck

Yours sincerely

Leslie L. Irvin

---

[126] George Forty, 4th Armoured Division in World War II, 2009, page 11

Note 2.

If Morecombe in the winter of 1944 had been anything like the cold, dingy place Daphne and I visited in the winter of 2014, I can understand why my father never mentioned it. With parquetry clouds scudding in from the Irish Sea and tattered curtains of rain lashing the promenade, the town had all the soul of a dead kipper.

Note 3.

My father didn't talk much about Jock and Paddy's deaths, but following the demise of his own crew over France it must have hit him particularly hard.

It wasn't until author Max Lambert contacted him during the course of his research for his excellent book, 'Night After Night', an account of New Zealanders in Bomber Command, did Paddy and Jock's fates finally come to light. Max told my father, Paddy and Jock had been killed when their Lancaster was shot down over Denmark. The following is an account from 'Night After Night.'

Eight New Zealanders lie beneath the manicured lawn sloping away from Svino Evangelical Lutheran Church (Denmark's national church), eight of 62 in the British plot. Three of them are from 75 Squadron Lancaster captained by Wilson Hadley, 30 (Christchurch), shot down on 11 September 1944. Save English engineer Colin Fowler, the crew were all New Zealanders: Hadley (known as Joe), navigator John Gudgeon, 23 (Christchurch), bomb aimer Jack Wilcox, 24 (Matamata), wireless operator Paddy Giles, 21 (Christchurch), mid-upper gunner Vic Boyd, 20 (Nelson), and rear gunner Jock Biggar, 22 (Wanganui). Wilcox and Fowler were the only survivors.

The aircraft had dropped mines in Danzig Bay and was homebound when attacked by a fighter over Vordingborg at about 11.45pm. In 1990, Wilcox, a dairy farmer, wrote about what happened for a Danish researcher. He said they had been on track and just about to cross the coast at 20,000 feet when they were hit by cannon fire. 'The plane became an inferno ...the heat was terrific.' He jettisoned the hatch cover but the heat was so unbearable he only had time to snap his chute onto one harness clip before throwing himself out. He hurt his right shoulder landing and found himself covered in blood. He woke an elderly farm couple to get help. 'They were darlings and most helpful bathing my face and giving me a drink.' Wilcox was taken to the local hospital, where he was picked up by the Germans. Fowler escaped the clutches of the Germans, was spirited to Sweden and got back to England.

Gudgeon, Giles and Boyd apparently jumped from the Lancaster but too low for their parachutes to open. Their bodies were taken to Svino for burial. Hadley and Biggar were still on the bomber when it crashed - on a farm house at Orslev, 10 miles from Svino. The gasoline-fueled explosion and fire burned the house to the ground, incinerating the flyers and five Danes, members of one family - the farmer, his wife and three of their grown children. Despite the devastation and tragedy, surviving children insisted Hadley and Biggar be buried in the village churchyard alongside their parents and siblings. 'They died together, so they belong together,' one Dane wrote years later.[127]

Chapter 34 - Final Days

More than 60 years after the end of the second World War, my father remained irritated that Winston Churchill had made no mention of Bomber Command in his victory speeches, choosing to ignore the contribution of thousands of young men, many who gave their lives, while thanking the other armed services for their devotion to duty.[128]

Indeed, following the bombing of Dresden, a raid often seen to tarnish Bomber Command's reputation, Churchill, in the name of political expediency, distanced himself from any responsibility

I once asked my father for his opinion of Winston Churchill.

'He was a warmonger,' he declared. 'A man for the time, most certainly, but a warmonger all the same. I never liked him.'

'Because he ignored Bomber Command after the war ended?'

'That might have been part of it, but I still never liked him, and I wasn't surprised when he was kicked out of office after the war. He wasn't a peacetime politician, that's for sure.'

There wasn't much about my father's time in Bomber Command that annoyed him, but Churchill's disregard of the bomber and ground crews certainly did. Missing out on the Aircrew Europe Star, a campaign medal awarded to men who had flown operations over Europe also irritated him. Only aircrew who had operated over Europe prior to the D-Day landings on 6 June 1944 were eligible for the award. Missing out, he bemoaned later in life, meant he didn't have anything to show for his time in Bomber Command, unlike those in Fighter Command who had flown during the Battle of Britain and were honoured with a 'Battle of Britain' clasp to attach to their 1939 - 45 campaign star, or those who served in the Eighth Army and were given an 'Eighth Army' clasp to attach to their North Africa Star.

When an unofficial Bomber Command commemoration medal came out in 1985, for members of Bomber Command or their next of kin, my father promptly applied for one. When it arrived, he unexpectedly gave to me. 'I got it for you,' he said, handing it over in its presentation box. 'As long as I can wear it with my other medals on ANZAC Day.'

---

[127] Max Lambert, Night After Night, New Zealanders in Bomber Command, pg 443-444.

The unofficial Bomber Command medal is meant to be worn separately from other gallantry and campaign medals, but my father argued that since he and his fellow members of Bomber Command had had to wait so long for any recognition at all, he would wear it alongside his other decorations because believed it deserved equal status.

Chapter 35 – Heroes

Jim's meeting with Elva resulted from of one of those mysterious coincidences that occur every so often in one's life. At the time, I worked for a friend in his music store where he introduced me to his girlfriend, Jackie Crowe. A couple of years later at my 30th birthday party while inspecting some photos on the wall, Jackie exclaimed, 'That's my uncle Frank!'

She started to tell me all about her great uncle, Frank Jenkins. Terribly excited by this amazing coincidence, she arranged for her mother and grandmother to meet my father. He enjoyed meeting Elva and remained in touch with her for many years until her death. As for Elva, I believe meeting my father gave her some closure regarding Frank, and she found some peace knowing he hadn't been alone when he died.

I met Fred Climo's nephew, Paul, in 2009. I had spoken to Fred's brother, John Climo, a few years earlier, and again more recently in 2009, but as Paul explained, John's health had deteriorated and he was now often fuzzy regarding the past.

Paul told me he had visited a clairvoyant/medium. 'Not that I ever believed in that sort stuff,' he said. 'I was always really skeptical. But this woman told me she could sense a presence. Then she told me she could see a man in flying gear wearing a leather helmet and goggles, and he was clutching his chest. Of course, when your father told me that Fred had been hit in the chest when that night fighter hit them it made perfect sense. I've been back a couple of times since and been told other things that only the family could have known about Fred.'

Paul's story reminded me of something my father had told me about Fred's wife, Margaret. After he returned from France, my father wanted to see Margaret, but she had returned to the Wrens and he couldn't find her. When he arrived back in New Zealand, he visited Fred's mother in Timaru. She related how Margaret had told her about a dream she'd had about Fred. In the dream she saw him getting into the Lancaster and then the next thing it was on fire. She said she'd woken up and checked the time. It was the exact time her husband's Lancaster had been shot down. She had been so convinced that Fred had been killed she took immediate leave and went home. My father put it down to one of those unexplainable events, like the night he went to meet Jock at the station only to sense his friend wouldn't be on the train.

I have been unable to trace any of Ronald 'Oscar' Spencer's family. I did receive a letter from a man named Spencer living in Walsall, but it was only to inform me that he wasn't related to Ronald and, unfortunately, he didn't know any other Spencers in the area who might be. The search there continues.

I haven't had much contact with the Blance family except for an email from Sandra Blance in Australia. Another member of her family had read a story I'd had in the Christchurch Press about the crew and they had sent her a copy. She couldn't impart any information about Ian. Indeed, she just wanted to say how much she and the family appreciated finally knowing what had happened to her uncle. They knew he had been killed during the war, but reading an account of his last operation provided closure on a family tragedy. As I once told my father, this is why he had to tell his story.

My father didn't make it back to France until 1984. He went to Pompey to find his crew's graves. Unfortunately, despite his visit being reported in the local paper, he didn't make contact with M. Hugot (Ugo).

Did Marie's fiancée come back after the war? Did she stay in the village? If she is still alive, Marie would be in her nineties. Maybe one day a quirk of circumstance will provide me with the answers I seek.

I found Captain Williams an interesting character. On one hand my father painted him as an aloof, pompous character, but on the other hand it's difficult not to admire his tenacity, fortitude and downright determination. To be fair, Williams and my father came from social upbringings that were probably poles apart which may have accentuated the friction that existed between them, as it often did between colonials and British officers.

As pompous as my father found Captain Williams, and as unwilling as he might have been to do anything for him, he did concede that in hindsight he may have been doing his duty in a way to which he wasn't privy. I chuckle when I think about him reminding Captain Williams of his duty to escape, especially after everything Williams had been through to that point.

Author's Epilogue

My father remained a reserved, modest individual in most regards as I was growing up, so sometimes I had difficulty reconciling the man I knew as my dad with the man who had faced the horrors of war - the man who had jumped from a burning aircraft; the man who had tackled enemy tanks - but every so often he would display an impetuousness more akin to the young man who had been so desperate for adventure. The more I learned about his experiences, the higher the regard in which I held him.

He was never been reticent when it came to talking about his experiences that took him from being a Lancaster rear gunner to a maquis fighter. Over the years, students from a number of high schools turned up on his doorstep to interview him as part of their history studies and he always welcomed their interest and questions.

Although always agreeable to helping out the students who came to his door, whenever I suggested to him that we should write down his experiences, he deflected the notion with a diffident, 'I didn't do much. Write a book about Somme.'

Somme was my father's cousin, Edgar Sanders, who had been the only New Zealander to serve with Popski's Private Army in North Africa and Italy, and had been awarded the Military Medal while fighting with the Long-Range Desert Group in Libya. Often regarded as the best gunner in the LRDG, he was also said to be the scruffiest man in the British Army.

'Somme was an adventurer and hero,' my father said, with a typical veteran's self-effacement. 'I didn't do much at all.'

My father would never countenance the mantle of hero. The heroes, he maintained, were the aircrew who made the absolute sacrifice - over 55,000 of them - and the French people who selflessly aided him during the most perilous time of his life. At my father's funeral one of my cousins told me, 'There have always been two heroes in our family – Uncle Jimmy and Sanders.' Far be it for me to contradict my father, but to my mind he remains a hero, as were all the young men who night after night climbed into their cold, dark battle stations to fly into hostile skies in the face of violent anti-aircraft fire, enemy fighters, and the affliction of their own inner fears.

After a great deal of benign persuasion, my father finally submitted to writing down his story. It resulted in a brief memoir somewhat devoid of colour, personality and essential background, and there were a number of anecdotes and stories that he had either brushed over or inadvertently omitted. Whenever I mentioned such oversights, his response remained characteristically unassuming. 'Oh, I forgot about that,' he would say. 'Maybe one day when you write that book you can slip it in somewhere for me.'

255

Printed in Great Britain
by Amazon

77886861R00149